Desires of the Heart *captures in powerful detail not only (the*
fumbling) ventures into some of the first long-term, sustained, cross-cultural interactions
of our time, but also the conflicting sentiments common to many raised as missionary
kids. The story comes full circle as Frerichs makes her 'journey of clarification' and
returns to the land of her upbringing to reconnect with it and her past.

> —Ruth Van Reken, co-author, *Third Culture Kids: The Experience*
> *of Growing Up Among Worlds*

Weaving together vivid recollections, reflective analysis and excerpts from family
documents, Frerichs delivers a moving memoir. This book crosses time and distance
to connect mind and heart.

> —Nurya Love Parish, Executive Director, Grand Rapids Area
> Council for the Humanities

Catherine Frerichs's journey is compelling. Her insights are valuable for all who are
perched at the intersection of cultural relativism and a belief in the righteousness of
western belief and culture.

> —Cindy Hull, Department of Anthropology, Grand Valley State
> University, author of *Katun: A Twenty Year Journey with the Maya*

Successful mission fields are not just the Lord's work; they can be the result of dedicated
single-minded missionaries. This story is a daughter's search to understand what
propelled her father, and later her mother, to require such emotional sacrifices from
their own family to do God's work in New Guinea.

> —Lowell Johnson, Professor Emeritus of English, St. Olaf College

Desires of the Heart *is more than a scholarly and well-researched account of the life*
of a missionary family. With what is obviously some tenacity, Frerichs comes to terms
with how her parents' ministry in New Guinea also shaped her and her siblings' futures
as children of no earthly countries, but only of the Kingdom of God. A genuine and
heart-felt tour of duty.

> —Diane Herbruck, CEO, The Wordsmiths

...a marvelous reminder of the sacrifices the missionaries and their families made to
spread the gospel around the world. God bless you, your book and all who read it.

> —Nancy Fritz Christian, former Vice President, Women of the
> Evangelical Lutheran Church of America

DESIRES OF THE HEART
A DAUGHTER REMEMBERS
HER MISSIONARY PARENTS

Catherine E. Frerichs

COLD RIVER STUDIO
NASHVILLE, TENNESSEE

Cold River Studio is an independent press committed to introducing fresh, exciting voices to the reading public. It is our mission to take a chance on deserving authors and achieve the highest quality when bringing their words to the marketplace. We believe in the power of words and ideas and strive to introduce readers to new, creative writers.

Published by Cold River Studio, Nashville, Tennessee

First Edition: January 2010

Printed in the United States of America
ISBN-13: 978-0-9842298-3-3

Table of Contents

Maps

Papua New Guinea, 2010, in the South Pacific

Map created by Roy Cole

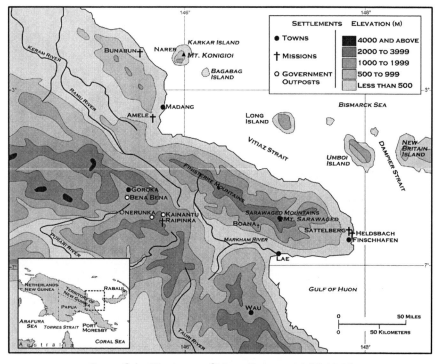

Part of the Territory of New Guinea, 1946-1975

Map created by Roy Cole

Introduction

I thought we two were their favorite children, and yet our parents left us behind. Albert and Sylvia Frerichs were departing for another term as Lutheran missionaries in New Guinea, taking only our five younger siblings with them. I was 18 and my brother David, 19. He and I were to remain in Minnesota, to attend St. Olaf College in Northfield. That bleak January day in 1964, as the train left, I thought I would never see my family again. New Guinea[1] was too far away, and their seven-year missionary term was too long. I would see my mother twice in that seven years. But I would not see my father again until I was 25, one month before my wedding.

After their deaths, when I began to read the thousand or so letters my parents had saved, one question overrode all the others: "Why did our parents become missionaries?" As children, we had always known their answer: "We were doing God's will." Growing up, we had no thought of second-guessing the fundamental choices our parents had made. That answer was enough. But as adults, we needed more. How did a Nebraska farm boy, none of whose siblings had attended high school, go on to college and then seminary? Why was he willing to go halfway around the world,

---

[1]   The country I am calling "New Guinea" is actually the northeast quadrant of the turkey-shaped island just north of Australia. For the forty-year period that my parents lived there, it was the Territory of New Guinea, administered by Australia, first for the League of Nations and, after World War II, for the United Nations. The southeast quadrant of the island was Papua, an Australian colony. The western half, Netherlands New Guinea, was part of the Dutch empire and is now part of Indonesia. In 1975, the Territory of New Guinea and Papua formed the independent nation of Papua New Guinea.

against the express wishes of his newly widowed mother, "to save the souls of black people he knew nothing about" (as she put it)? Why would our mother, a woman of such beauty, sparkle, and imagination, leave her family, send her young children off to boarding school, and endure years of loneliness on isolated mission stations?

There was also the most basic question: how could they have chosen God over us? The letters make plain the irony of our parents' lives. Their devotion to a God of love and to bringing that God's message to those who had not heard it meant they could not give their own children the love we craved and needed. Their letters make plain the further irony that they considered the unknown people to whom they were carrying this message to be inferior to their children.

For many years as an adult, I was ashamed of my parents and their choices. In the academic world where I live and which I love, missionaries are often looked on as misguided do-gooders who impose their religious ideas and materialistic American values on vulnerable "natives." While I knew that that view was a caricature, I also thought that it held some truth. I did not admit to myself, let alone to anyone else, that my parents had sent me away at the age of six to attend boarding school. My saying so would show clearly that my parents had chosen God, an abstraction, over me, their daughter. I attributed my discomfort with African-Americans to the superiority I felt as a child towards New Guineans, a superiority that I believed I had learned from my parents. I avoided talking about my background. People would ask where I was from, and I would say, "My father was from Nebraska, and my mother from Minnesota." Neither did I think too much about my past and the choices my parents had made. I was in my thirties before I realized that the seven years during which I had not seen my father was a long time not to have seen one's father.

The letters show me the power and allure of what my parents were doing. Reading them has been like getting to know the other woman in your husband's life. If you were writing the script, she never would have been there. You feel jealous and betrayed. But there she is, and in the moments that you can open yourself enough to see her, you understand why he made the choice. Understanding actually heightens the irony: seeing more fully, you feel the tension more deeply.

The years I have spent with the letters, carrying out other research, writing and discussing chapter drafts, and then revisiting Papua New Guinea, have been gifts—a many-faceted window into my parents' lives, letting me grasp a roundedness, depth, and complexity that cannot be available to a child growing up.

This is a story about what a daughter has come to understand about both her parents and their choices.

Chapter One
An Autobiography of a Piece of Chalk

I: Katharine Lehmann School

The young piece of chalk in the box is the largest, widest, most beautiful chalk of all. It is even made president of all the pieces of chalk in the box. People who open the box are attracted to the chalk's rich, dark green color and want to use it. Being pressed against a blackboard is painful, but it passively accepts this function it is expected to perform. It thinks to itself: "I know I have to get used to it, or I will be in agony all my life." When the chalk is covered with dirt and worn down to half an inch, it considers trying to escape. It quickly decides otherwise: "The only way I can really protect myself is to work my way down to the bottom of the box where I won't be noticed." That is what it does.

So goes a summary of an essay I wrote as a seventh grader at a boarding school in Wau, New Guinea, in 1958. I called it "An Autobiography of a Piece of Chalk." If you had asked me about it when I wrote it, or even in the next few years, I would never have recognized myself in it. The worn-down piece of chalk at the bottom of the box was an embarrassment. Who would want to be that way? I was good at most things, acknowledged as a leader by both peers and adults. I would not have admitted that I wanted to disappear. I would never have admitted to being almost an orphan. But I was. For eleven years, my parents kept sending me away, first to Wau and then, for high school, to Australia. They sent me and my siblings in as loving a way as they could, and they maintained regular contact with us, but they still sent us.

Katharine Lehmann School (KLS) was established in 1951 by the Women's Missionary Federation of the American Lutheran Church for the children of Lutheran missionaries. With this school, parents no longer needed to leave their children in their home country for their education, not seeing their parents for seven or eight years at a time.

My parents sent me to KLS for the first time when I was six. Except for two years in two different places in the United States, we would never again live together as an entire family. As was to be the usual pattern, I was sent with my older brother David, aged seven. It was February, 1952, the start of the school year in any Southern Hemisphere country. We would not be home again until July, for a two-week vacation, although Mother and Dad planned to visit us in May. A few missionary mothers home-schooled their children, but most parents eventually agreed that their children could not receive a good education at home. A missionary wife had too many other duties: caring for younger children, sewing clothes, baking bread, supervising the young New Guinean women who worked in the house, and, in the case of Mother, teaching a class or two in the local school. Besides, their children should be around other "European" (i.e., white) children their age. We played with New Guinean children all the time, but my parents, Mother especially, wanted us to grow up knowing that we had other identities besides the current New Guinean one. Mother and Dad could give us some of that, but being with European children was also essential. Even though this decision was not intended to imply that we were better than (just different from) our New Guinean playmates who attended the local village school, I drew the unspoken inference at the time.

My parents' decision was less clear-cut than for most missionary parents because the town where we lived, Lae, had a school for European children. Mother explained their reasoning to her parents:

> I'm sure it seems silly to many that we're sending them away from home when there's a school here, and we too have had our doubts and it was pretty tough to say goodbye that hot Sunday p.m. The school down here is pretty lackadaisical and many of the children are pretty rough—used to a lot of drinking etc. David has used Cathy for a crutch in reading and numbers and she was getting ahead of him. So at Wau, Miss Miller, using an American system, is working him very hard. *[12 March 1952]*

My parents felt they had no choice but to send us away. In an interview for Lutheran church archives after they retired, Mother said, "We had to do it [sending our children away], and we didn't fight against doing it."

They also knew that KLS was a much better choice than had been available to missionary families before World War II, when school-age children had to be left with relatives in one's home country. Given the length of missionary terms, seven or eight years might pass before parents and children would see one another. Sometimes, children even younger than school age were left in the home country. In one family, two boys, ages four and six, were left with relatives—the four-year-old so that he could keep the six-year-old company. The boys next saw their mother when they were twelve and fourteen, but they never again saw their father, who was killed during the Japanese invasion of New Guinea in World War II. Even before World War II, women married to British civil servants in colonial Nigeria faced more difficult futures than the wives of missionaries. British wives routinely returned to England to have their babies, delivered, and then left them there with either relatives or a paid nanny. Wifehood was far more important than motherhood.

As a six-year-old, I never questioned my parents' decision to send us to boarding school because it seemed the logical thing to do. Mother said in an early letter to us that we were at Wau "to learn all the things boys and girls must learn to grow into good, useful men and women" *[25 February 1952]*. I believed I could take care of myself away at school. I already thought that I was smarter than David because I had learned to read faster than he had, and I sensed that my parents also considered me more advanced. When I was five and David six, our parents gave us each one 78-rpm record for Christmas: a recording of Tchaikovsky's *Nutcracker Suite* for me, and a recording of Walt Disney songs for David. My parents put my record on the record player first. Could a child ask for better proof? I had proved myself in other ways as well. I watched Mother sew on her Singer treadle sewing machine and asked her to teach me. She liked teaching me, and I liked learning from her. Just before we left for school, I sewed my own skirt—blue with white polka dots and an elastic waistband.

MOTHER WAS CRYING as she hugged and kissed us one last time before we boarded the plane. "I love you. Be good." "I love you too," I replied obediently. Her tears embarrassed me since I wasn't crying and wanted only to find a seat on the plane. During the six years I spent at Wau, I made it a point of honor never to be homesick. It seemed the safest and therefore best way to be. My parents may have unknowingly encouraged this response. After all, if Cathy did not cry when she left, and if she never asked to come home, and if she did well in school, she must be okay. Therefore, it cannot be so bad to send one's children away.

I do not remember David reacting differently to our leaving, but years later, Mother told his wife that he had hidden at the airport so that he wouldn't have to board the plane. A photo taken in front of our home the day we left makes the same point. I'm smiling, swinging my little suitcase, and looking directly into the camera. David stands stiffly, knees together, looking down, holding back tears. *(See photo on p. 144.)* I never wrote letters about missing my parents or wanting to go home, but David did. "Let me come home," and "I want to come home because the other boys don't let me play with them," he wrote during our first year away. In 1953, Mother was the temporary matron (caretaker) at Wau for several months. When she left, David's letter began simply, "We are very sad you left." Somewhere in the middle of my letter, written at the same time, one plain sentence said: "Thank you for all the things you have done for us." I was distancing myself, as if writing to someone I barely knew.

Going to Wau was not my first flight, although all the other times at least one parent was with me. The DC-3, our plane that day, felt big and solid. It was one of my favorite planes. We sat on fold-down seats that lined both sides of the plane. Four other missionary children, who were German, older, and whom we hardly knew, sat away from us. What if they didn't like us, I wondered. It was the first of many times that I felt thin and exposed, no matter that I put up a carefree front.

Even though I felt I could take care of myself, I also knew that I had no choice but to do so. I changed my focus by looking around me. The plane's cargo was right up against our knees, a heavy net securing it: our luggage, supplies ordered by people who lived in Wau, and chickens in a crate. The propellers started up, and the plane lumbered down the airfield. I was on the side of the plane away from the hangar, and so I could not wave to my parents, and then we were airborne. Taking off from the Lae airport was always scary because the runway literally ended in the ocean. Off to the left I could see the rusted hulk of a Japanese ship, just one of many reminders that the war was not long gone. My new life on my own had begun.

AFTER HALF AN HOUR'S FLIGHT, fifty miles up the Bulolo River valley, we landed at Wau. The house-father for the boarding school met us at the Wau airstrip and piled all of us in the back of the school's truck, a weapons carrier with seats in back, that the US Army had abandoned. The road was dusty and bumpy. If you were so unlucky as to sit at the very back, which was wide open, you would be covered in dust by the time you reached the school.

We drove through the small town of Wau, then followed the road curving out of town until we reached the hill on which Katharine Lehmann School stood. I felt numb, a little light-headed from the lurching ride and queasy in the stomach, trying at the same time to take in the details of my new home. Small guest houses for visiting missionaries and, most especially, for parents lined both sides of the road up the hill. As we approached the top of the hill, we saw the dining hall and a large meeting room to our right. Across an open grassy area the dormitories formed a right angle: two long rooms with Little Boys and Big Boys on one side and Little Girls and Big Girls on the other, with housing for two matrons in between. The two-room school was on the left. The grounds and buildings were a manageable space for a six-year-old to navigate. The sooner I knew my way around, the better.

During the six years that I was there, as many as 40 children attended the school. But that first year there were just 31. We came from various backgrounds. The German missionaries to New Guinea and their children—who had been forced into internment in Australia at the start of World War II because their country was at war with Australia—had been freed only recently. The American and Australian children of young parents such as Mother and Dad were just becoming old enough for school.

There were usually seven European staff at the school: Germans, Americans, and Australians of varying occupations. Two house-parents had overall responsibility for the school. The cooks for many years were Australian women, first, Miss Radke, and then Miss Jericho. Several young New Guinean men assisted them. The mission had trouble recruiting matrons, young women who served as our primary caregivers. Mother was one of four missionary wives who helped fill this role. An American always taught the younger children, since they were mainly American. An Australian teacher taught the older children, whether American, Australian, or German, since they would all soon be attending high school in Australia.

I loved the pattern of the school day because there was both structure and freedom, with plenty of time to be outdoors. Mornings could be cool at 3500 feet, and the grass was usually wet from dew, so we had to wear shoes until morning recess. All of us had grown up almost never wearing shoes; having to do so was an imposition. Girls also had to wear skirts to class but could wear shorts underneath so that we could take the skirts off in a moment to play Kick-the-Can, Dodge-Ball, or Hide-and-Seek at recess. After lunch, we all had to rest quietly in our rooms for half an hour. Shoes went back on for dinner. So near to the Equator, darkness comes on quickly, and the staff were concerned that one of us might step on a snake in the dark, as in fact a few of us did each year.

After dinner, there were always devotions. We sang hymns, and one of the adults read from the Bible, followed by brief comments on the passage. By the age of 10, I could play the pump organ well enough that I, along with a few other older children, took turns accompanying the hymns. Devotions always ended with the same ritual, a German custom: we formed a line and went around the room of adults, including any visitors, shaking their hands and saying goodnight. I liked this orderly way of ending the day, but now, I'm also aware that a handshake, not a hug, was my only regular physical contact with an adult.

Saturday morning we changed our sheets and made our beds, carefully tucking in fresh linens, blankets, and bedspreads. All of our clothes had to be neatly folded. We took great pride in cleaning our shoes, perhaps because it was easy to be successful in such a small job. Most of the time we wore flip-flops, using discarded toothbrushes and soap to scrub away the dirt that our feet had worn into them. We cleaned our canvas shoes by scrubbing them with a brush under running water, then by applying liquid white polish. To dry our shoes, we propped them up against the screen enclosing the porch that ran the length of the two dormitories. After one of the matrons pronounced our work satisfactory, we were free to play.

Saturday afternoons, twice a month, we could go into Wau to shop, spending our weekly allowance of one shilling (about a quarter). Usually, we went to the trade stores run by Chinese merchants. I might buy a paper fan or some candy or try to figure out what Mother would like for her birthday. Another place we loved was the town swimming pool, which was roughly Olympic-size. Many of us learned to swim by being pushed into the deep end, in my case, by one of the older German girls. With the water depth way over my head, I had to kick and paddle furiously to reach the side of the pool and safety.

I don't believe I ever pushed anyone in who couldn't swim. When someone else did, I stood by silently, not protesting but also ready to jump in if necessary to help the non-swimmer. It was good to be tough, I thought, and I believed that learning to swim this way helped to develop this quality. I have helped my own children and grandchildren to swim in much more conventional ways. It matters to me that, as individuals, they are resilient, not tough.

Our other favorite swimming place was the Bulolo River, which was still being dredged for gold (Wau had been a gold-mining town) and was only a few miles from the school. On weekend afternoons, we sometimes swam and picnicked there. Just as with the way most of us learned to swim, the river was an opportunity to push the bounds of authority that usually reined us in.

Once when the river was in flood, it was obvious we could not swim in the roiling brown water, which hurled trees along as if they were matchsticks. But my daredevil brother David decided that he was strong enough to swim to the opposite shore and ended up downstream a hundred yards or so. Climbing up one of the big boulders we ordinarily jumped from, he saw what was obvious to the rest of us: he couldn't get back without being swept even farther downstream by the current. David couldn't hear any of us over the roar of the river and had to come up with his own return plan. He made his way downstream along the river bank until he found a fairly shallow place. From there, with the help of a New Guinean, he crossed the river and was back at school several hours later, dry and in clean clothes. The other children and I admired his bravery. I had not been overly concerned. He and I were used to taking chances and always, somehow, getting through.

Church services fully occupied Sunday mornings. I don't remember ever questioning why we had to attend. I took my identity as a Christian for granted. Even though my beliefs have evolved since then, having Christian rituals and study woven seamlessly into my life as a child, both at school and at home, may be the primary reason why I have been able to continue as a Christian. My experience of religion and faith was a natural part of my life.

WE COULD NOT APPEAR at supper on Sundays unless we had written a one-page letter to our parents. It always began "Dear Father and Mother," even though we actually called them "Daddy" and "Mommy" (or sometimes the Australian "Mummy," the sound of which Mother hated). Perhaps one of the matrons had told us that that was the proper way to address our parents. During the week, we probably would have received a letter from them. Dad never missed a week, but his letters were rarely interesting: they were so matter-of-fact, and they always began with a Bible verse. Now I appreciate the faithfulness those letters imply. Mother's letters were the ones I waited for, even more so because she did not write every week, or she might add a quick scrawl at the end of Dad's letter. Her letters always took us into the middle of what was happening at home: "Do you remember the picture in your Calvert Course Science book where a cow is flying? Jonathan [our two-year-old brother] looked at it this morning and said, 'Cows don't fly. Butterflies fly'" *[30 September 1952]*. She could make me feel that I was special, that she was thinking about the very particularity of my life. Did the cookies that she sent crumble en route? Did the dress fit that she made? Was I practicing the piano every day? My hunger for Mother's letters shows me now how much I missed her, although I do not remember making that connection.

Our parents must have been frustrated by the snippets we conveyed of our lives. This third grade letter is typical of my letters, errors and all:

> Dear Mother and Father,
>
> This coming Friday we are going to have the criket match. I am going to be in the match, and so is Roswitha and Rosalind. But I can't play it very good.
>
> Yesterday we didn't go swimming because Mr. Wagner and Miss Miller took us for a walk to the dredge [an abandoned gold dredge] and then into the bush. Mr. Wagner told us about different kind of plants and stones. I liked it very much.
>
> As you might know that last Tuesday was a holladay. That was fun to. We went somewhere near the dredge.
>
> Some of us let ourselves foat downstream with the river. After we had done that we made a sandcastle and found flowers to make it look nice. Then we had lunch. After that, Heidi, Irmgard, Roswitha, Erica, Elsbeth and I lay out in the sunshine and got sunburned. All of the children did get sunburned.
>
> Now our skin is peeling because we were sunburned. Mine has patches on it. But it doesn't hurt.
>
> When is your birthday, Mommy? Love, Cathy

My parents knew that, having chosen to become part-time parents, they were missing out on the day-to-day events in our lives. They could not swim with us, put salve on our sunburns, or admire an essay we had written. They could not guide us, except from afar.

Nor could they help us when we were afraid. The school was no less safe than other places in New Guinea, but our parents were not with us. Every few weeks, an earthquake occurred, and we all ran outdoors. One boy, reminiscing on the 40th anniversary of the school, described an earthquake where he was unable to get out of the swaying top bunk in which he had been sleeping: he felt "totally abandoned." An ongoing concern for us girls especially was being watched at night through our dormitory room windows. Sometimes we actually saw New Guinean men; at other times, I am sure we imagined them. When we were in our rooms at night, we were always conscious that someone might be watching us, trying to look through a gap between the curtains. Sometimes we would pretend that we weren't sick so that we would not have to stay in the "sick rooms," two rooms in back of the matrons' quarters that were isolated from the rest of the school, their windows close to the ground, therefore making us more vulnerable to unknown eyes.

Unanticipated events frightened us. The kunai grass (tall, sharp grass that grows throughout the Highlands) on the hillside around the school caught fire during our first year. A lightning spark might have started it, or a New Guinean burning off grass to prepare his garden. The adults put out the fire, pouring buckets of water on it and beating it with sticks and blankets. We were not in any great danger, but the fire could easily have engulfed the entire school. I felt helpless, at the mercy of the fire and uncertain whether the adults would defeat it. Another time, when I was about ten-years old, I was sitting in the second of three stalls in the bathroom. I looked up at the partition on my left to see a six-foot python draped peacefully over it. "Snake!" I screamed, running out of the stall, stumbling over my pants, which were still down at my ankles. Even though I knew that pythons were interested in rats and chickens, not humans, I was still terrified. One of the

New Guinean cooks removed the snake later, using two sticks, but I had only my ten-year-old self to help me stop trembling.

Our parents learned about such incidents from our letters. By the time their alarmed letters reached us, expressing concern, several weeks had elapsed. Whatever feelings we had had about the event were gone as well. I fell into a pattern, which I continued to refine through high school and college, of telling my parents about my concerns only to make them feel needed and useful. I knew that the problem would have long vanished before I heard back from them. Overall, I could see that I was growing into the "good, useful" woman Mother had urged me to become, self-contained and considerate of others.

IT WAS CRITICAL for all of us—staff, students, and parents—that KLS feel like a home. The staff of the school put considerable energy into making this happen.

Birthdays were an important ritual. Mother visited if she could. We followed the German custom of opening gifts before breakfast. The night before, everyone drew cards and colored them, the ideas for the cards deriving from coloring books. It was cheating to trace over a book's drawing but worth admiring if we copied the original well and then colored it in. The European cook always baked and decorated a cake, and one of the matrons put any gifts from parents and all the cards around the cake on a small table in the main recreation room. We sang "Happy Birthday" and the birthday boy or girl opened the gifts and cards. At afternoon recess, we ate the cake with ice cream made with powdered milk, its thin sweetness not tasting at all bad if you had nothing with which to compare it.

My favorite celebration each year was Easter. The cook made Easter "eggs" about six-inches long and four-inches in diameter for each of us, a trick she performed by making a heavy chocolate dough, then using a form to shape the egg halves into a shell half-an-inch thick. Next, she frosted the halves together and decorated them. These masterpieces were placed in large, flat soup bowls, along with candy and decorated hard-boiled eggs. The staff arose before dawn on Easter morning to hide the bowls all over the school grounds. The bowls for the younger children were hidden close to the dormitories and school, while those for the older children might be in a bed of long grass, or behind one of the big posts holding up the dining room and kitchen—or almost anywhere. It was important to find our bowls as quickly as possible—to show how clever we were but also to keep ants from finding the sweets first. We made the treats last as long as possible, especially those enormous chocolate eggs. The excitement of the hunt and the taste of the sweets delighted me each year.

I was in college before I understood that what really mattered was the time, thought, and affection that the staff had baked into the chocolate eggs and then put into hiding the bowls. I don't think Mother and Dad sent us anything for Easter. They knew we thought our celebrations were perfect. We didn't expect anything more.

We were also required to participate in events outside the school, a demand that helped me to understand who I was and where I was, beyond being part of a missionary family in a land that I knew I could never call my own. I was American, but I also liked feeling connected to Australia and, through that country, to the entire British Commonwealth. My second year at Wau, all the school children in the area, along with hundreds of adults, both European and New Guinean, gathered in the large sports oval in Wau to mark the coronation of Queen Elizabeth II. Several years later, the Duke of Edinburgh visited New Guinea, and we traveled 30 miles to the gold and lumber town of Bulolo to cheer him, waving our Union Jacks as he walked almost within touching distance.

When we competed in cricket, softball, or swimming against teams from the government school in Wau, we saw that we measured up to them, sometimes even winning. Once a year, the Wau District Show was held on the sports oval. Much like a state fair, it was an occasion for sporting events and for any European children within a 30-mile radius to display their art or handiwork. I always entered the embroidery and drawing competitions. My stitches on little doilies were never tiny enough or uniform enough to win me better than a third prize, although for a hand-drawn map of Africa, about twelve inches by twenty inches, I won my only first prize. I won it, I thought, because of how well I shaded in the ocean around the entire continent and because of the wild animals I drew at strategic places on the map and then colored in.

We were at Katharine Lehmann School to get an education, of course. I quickly saw that I could be one of the pets of my first teacher, Miss Miller, from Des Moines, Iowa, if I did all my work and behaved in class. Her idea of how to motivate us would not go far today. She cut out pictures of big American cars, which none of us had ever seen, and pasted them on cardboard, each car bearing a student's name. She arranged them in the form of a racetrack across the front blackboard, so that the students who were doing the best work were out in front. I was always there. Miss Miller also freely expressed her political opinions. There was a race for president going on in America, she told us, writing "Eisenhower" and "Stevenson" on the blackboard. "We want Eisenhower to win," she said. In fourth grade, I received my first and only formal education in American history. Our textbook was red, and I remember studying Leif Ericsson, John Cabot, Christopher Columbus, the Virginia colony, and the Pilgrims.

Because many of the students and some of the staff were German, the Australian and American children heard the language daily and felt comfortable with it. Our classes in German were taught from a book printed in old-fashioned, black-letter Gothic type that was so difficult to read. The best part was singing German folk songs, which we did over and over.

Most of us also became serious stamp collectors. Particularly during the year when Dad was Acting Superintendent of the mission, people wrote him from all over the world, and he would send us the stamps. Trinidad, Tobago, Togo, and Tunisia were unknown to me except through these stamps, and I was curious about where they were and what they were like. Collecting stamps was also a way to learn more about New Guinea. The current stamps from the independent country of Papua New Guinea are brightly colored, featuring shells, butterflies, birds, flowers, and New Guineans in traditional dress, but I prefer the older stamps: understated drawings in a single color of a beautifully carved shield and arrows, a handmade catamaran, or a decorated *haus tambaran* (spirit house).

Our Wau education must have had some substance, even though I can describe it in only fragmentary ways now. Several years ago, one of the teachers at the high school we attended in Australia told me that the presence of New Guinea missionary children at their high school raised its standards because we were taught to excel inside and outside the classroom. Music and art were essential, not just add-ons if you had time. Another teacher agreed, saying that our parents were well-educated and had the "initiative and strength of character" to do mission work under difficult circumstances. Our parents passed on these qualities to us (he felt), and we brought them to the school.

No DOUBT, we received the school learning that KLS was supposed to give us. I have no idea, however, whether the staff or our parents thought about guiding our emotional development. How to have relationships with other people cannot so easily be taught in groups when significant adults are available only irregularly. But we often developed close and loving relationships with other children. At least to some degree, the closeness that we had with one another replaced the closeness we might otherwise have had with our parents, and it probably helped convince us that we really did not need our parents. We made our own world with its own values. When I first read William Golding's *Lord of the Flies* in college, I instantly accepted its credibility: I had come from just such a world. True, we were not marooned on an island, were not petrified by a beast (real or imaginary), and did not kill each other. But we did create our own order that the adults seemed unable to control. At its best, it resulted in long-lasting friendships; at its worst, it seemed to confirm that, left to their own devices, humans were callous and harshly competitive.

The relationships among us were complicated. For starters, the 40 or so of us represented four nationalities—American, Australian, Canadian, and German—one of which had recently been vanquished in war by the other three. None of us could remember the war, but our parents lived with its effects, whether they were forced out of New Guinea because of it, knew people who had been killed, had been interned in Australia, or had supported Hitler. When David and I arrived, the older children were Germans, so they had the upper hand. It was no small satisfaction to me that, by the time I left, the balance of power had shifted decisively toward the Americans. Often, how you were treated—whether you were locked in an outdoor toilet at night or had your bed shortsheeted—depended on which nationality happened to be the most powerful at a particular time. The matrons punished the guilty parties if they found out, but they didn't always know, and the older children got away with a great deal.

On the outside, I was hotly pro-American. Inside, I was not so sure, not even sure what it meant to be American. When my family went "home" on furlough in 1954-55, or when we ourselves met missionaries just arriving from the United States with their children, we could see that we were not typical Americans. Americans had won the war, and now they had more and bigger things, but beyond that, I could not see much advantage to being American. They talked loudly, did not pronounce their words carefully, and chewed gum whenever they wanted to. When the ocean liner on which we were crossing the Pacific stopped in Hawaii, I, at the age of eight, was shocked to see the customs officer chewing gum. Americans were also fussy eaters. They were upset when Australian "tomato sauce" did not taste like American ketchup. Peanut butter in both countries was different, and the Americans thought the Australian kind was inferior. If Americans thought Australia and New Guinea should be just like America, I wondered why they bothered to come to either country.

Our nationalities were fixed, but almost nothing else was in our relationships. We were intensely competitive—more so, I believe, than children usually are. Perhaps being the best in something was a way to cement our identity. At birthdays, we always compared the cards we had drawn. We judged the presents as well. Was Mary Esther's new dress from the Montgomery Ward catalogue prettier than any of ours? Who had stamps from the strangest place? We even compared our parents. A few fathers who visited were gentle and at ease with their children. Sometimes, I allowed myself to wonder what it would be like to have such a father. As a somewhat remote and strict person, Dad came in about average, although he got extra points for status the year he was Acting Superintendent of the mission. Mother, however, was one of the best. She was pretty, dressed more stylishly than many missionary wives, baked good cookies, and was warm and friendly. I benefited from her acknowledged superiority, but I wanted more from her even though I knew that I had to be satisfied with less.

We competed most overtly in three areas: sports, music, and art. Only a few children were good at all three. Even if you were deficient, as I was in sports and art, you could gain credit in other ways. My credits were being tall, nice, and a good student. The skills we valued also served as passports for two biracial girls (their mothers, New Guinean; their fathers, Australian) who entered KLS in 1953. Barbara and Alice both earned their acceptance many times over by how fast they could run and swim, how quickly they learned to play the piano, and how well they could draw. Their young mothers, abandoned by the girls' fathers, thought their daughters would be better off if they were reared "white," that is, if they could receive the superior education available in New Guinea to white children. Separately, the mothers approached an American missionary family about "adopting" their daughters.

Coincidentally, the Lutheran Mission had begun to discuss whether it could help these "half-castes" (as they were then called) who would never fit into the home villages of their mothers. Even with the mission's agreeing to help children such as Barbara and Alice, the girls were admitted only after a discussion among all the parents whose children attended the school. A minority of parents did not see the irony in the situation. They were in New Guinea to save souls, but the souls they saved were inferior to theirs. Was it appropriate to educate children who were half New Guinean in the same way that European children were educated, thus implying there was no difference between them? I do not recall that we ever discussed the matter explicitly. But we knew that the races were separated, and we took the separation for granted. Barbara and Alice would have to prove that they too could be white. Somehow, we sensed that our skepticism should not be obvious.

Our relationships with the staff were complicated in different ways. Some of the boys on the island in *Lord of the Flies* long for "grown ups" to come along and fix everything. We might have done so too if we had none at all, but we had just enough of them that they intruded more than we wanted. The school was ours, we thought, much more than the staff's, many of whom had not been there as long as the older children.

Some of what we did was harmless, although it showed the staff the control we had if we chose to exercise it. Most of the students lived on remote stations, accessible only by air, and every few weeks, a mission plane would fly into Wau, usually carrying parents or other visitors. We became expert at identifying a plane by the sound of its engine. We could tell a Cessna 172 from a Cessna 180, a DeHaviland Beaver from a DeHaviland Otter. And nobody would mistake a noisy DC-3 for any of those others. When we heard a plane coming and were sure that it was a mission plane, we ran outside to wave, whether we were at a meal, in school, or resting quietly after lunch. The pilots, who were our heroes, obliged us by "buzzing" us, flying over us low enough so that we could sometimes tell who the pilot was and whom he was carrying. On the school's 40th anniversary, one teacher remembered, "You could do what you liked; the children just raced out."

We knew the adults were supposed to be in charge, and we also knew we needed them. At the same time, there were not enough of them to monitor our behavior very closely, and most of them were young and single. We felt strong enough in our own self-involved world to take advantage of their lack of experience with being parents. If we sensed any weakness— which we usually found in the young, single women—we set out to bring them down. By paying no attention to a request, we would make them ask us two or three times to do something. The more brazen of us, I included, were cheeky, answering back. At night, when we were supposed to be in bed, both boys and girls would sneak down the porches to each others' dorms, an act that required us to cross directly in front of the matrons' windows. Our ingenuity at breaking rules easily surpassed their resolve not to be rattled. If we saw them cry, we knew we had won. Some of them remained only a year or less. We were not murderously ruthless in the way that Jack and his group of hunters are in *Lord of the Flies*, but we lived by our own rules much more than was good for us.

David must have been ten or eleven when he pushed one of the matrons into the deep end of the town swimming pool, knowing that she could barely swim. She was quickly rescued. The rest of us were shocked, but we also knew that he would somehow get away with what he had done. We thought this matron, who was young and single, had a crush on David (strange to say of a pre-adolescent boy and a woman in her twenties, but so we thought and said to one another). We viewed his pushing her into the pool as a kind of flirting, taking a liberty with her that was far beyond the bounds of an appropriate adult-child relationship.

I was daring in different ways. The April that I was 11, we girls learned that new curtains were being hung in the two rooms of the boys' dorm. As one of the Big Girls who had seniority over almost everyone else at the school, including the adults, I knew that the curtains in the Big Girls' room were older than any the boys had. My friend Roswitha remembers fingering the faded limpness of a curtain and how easily it tore. She and I and Erika, another of the older girls, soon devised a strategy for getting new curtains. We slipped the threadbare curtains off their rods and tore each of them into strips a few inches wide. To announce what we had done, we wove the strips from one shredded curtain into a giant braid, and then we again hung it up on its rod.

Within a few hours, a matron on a routine walk through the dorm rooms noticed the novel curtains. A visiting mother remembers seeing the matron shortly thereafter, gasping as she spoke: "You can't imagine what the Big Girls did today!" The staff met that evening to decide our punishments, intending to hurt us in the worst ways they knew how: we could not go shopping in town nor could we swim in the big town pool for the rest of the term. Since we were only half-way through the five-month term, the punishment might as well have been for eternity. And there was a clincher: when we went home on vacation in July, we had to tell our parents. I waited until the last night of vacation to do so, and they had no idea how to respond. This was their Cathy, whom they had sent away to become a "good and useful" young woman? "You what?" "But why?" They did not add their own punishment. We were not given new curtains until the following year, which meant months of crouching between beds or turning off lights whenever we dressed or undressed.

As I look back on the outcomes of the curtain incident, I see that it contradicts two images I have carried with me about life at KLS. First, if the staff wanted to, they did indeed have the upper hand. And second, whether or not they were aware of it, they favored the boys over the girls, at least in extreme situations. We girls had a long and harsh punishment for destroying our rotted curtains. Was David ever punished for pushing the matron into the pool or crossing the flooded Bulolo River without permission? Not to my knowledge.

I CAN WRITE LESS CLEARLY of life with my "real" family than I can of life at KLS. The constant separations stifled us, preventing what we could have made of ourselves as a family. I still grieve for not having lived with my family for any significant length of time after the age of six. I have come to know my five living siblings only as adults. Angela, three years younger than I, was at Wau for my last two years, but I thought of her then mainly as an irritable bother. Had we lived at home, I would have had a chance at a better relationship with both her and David.

At Wau (and later in high school and college), David was a perpetual frustration to me. Tall for his age, with a natural magnetism and a handsome face, this brother did not need me. I could, however, make him talk to me by exchanging letters from our parents, or returning the canvas shoes that I cleaned for him, hoping he would pay more attention to me. David was killed in a plane crash when he was 30-years old, just as we were beginning to be able to relate as adults, and so I'll never know whether his treatment of me was intentional or simply an oversight. I never told him in a clear, direct way that I wanted to spend more time with him, and by that omission, I denied myself a family connection that could have been invaluable.

The relationships David and I spoke least about were those with our parents. I did my best to follow the script: I was to show that I was developing the traits necessary to be a "good, useful" young woman, and I was. I was polite, I did well in school, and I was learning to sew and to play the piano and organ. I must have been in trouble for more incidents than tearing the curtains, but I don't remember them. There were not many. It never occurred to me, as it does now, to view my part in tearing the curtains as a healthy attempt by a young girl to express herself, to gain equal treatment with the boys.

Just as I did not play my part consistently, neither did my parents. It hurt that I couldn't rely on them as completely as I wanted to. Dad wrote every week, but Mother did not. They visited us once a year, Mother more often if she could. But because of his work, Dad could visit for only part of a vacation or was gone for part of the time that we were at home, thereby intensifying the already great difficulty of relating to him as our father. Yet, packages from home showed us that our parents were thinking of us. We counted on the cookies, the candy, the tins of Milo and of Nestle's powdered milk, both of which we mixed together in a mush. They also sent cans of sweetened condensed milk, which we ate straight out of the can with a spoon.

On our ritual visits home, our parents treated us like little princes and princesses. We walked into a gleamingly clean house with our favorite cookies waiting for us. Mother planned picnics. Once, Dad took an uncharacteristic amount of time away from his work to climb a mountain with us older children and to spend the night in a New Guinean hut. There we huddled around the fire, first eating canned beef and rice, and then taking turns reading *Robinson Crusoe* out loud. They wanted our time together to be special, and I wanted to please them. But how could we have relaxed into the normal ebb and flow of family life, especially during the July vacation, which was so short? What could they have taught us that mattered?

In retrospect, I see that I protected myself by not expecting very much from my parents, and that that is what I received. For their part, they accepted their diminished role as the price they had to pay for the choices they had made. They could see that they had only some of our loyalty and could influence us only so much. We were never home long before we began talking about how much we missed our friends and the fun we had together. Nor could they say much about their feelings about continually sending us away. In later years when Mother and I talked about boarding school, she told me that she often cried herself to sleep at night. She cried again in the re-telling without explaining herself. I did not understand her tears, nor did I understand what I could have said or done in reply. It seemed best not to bring up the topic. I could never bring myself to say to her, "If you really loved us, how could you keep sending us away?" A part of me is dead, shriveled up from so many years of refusing to acknowledge the effects of my parents' actions.

Mother wrote about one farewell for an article in the November 1953 *Lutheran Missionary*. I was seven, and David had just turned nine. My parents were living at a new station in the Highlands, one that did not yet have an airstrip. David and I had to walk six miles to the nearest airstrip to meet the mission plane that would return us to school after our mid-year break. Mother and our two younger siblings, Angela and Jonathan, walked halfway with us, until we reached a river that we had to ford. Then they turned back toward home, saying goodbye at the water's edge. Dad, David, and I continued on to the airstrip, the New Guineans who carried our two suitcases accompanying us, as was customary for Europeans who were traveling by foot or horseback. In the article, Mother describes the walk and the river in great detail, but her feelings are only obliquely present. She knows the exact number of days, 17, that we were home. When she and the children returned home, Angela began trying out the organ. Mother writes: "Jonathan [age three] ran quickly into the room, but stopped dead. His voice was flat. 'Oh, I thought it was Cathy playing.'"

On that return to Wau, I probably felt the way I always felt when we went back to KLS, eager to see my friends and missing the familiar routine. When I was 30, my then husband and I adopted a six-year-old boy, small and vulnerable. I saw how much he still needed me to hold him on my lap. How much like him I must have been! And yet I have no memory now of any of those feelings in Wau. The most difficult part of writing this book has not been doing the research or grappling with my fading memory. It has been trying to say how I feel about what happened to me, about what it was like to be the chalk at the bottom of the box.

II: St. Peter's Lutheran College

I LEFT KATHARINE LEHMANN SCHOOL in December 1958, having completed seventh grade. I could have stayed one more year, but my friends and I believed that we were ready for something bigger: St. Peter's Lutheran College (actually a high school) in Brisbane, the capitol of Queensland, the Australian state closest to New Guinea. St. Peter's was a place in which I prospered, once I learned my way around, as I had at KLS. St. Peter's, now 1800 students, is considered one of the best private schools in Australia. Children can attend for the entire twelve years of schooling it offers, and they arrive from everywhere in Southeast Asia and China, as well as from Australia and Papua New Guinea. When I entered in 1959, it was a school of about 400 students for grades seven through twelve, drawing children almost entirely from Lutheran homes in the Brisbane area.

Unlike almost all private and public high schools in Australia at that time, St. Peter's was coeducational. Perhaps its Lutheran founders made it coeducational so that they would have to build only one school, not two, since there was already a Lutheran high school in South Australia, designed along the same lines. Carson Dron, a former teacher and head-master, acknowledges that St. Peter's then was more accurately described as "coinstructional." Boys and girls were strictly separated. Our dormitories were far apart, and there were no social occasions, such as dances, when we could mingle. There was no way to continue the easy friendships we had with boys at Wau. We developed crushes on boys, but could never get past the infatuation. Because David was my brother, I was allowed to talk with him for 15 minutes in the morning and 15 minutes in the evening, in one specified place outside the dining hall. One girl who sneaked out of her dorm in her shorty pajamas to meet a boy was promptly expelled.

Every new student had to learn all the rules before anything else, most of them enforced by sub-prefects and prefects, who were Sub-Senior (eleventh grade) and Senior (twelfth grade) students selected for their good character. Any *Lord of the Flies* impulses remaining from Wau had no chance for being expressed, in part because some prefects and sub-prefects used their positions to harass younger children, their "good character" notwithstanding. Most of the time, boys and girls had been equals at Wau. Here, we girls were equal academically but not socially. Our clothes alone reminded us of our regimented lives. Our uniforms were maroon tunics having no waist but with three box pleats, front and back. Only a belt held the pleats in place. We had to learn how to sit down without crushing the pleats, which required ironing each day, regardless of how carefully we sat on them. The boys in their shirts and shorts or slacks moved much more easily. Those of us from New Guinea had to become accustomed to wearing "hard" shoes all day long. Going barefoot, a freedom we had taken for granted, was gone forever.

When we played basketball or ran track, the girls' uniform was the same as for classes except that the tunic ended about six inches above our knees, and we wore maroon bloomers underneath it. Girls in the United States may not have had to put up with such quaint uniforms, but at least in Australia we could participate in athletics to a far greater degree than was possible in the States before Title IX was enacted. We wore "street dresses" on Saturday mornings to breakfast and lunch. Sundays, our only other opportunity for individual expression in dress, we wore white dresses. My confirmation picture shows me in a white dress that Mother made for me, scallops all around its hem. The crinoline half-slip from my Aunt Genevieve made me happy by allowing my skirt to billow out. *(See photo on p. 145.)*

We lined up by grade to enter the dining room for our meals, and then we sat in assigned seats, boys on one side of the dining hall, girls on the other. A prefect or sub-prefect sat at each table, as did any teachers who happened to be eating in the dining room. All of us ate the same food on the same days all year round, and because there was usually not enough of it, we filled up on bread, jam, peanut butter, and honey. Fried rice was served on Thursday night; bologna sandwiches, salad, and blancmange (a white or pink pudding) were served Saturday at noon, and so on. Several years after I left, students held a food strike. My brother Paul, a student at the time, says that boycotting a single meal was sufficient to end the strike. The food improved immediately thereafter.

The excessive emphasis on rules is apparent in the way that girls were required to eat bread, an example that also displays the double standard that confronted girls at St. Peter's. The procedure was this: girls had to place a piece of bread on our bread-and-butter plate, cut it in half, and put one half off to the side. We were to cut the remaining half in half again, again placing one of the halves on the original half. We were then to cut in half again the remaining one-quarter piece of the original, separating the two new halves. Finally, we were free to take up the one-eighth piece resting in the middle of the plate, butter it, and add jam before eating it. There was one more rule. The one-eighth piece of bread had to be eaten in two bites, slowly and thoughtfully. The boys, on the other hand, had only to cut their bread into quarters that they could eat as they wished.

We girls complained about rules such as these, but I don't remember disobeying them in any significant way. The spirit I showed in tearing curtains for equality was now completely redirected to excelling in conventional ways—academically and musically. Although I was never a good athlete, I wanted to be physically active, and the approach to sports at St. Peter's included a place for people like me.

MOST OF OUR TEACHERS were well-educated and loved to teach their subjects. Electives were not offered. Through my three years at St. Peter's, I had the same schedule: English, German, Latin, History, Mathematics,

Chemistry, Physics, and Religion. Music—choir and piano—was an extra and not for credit, even though taken seriously, with choir competitions and state examinations in piano performance and theory. All the teaching in our academic courses was directed toward passing the Junior (tenth grade) and Senior (twelfth grade) examinations, which the state administered.

Mr. Lohe, the headmaster, taught German and European History. Mr. Schneider taught Latin and Mathematics. Mr. Dron taught Chemistry, and Miss Bryant, English. Whatever the subject, each teacher stressed memorization and careful attention to the text. I learned that there were 12 reasons for World War I to erupt. I can still recite the German prepositions that take the dative case. The Shakespeare play for the Junior exam the year I sat for it was *Julius Caesar*. Fifteen years later, when I had a weekend's notice that I would be substituting for an ill professor who could not teach his college-level Shakespeare class, I could walk in to teach that Monday morning class with some confidence because, although Shakespeare was not my special field, *Julius Caesar* was the day's topic. I still felt familiar with it because of what Miss Bryant had taught me.

The teachers cared about us as people. Most of them had duties outside the classroom, probably without extra remuneration. That was just the way things were. Mr. Dron coached football. Miss Eckert, who had taught us Scripture in eighth grade, and Miss Heck, my piano teacher, collected the girls' swim team at 5:30 in the morning and drove us to the pool in the nearby suburb of Toowong so that we could train. Some of the staff made a point of paying special attention to the children from New Guinea, who were so far from home. David and I were fortunate that Miss Eckert took us under her wing. David, who had come down a year earlier than I, had already met her parents and brothers and sisters. To me, she gave a white dress to wear on Sundays, its deliciously full skirt forming a complete circle that whirled as I moved. I owe to her generosity my memory of hearing Daniel Barenboim, then a 16-year-old prodigy, play with the Queensland Symphony Orchestra.

When later I spent one semester in an American high school and then entered St. Olaf College, it was natural to compare myself with American students. They seemed much freer and more creative in their work than I. They had also acquired practical skills such as typing, which you could learn at St. Peter's only if you were on the non-academic track. On the other hand, I had been required to read and write a great deal, and studying came easily. The state exams in Queensland for high school students were six or eight hours long (divided in half over the course of a day), depending on the subject matter. The only way to do well was to begin studying three months in advance, pacing out the memorizing of huge amounts of material.

In spite of some silly rules and dowdy uniforms, St. Peter's was a good place for me. I fit in. There were always other missionaries' children, and almost everyone was Lutheran. The pain that I remember—the same thin, small feeling of being on that plane in Lae when I was six—arose during vacations, the problem that missionary kids could never avoid. The school year was divided into three terms, with two short vacations of two weeks each and then one of six weeks over Christmas. Recognizing that there were no high schools in New Guinea, the Australian government paid for our flights home, but only for the longer vacation. Nor could parents afford to fly down during the year to see us.

We dreaded the short vacations because, with the buildings closed and no meals served, yet again we had to find some place to stay, usually with people we did not know. Carson Dron remembers us as "cast adrift." Our parents couldn't help us because they didn't know anyone in the area. School authorities urged families in Lutheran churches to take us in, and some did. David came to know Miss Eckert's family when he asked whether he could spend a vacation there rather than at another home where he felt that he was expected to work unreasonably hard. I too spent one vacation with a farm couple who seemed interested in me mainly for the work I could do for them. My friend Carolyn twice invited me to her parents' ranch in western Queensland. A young kangaroo lived in the house with them, and I quickly learned to stay away from him to avoid a kick from his long back legs. My friend Barbara from Wau once came along with me. Neither Barbara nor I had ever been taught how to ride, but Carolyn could ride horses bareback. Barbara remembers one of our rides:

> As we were heading home with the horses, they suddenly took off with a gallop. Both Cathy and I, inexperienced riders, hung on for dear life, while they made their way through the undergrowth. As the horses rounded the bend, Cathy could feel the saddle slipping. The next second, she landed smack into the middle of the slimy green duck pond. Lilies and roots draped from her face as she scrambled quickly out of the mire.

Barbara could not help laughing, and I hope that I laughed too. My most searing memory of that vacation is of being in a place where I did not have the skills that those who were otherwise my peers took for granted.

Vacations were often a reminder of another set of skills I had had no chance to develop once I left Wau: the ability to relate easily to boys. Small-town, Saturday evening dances were a feature of farm life in the Queensland countryside. I always packed a pretty dress with a full skirt for these occasions, always hoping to have fun. The problems began with my dresses, which were never quite right. Usually, an American relative had sent them, and the styles didn't fit what everyone else was wearing. At the dance, all the girls sat along a wall, waiting to be asked to dance by a boy. Sometimes, a boy in my host family would ask me; otherwise, I would sit the entire evening. At the same time that I desperately wanted to be asked to dance, I also dreaded the experience. I could count on being taller than my partner. Worst of all, I didn't know how to dance. I could never get the feel of following my partner, whether I was relaxing into a waltz, or swinging into a polka.

Had I been capable of reflecting on my experiences as a teenager in Australia, I would have seen that my academic development was far ahead of my social development. My missionary children friends and I had done well in the contained life of KLS. When we then had to function on our own in a larger, more complex setting, the intellectual parts of us transferred much more easily than did the social.

RECENTLY, I DISCOVERED the category of "Adult Third Culture Kid," and that I am one of them. It means that I lived with my parents in a culture different from that of their country of origin, and that I do not feel completely at home in either one. It means that I can never easily tell people where I am from let alone tell myself where I belong. It means that I have both the advantages and the ambivalences of being forever in-between. Ordinarily, I dislike labels. They confine people in boxes and limit the way we see one another, but this label I don't mind. It broadens my view of myself. Knowing that hundreds of people have grown up in cultures other than their own, in a great variety of circumstances, and that their adult lives exhibit similar patterns, I can see connections with my own experiences. I feel typical rather than alien. I feel freer to step back and acknowledge the advantages of my upbringing, and I can also be honest about its shortcomings. So doing, I find a peace that is more meaningful than being told that my parents were doing God's will.

The most obviously distressing aspects of being a Third Culture Kid may occur in the borderland experiences as one crosses from one culture into another. The half-year I spent as a high school senior in Northfield, Minnesota, in 1963, is a case in point. At the end of 1962, the family was due for our second furlough. It made sense to my parents to leave New Guinea in December, at the end of the Australian school year, but for me, the timing could not have been worse. I had completed eleventh grade at St. Peter's, but by leaving then, I could not sit for Queensland's Senior

Examinations. I did not really miss all that studying, but I did miss the sense of closure and the pride I would have from successfully completing a rigorous program of study. I also lost my chance to be Girls' Head Prefect, as David had been for the boys. Most of all, I was leaving my friends, almost all of whom I knew I would never see again.

And so, in the dead of winter, I accompanied my family to Northfield. Some of Mother's family were close by, we had the use of a missionary furlough house rent-free, and David could begin his studies at St. Olaf College in the same town. To my parents, looking at the big picture, they had made a good choice. For me, having lost my secure place at St. Peter's, I had nothing to hold onto. I could have persuaded my parents to allow me to remain in Australia, as did some American missionary children, but that would have meant missing my family's entire year of furlough as well as the chance to begin college on the same schedule as other American freshmen. Instead, I came to the States with my family to find out whether I wanted to be an American. I wanted to give a chance to the country of my birth and my parents' by attending college there.

I was ill-prepared for this project of discovery, coming as it did when I was entering young adulthood. My parents were with me that year in Minnesota, but I had to share them with six other children. And, as always, Dad was often away on speaking engagements for the church. I was keenly aware of all the ways I did not fit. I was somewhat overweight from eating all that bread at St. Peter's. Having worn uniforms for four years, I had no sense of how to dress and few appropriate clothes.

Neither did our parents have the money to buy clothes that might have made a difference. Dad had found a good buy on parkas made in Hong Kong, and so all seven of us—four boys and three girls, ranging between the ages of four and 18 years—wore the same style of parka: its collar wide-open, and no lining where the two front halves of the jacket overlapped. I remember wearing a cotton dress that I had made: my legs were bare, I had no gloves, no hat, and nothing but socks and tennis shoes on my feet. Only that parka protected me from the icy Minnesota winds. They blew right through. I did not know how to become and stay warm, and thought I might never again be comfortable. I'm sure my parents told us to dress as warmly as we could. The problem was, wearing so many clothes didn't feel good. We preferred to shiver.

I graduated from high school that spring, having met a social sciences requirement designed as a tenth-grade course. One unit was about preparing an income tax return, and a certain form asked for my social security number. Not having one and not knowing what social security numbers looked like, I scribbled a random line of numbers—say, 409310. The teacher, passing by, looked over my shoulder and spoke loudly: "What, you don't know what a social security number is?" All the students could hear him. I knew I had much to offer, but in that class, to that teacher, I was stupid. He may not have known that I had just arrived in the United States. I would never have drawn attention to myself by asking for help on something that everyone else knew. I just wanted to fit in.

III. St. Olaf College

My four years at St. Olaf College were easier. When I was a sophomore, I was finally able to walk on icy sidewalks without slipping and falling down. My courses built well on the work I had done at St. Peter's. They developed the skills I have always used as a professional: analysis, reflection, and deliberation with others about things that matter. I benefited academically from the attention professors were expected to give their students. Lowell Johnson, my advisor in the English Department, told me about a fellowship that would pay tuition and living expenses for a Master's degree. I applied, was awarded it, and thus had a much more focused and profitable beginning to my career than would have been the case had I proceeded without direction.

The required religion courses enabled my faith to develop even as I was growing intellectually. What professors taught us in religion classes made sense. Stories like Noah's ark or Jonah in the belly of a whale were "myths." That didn't mean they were false, as one meaning of "myth" implies. They were figuratively true: studying them, I could learn about human nature and God's continuing love for us, regardless of our actions. I could also recite arguments for and against the existence of God and had a context in which to put the "God is Dead" movement of the late 1960s. I admitted to myself that having my parents half-way around the world was sometimes an advantage. I didn't have to think about how I would tell my father that I no longer believed the world was created in seven days.

As I remember it, my experience of the spiritual, of a presence infinitely larger than myself, came primarily from music. I wasn't in the First Choir, the one that toured internationally and put St. Olaf on the musical map. In the Second Choir, then led by Kenneth Jennings, we sang the large pieces that possess the heft and beauty to carry one through a lifetime of worship. Bach's *Mass in B-Minor* and *Saint John Passion* were my favorites. When we finished singing them, I wanted more than anything to sing them again. They filled my world.

My social life at St. Olaf was an easy transition from St. Peter's. The people who made the rules at both places might as well have been talking to each other. Freshman girls had to be in their dorms by 9:00 p.m. on weekdays. Boys were never allowed past the lounge in a girls' dorm except on special open-house days. Girls had to wear skirts to all meals, classes, and the library, except for Saturday mornings, when they could wear slacks. St. Olaf administrators were proud that weekday chapel was well-attended although voluntary; but with no classes scheduled and the library closed during chapel time, there wasn't much else to do. On the whole, I felt comfortable. I didn't have much in common with the upper-middle-class students from Minneapolis and St. Paul, but David was there, and there were two other missionary daughters in my class. I rarely had to explain myself, in the way that I have frequently had to as an adult.

The social handicaps I brought with me from St. Peter's had harsh consequences at St. Olaf. My first experience with a boy at the beginning of my freshman year set the tone for all my college years. Someone thought everyone should have a date for the first concert, so the dorm mothers (all widows of Lutheran pastors) lined up the boys and the girls according to height. Two hundred girls in line, shortest to tallest, and I was at the very end. Tom, my date, was a big football player. We hardly spoke the entire evening and never again after that. I had one other date during those four years. A young couple arranged for me to go out with the pastor of the local Moravian church. Neither of us knew how to make small talk or to tell a good joke; we were incapable of beginning a relationship. I knew I had no chance to succeed at one of the unadvertised purposes of college—finding a life mate.

As best I could, I made up for not having a home or parents by developing a network of relationships that have continued to the present. While I was in school, I was often in professors' homes, taking care of their children. Being there meant I could also observe adult relationships besides that of my parents, something I'd seen little of. I spent Christmas at my cousin Rosanna's, Easter at Aunt Nancy's, and Thanksgiving at Aunt Margaret's. This pattern was comforting, and I learned I could count on it. My relatives always welcomed me; I liked having several places I could call home. Summers were more of a challenge because I needed both a job and a place in which to live. The first two summers, I worked as a mother's helper on the North Shore of Long Island, and the last two I worked as a Kelly Girl in Minneapolis while sharing an apartment with another missionary's daughter.

HAVING LIVED IN THE STATES NOW for more than 40 years, I see that growing up in the culture of a developing country was the greatest single benefit I received as a child. I know how to live simply, not taking up much space. I can walk into new situations and come to know people who are not like me. I can travel cheaply and love every part of it. At my first live butterfly exhibit in the United States, I saw quickly that almost all the butterflies were native to New Guinea, and I knew how fortunate I was to have lived in a country that was home to these beautiful and fragile creatures.

Even though I have memories of feeling superior to New Guineans, I must somehow also have learned to empathize with them. As an adult, when I visited Palestinian villages in the West Bank and pueblos in the mountains around Oaxaca, Mexico, I felt immediately at home, no matter that I could not speak the language. I sat easily with the people of these countries, eating their food and playing with their children. Growing up in New Guinea and going to boarding school made me confident that I could take on what has been the most challenging and rewarding experience of my adult life: for six years, I was the foster mother of three teenaged siblings who spent eight years on their own in a refugee camp in Kenya, having fled the civil war in their native Sudan.

I have been healed in simpler ways as well. A piece of chalk cannot regenerate itself, but humans may. My brother Paul, ten years younger than I, figured out how to help me. Since we were never in school together, we did not know each other well. But several years ago, I mentioned to him that I had rarely celebrated my birthday in high school or college. The date always fell during a vacation. Because I was usually with people I barely knew, I felt it unseemly to ask them to celebrate my birthday with me. Paul decided he and I would celebrate now. Each time I was with him in the next several years, he gave me a birthday party, complete with a cake or pie, candles, and a gift. We have at last made up for all the lost birthdays.

My parents went to their graves believing that the richness of our upbringing made up for all the loneliness of the separations. For most of my adult life, I too accepted this view, refusing to acknowledge the high cost of their choices. Once I began to read my parents' letters, I could look more openly at them and their decisions. To lay out what I have learned, I begin with my father and his passion for winning people to Christ.

Chapter Two
Won't you let me follow the desire of my heart?

In my father's preliminary application to the Board of Foreign Missions of the American Lutheran Church, he was asked, "What prompted you to volunteer for foreign mission work?" He answered, "An 'inner call,' which became so pronounced that I had to volunteer." He never once gave or needed a fuller answer than that, and I lived many years believing that there was no other answer. Now, I see that a look at his background, his personality, and the experience of his call does much to explain his response to it and other important decisions in his life, including those that affected the family that he and my mother created together.

Being a missionary to a foreign country in the 1930s was not so different from being a 19th-century immigrant from Europe in the American Midwest. Both were going to alien countries they knew little about, hoping to make new lives for themselves and their families. To be successful, they had to endure great physical hardship and even danger. The geographic isolation was compounded by the emotional isolation of being separated, perhaps permanently, from the families they had left behind. When my father went to New Guinea in 1937, he was living out a version of the 19th-century immigrant experience that was no longer available to young men and women in the Midwest. This experience was not good or bad in itself, but it must have seemed heroic to someone like Albert and therefore worth emulating for better or for worse.

My father's father, Fred, was five years old when his parents, Abraham and Gretje Frerichs, immigrated with their family to the United States in 1857 from Etzel in East Frisia, the northwestern-most part of Germany. His parents were in their 40s, and the youngest of the five children was not even two years old. Accounts in the *Frerichs Family History* as to why they immigrated all agree: economic conditions at the time left them little choice. In the mid-1840s, the potato crop failed, and then the rye crop. Starvation was widespread. As a younger son, Abraham could not inherit the family farm, and little other farmland was to be had. "America fever," as it was called, undoubtedly infected him. Letters home from earlier immigrants, which were widely reprinted, fed the condition by extolling the good land to be had at cheap prices in the Midwest.

The Frerichses were among an estimated 40,000 to 50,000 East Frisians who immigrated to the Midwest between 1845 and 1890. They sailed from the north German port of Bremerhafen for New Orleans. Their 11-week trip could not have been easy. They were probably on board a sailing vessel. If they traveled steerage (as their lack of money suggests), men, women, and children were all thrown together in the same over-crowded compartment. Often, there was not enough food, and water ran low. Only those who could afford cabin class would have been above deck with better food and the opportunity to move around more. From New Orleans, they traveled up the Mississippi, landing in Alton, Illinois, which, along with St. Louis, was a common destination for Germans entering the country at New Orleans. By 1865, Abraham could afford to buy 175 acres of land near Talmage, in the lush, rolling hills of southeast Nebraska.

In 1891, at the age of 39, Fred married 18-year-old Anna Fahrenholz. My father Albert was born in a farmhouse near Talmage, on June 8, 1910, the second youngest of 10 children, two of whom died soon after birth. His older brother George remembered that, as a child, Albert "was quite set in his ways. When he once started a thing he would generally stick to it until it was finished. He believed in living very conservative, doing trapping and raising poultry for spending money. The teachers thought a lot of him. He was very puncil [punctual?] in his work and going places and going to school. God seemed to have called him early in life for the work which he was to do."

Part of preparing for the call, as we heard the story growing up, was learning all the skills a farmer's son had to know. Albert could take care of a sick pig and teach a horse to pull a plow. He milked cows by hand, and he planted corn, rye, wheat, and soy beans. He could build things and fix them and make things work. In general, he knew what needed to be done, and how to do it, and he wasted no time in getting it done. He must have grown up feeling at ease in the out-of-doors and knowing that he could count on himself, qualities that would be essential to his success as a missionary in New Guinea. Missionary families typically lived in isolated areas and, at least in the second quarter of the 20th century, traveled usually either by walking or riding horses.

But life on the farm was a closed world; the community was suspicious of anyone who was not German. Until the 911 emergency system required that all roads be numbered, there were no signs on the straight gravel roads that mark out mile sections between Highways 67 and 2, which bisect the part of Otoe County in which Talmage is located. If you live there, you don't need signs. And if you lived there, you were expected to stay. Older children were needed at home to work. All seven of Albert's brothers and sisters settled on farms within seven miles of the original homestead. Reinhard Beckmann, a Lutheran pastor who attended college and seminary with Albert, commented that you could persuade your parents to let you go to high school and perhaps college "only if you wanted to be somebody." Even going off to high school increased the possibility of being "contaminated" by "English" culture, perhaps even leading to marrying "out."

There may have been some truth to this. Alone among his siblings,

Albert attended high school, riding a horse five miles each way to do so. He graduated with his class of nine in 1927, then signed on for a two-month course with the State Department of Education. The certificate allowed him, at the age of 17, to teach kindergarten through eighth grade. He taught for two years in District 88, the same one-room country school he had attended as a child.

Albert would have tried to teach well, and he wrote to Mabel Nigh Ranum, who had been his high school mathematics teacher and who later moved to Alaska, asking for help in how to teach mathematics. She clearly liked him, thinking he could go far ("Remember, you are still one of my boys even though you are now meeting the world face to face. . . . I am so proud of you from all the reports I have heard of you."). Her assistance was forthright while gently admonishing: "You did not take arithmetic reviews with me or you would have had it impressed thoroughly upon your mind that only practical problems, and those which most of the class will some day need to meet, should be given" *[8 March 1928]*. Albert wrote again, asking about the possibility of his going to Alaska. Mabel advised against it unless he wanted to teach there more than anywhere else. She suggested college instead: "You will regret it all your life if you do not. . . . I shall be so anxious to hear from you and know what you have decided" *[17 January 1929]*.

Albert loved the farm on which he was raised. He was proud of the many skills he learned there and thrived on physical work and being out-of-doors. He also always felt close to his brother George, who took over the family farm after their father died. And yet, by going to high school, Albert started down a path that took him inexorably away from the farm. It represented values and skills that mattered to him, but he also wanted more.

ALBERT SOMEHOW PERSUADED his parents to allow him to attend Wartburg College in Iowa, perhaps by telling them that he wanted to become a pastor. His father must never have fully approved of his son's decision. Fred's will, filed in 1933, only three years after Albert entered Wartburg, gave Albert's two older brothers the right to live on and work sections of the family farm while their mother was alive, and then to buy the land when she died. At her death, each of them would also receive $1,000. Albert would receive $500. The remainder of the estate was to be divided equally among all the children.

Wartburg was then a small, two-year college of the American Lutheran Church in northeastern Iowa, located 400 miles from home. Later in life, Albert recalled how homesick he felt. His weekly letters home, however, were usually matter-of-fact descriptions of the food the students ate, the cakes, cookies, and fruit his sisters sent him, the weather and crops, going to church, and news about his job. He rarely wrote about what he was learning, probably because, like many students, he felt that his family would not understand. He segmented his life from his parents just as I did later in boarding school and college. This typical letter from Albert's first month at Wartburg begins (mistakes in the original):

Hello everybody,

Another week past and I must write you a little news. This is Sunday Afternoon. We had dinner at about 1:00 o'clock but it was a good dinner. Watermelon, Fruit Salad, Beef, mashed potatoes, peas, Cranberry Jam and several other things as bread which we always have. We had fish for dinner Friday.

I went to church and Sunday school this Morning. They have two church services here, German at 9:30 and English at 11:00 O'clock. A thing that seemed very different to me at first was when everyone comes in church, he or she remains standing and says a little prayer to himself. Of course, they say it silently. All the other boys and I do the same when we come in church. There are lots of other things different, which I can tell you about when I get home. The Annual Mission Festival is to be celebrated here next Sunday.

I got a bouquet of flowers from Mary yesterday [his oldest sister, who was married and had left home]. They were surely fine. I put them in water and they look real good today. I did not expect anything like that, but it was surely fine of her to send them to me. I am writing her a letter thanking her for them.

And the letter went on from there *[29 September 1929]*.

A flash of Albert the pious Christian emerges in just one letter, about working in a garage on Sunday:

Well I worked Sunday all day from 8 O'clock in the morning to nine at night. I liked the job fine. I sold about seventy-five gallons of gasoline and about six quarts of oil. I ate dinner and supper at the bosses house. They treated me very good and I had two good meals there. But they had a dog in the house. I earned $2.25 (that isn't near enough) for working Saturday night and Sunday. But so much for that, I'm never [underlined five times] going to work on Sunday again. It has hurt me ever since Sunday to think I did it. I did just exactly what I learned not to do five days out of the week in Bible class. I don't care how much money or what kind of a job I can get, if I have to work on Sunday I'll not take the job. *[22 October 1929]*

Albert repeats the phrase three more times in the letter. Deviating from what he thought was right was deeply distressing to him. Sunday was the Lord's Day, a time for rest, and it should remain that way. As he taught us children, rules were important, not for their own sake, but because people needed guidance from outside themselves if they were going to grow and develop in a Godly way.

Neither Albert's letters nor the people who knew him are clear about when he decided to become a pastor. In the fall of 1931, he enrolled at Wartburg Theological Seminary in Dubuque, Iowa. The cost made it easy to attend: tuition was free, and room and board were $180/year. The beauty and isolation of the setting, on the bluffs above the Mississippi River, would have encouraged Albert in his seriousness. Here, finally, he could concentrate on the study that most mattered to him. The small student body of 68 men, taught by five faculty, meant that he could come to know the people there well. The sudden death six years later of Daniel Spier, one of his fellow students, became the occasion of Albert's call to be a missionary.

Albert first preached at the seminary during his second year. It's tempting to think that he selected his own text. The one used embodies the no-nonsense way a German farmer's son from Nebraska might approach winning souls. In Matthew 25:1-13, Jesus tells the story of 10 young women ("virgins," in Albert's King James Version) who went out with their lamps to meet the bridegroom. Five were wise and took extra oil with them. Five were foolish and did not. When they ran out of oil, the foolish virgins had to return to get some. While they were gone, the bridegroom came and left. The door to the marriage feast was shut, and they could not enter. As Albert knew and believed, the Christian must be ready at all times for what Jesus might ask of his followers. Those who are prepared receive everything; those who are not, receive nothing: there is no middle ground. Albert's intent, always, was to be a wise virgin, and he usually succeeded.

The seminary students also went to towns nearby to give services. Unlike his younger self writing from Wartburg College and mechanically covering trivial topics, the Albert who wrote the following fragment speaks in detail about something of consequence. His attention to the little boy typifies the direct way in which he addressed individuals, particularly if he believed there was a chance to reach them with the Gospel:

Sunday two boys from Texas and I went to Wisconsin. It was a very interesting experience. At the first place, Burton, we were to have services at 3 O'clock in the afternoon. But when we came there we found only about 25 children. All the older people that generally came had gone to a funeral. Burton, Wisconsin is a very small place. It is nearly lost in the hills. When we came there, I saw a little boy, looking very dirty, roll a tire past the church. I stopped him and asked him if he wasn't coming to Sunday School. He said that he would be there and sure enough in about fifteen minutes he was back, dressed in a clean overall. The children surely were interested in the work. *[4 October 1933]*

Albert's older brother George, reminiscing many years later, wrote that Albert "seemed to be interested in people all along. He liked to go out of his way to speak to people. He always advocated waving at people. He would say what's a wave, even if you don't get one back. He always wanted to speak to people about their soul's problems."

While still at seminary, Albert began to advise his brothers and sisters, even though he was younger than all but one of them. It seems never to have occurred to him that they might not want his advice or that his extra education did not necessarily qualify him to give the advice. Nevertheless, he played that role for the rest of his life. When his sister Tina had an infection in her mouth, Albert wrote:

I was under the impression that you had tonsillitis. Then I thought it certainly would have been good if you would have had your tonsils removed. I didn't know that infection was very contagious. At the time, if you would have taken a mouth wash, probably you would not have gotten the disease. A mouth wash with Listerine is very good for killing germs.

You no doubt feel miserable because of the poison in your
system and because you have not eaten for so many days, but
try to cheer yourself the best you can. Then too remember
we had the first day of Lent yesterday. Think of how much
your Saviour suffered for you. *[15 February 1933]*

How much comfort could that final sentence have given Tina? Whatever
happened in Albert's family or his work, he believed his responsibility as a
Christian was to view the occurrence within the framework of God's will
and make the best of it. Abstractions always won out over feelings.

My siblings and I resented the consistency of Albert's singular point of
view on anything difficult, buttressed always by what he believed Scripture
asked of him. He could irritate adults for the same reason. My father
reminds me of the hero in Leo Lionni's book, *Frederick*. In late summer,
all the other mice in the family gather corn, nuts, wheat, and straw for the
winter—but not Frederick. When he's asked why he doesn't work, he says
he does: he gathers sun rays "for the cold dark winter days," colors "for
winter is gray," and words so the mice don't "run out of things to say." In
the dead of winter, when supplies are low and everyone is glum, the mice
turn to Frederick, who asks them to imagine the sun and the colors, and
who recites poems for them. Soon they all feel better.

In the short run, we might not have felt better, but we surely benefited
from our father's teaching us a clear message—built on prayer, study, and
reflection—that did not change, regardless of what was happening around
us. Like Frederick the mouse, collecting sun, colors, and words, Albert
always knew what the most important thing was.

WHILE ALBERT WAS STILL IN SEMINARY, the American Lutheran Church
recommended that pastors get a four-year undergraduate degree rather than
the two-year degree he had earned at Wartburg College. Thus, in 1934, after
he had completed his seminary work, Albert enrolled at St. Olaf College in

Northfield, Minnesota, a college of the Evangelical Lutheran Church. Why St. Olaf? He wanted to go to a different place. As a child, I knew only two things about Albert's year at St. Olaf. The first was that he barely met the graduation requirement of swimming the length of the college pool. The second was that he met his future wife, Sylvia Fritz, only two months after the year began. With some other students, he had gone to a local nursing home to sing and offer a service. The young woman accompanying them on the piano was Sylvia. He does not once mention her in the few St. Olaf letters that remain, and yet he asked for a commitment from her only a year later. She declined.

When Albert graduated from St. Olaf in 1935, his mother Anna asked him to remain close by, as had all her other children. Not acknowledging the depth of her feeling, then or later, he tried to assuage her by pointing out that Lincoln, the site of his first job, was a mere 50 miles from his parents' farm:

> You wrote in your letter that you did not like it that
> I am going to Lincoln and that you had hoped that I
> would be close to home. I think that your wish has been
> granted. Lincoln is certainly very close to home. I can
> come home often and see you during the summer. I think
> it is something to be thankful for that I am so close to
> home. *[27 May 1935]*

Anna was not pacified, and the issue was to plague her for the rest of her life.

Soon, Albert moved even farther away. That fall, he was ordained a pastor and accepted a call to his first church, St. Paul's American Lutheran Church, in Hildreth, Nebraska, 200 miles from Talmage. Even now, Hildreth is literally at the end of a road, nestled in rich, undulating prairie. Albert was excited about beginning the new life, telling Sylvia, "It's fun to be a preacher in a little country town. Hildreth has a population of five hundred and is located on the edge of the sand hills. It has running water and many other conveniences which the large city has—probably fifteen blocks of paved streets" *[27 October 1935]*.

He also felt confident enough to counsel Mabel Ranum, still far away in Alaska, about her soul's salvation. Mabel, who disliked his being a pastor, wrote that he should "do something worthy of [his] ability." Albert wrote Sylvia that he found Mrs. Ranum's letter "so disgusting that it hurts" *[December 1936]* and then a month later added, "I wanted to make her feel the seriousness of Christianity and the tragedy she will face at the end of the course of life, in other words trying to speak the truth in love" *[January 1937]*.

Albert was serious by nature, which may explain why his sense of humor inclined toward the obvious. During his second year in Hildreth he grew a mustache, which he saw as an expression of his manhood. He was proud of it, using it as a chance to be a little silly with Sylvia:

> Mustaches will always be—mine was—very cute. It added prestige, dignity and poise to my person. Women raved about it; men admired it etc. You would have liked it too—I know you would have. If a man can't grow a mustache, he isn't intact. It had a streamlined effect. In spite of all these advantages, I bade my mustache farewell when I arrived home. My friends might interpret wrongly. When I returned, I find that you disapprove. Anything to please you my dear! Why, I'd even wear my hair in a braid, if I knew you liked it. *[February 1937]*

Albert wrote faithfully to his parents every Sunday evening, ignoring whether they understood or accepted his choices, believing that he could win them over. He reported on the crops and weather. A "tramp" came to his door one morning, and he invited the man in for breakfast *[6 July 1936]*. He taught Sunday School, prepared sermons, visited members of his congregation, and encouraged by his presence all the ladies' bake sales. The autumn mission festival was the great event each year, attracting people from nearby congregations. The day-long gathering, punctuated by a large midday meal, raised money for mission work and featured a guest speaker at three services. When my family returned to the States on furlough in the mid-1950s and again in the early 1960s, mission festivals were always on the calendar for the speaking tours my parents made. They—and we, by reflection—were minor celebrities. A visiting missionary carrying the aura of the strange country where he ministered might easily have captured the imagination of a young man like Albert who had had even a small taste of life beyond southeast Nebraska. The hymns unfailingly sung at these festivals included this perpetual favorite:

O Zion, haste, your mission high fulfilling,
To tell to all the world that God is light;
That he who made all nations is not willing
One soul should perish, lost in shades of night.

Give of your own to hear the message glorious,
Give of your wealth to speed them on their way,
Pour out your soul for them in prayer victorious,
And haste the coming of the glorious day.

Thus were worshippers strengthened in their belief in the Great Commission that Jesus gave to his disciples: "Go ye therefore, and teach all nations, baptizing them in the name of the Father, and of the Son, and of the Holy Ghost" (Matthew 28:19). Ideally, one gave one's all, joyfully and unquestioningly.

Mission festivals nourished enthusiasm for the work of the church, but only for the parishioners who attended. Albert's primary concern as a pastor was persuading people to come to church. Truly knowing that you are a Christian rests upon being part of a community of faith: "It certainly is too bad that so many people in this neighborhood hardly ever go to church. There isn't much hope for such people. Everyday it becomes clearer to me that people must go to church" *[1 February 1937]*. Of the farmers who harvested on Sunday, he said, "[Doing so] will never get them anywhere" *[6 July 1936]*. He always pursued people forthrightly. He was doing it in the name of Christ: "Mr. Anderson and I were out to try to get some of the people who are attending services to join. Three parties joined. We are going out again tomorrow night" *[no date]*.

And yet, the faithful young pastor busily performing his duties was apparently becoming bored. In late 1936, he considered working for a master's degree. He wrote to William Goetz, the librarian at Wartburg Seminary, expressing his interest in the Roman Catholic and Lutheran doctrines of repentance, and requesting Goetz's assistance in writing a thesis. Two months after beginning his research, however, Albert reported to Sylvia that "my progress is about like that of the turtle" *[14 January 1937]*. His head was engaged but not his heart. Repentance is a key Christian concept, but it's not hard for me to understand that he had difficulty motivating himself to compare two doctrines on the topic, far away from anyone else with similar interests.

Albert was still looking for something that would engage all of his faith and energy: "It seems that mission work surely is hard. Now and then I think I'd like to go to a foreign field. Just last night I read that we need more men in our foreign field of New Guinea, but no one will volunteer. I'm not saying that I will go. I'll let the Lord give the answer. In the meantime I'm a preacher here—in this country—and I'm to work here" *[4 January 1937]*. He joined the Mission Auxiliary, a group formed within the church to promote mission work, and continued to wait for a sign: "Before I'll go, something will have to happen to cause me to make a decision to go. The inner urge will have to be stronger than the one I have at present" *[January 1937]*.

ALBERT WAS CLOSE to his sister Genevieve, whose two-month-old daughter died suddenly in February. He wrote to Sylvia: "An indescribable emotion came over me when with tears streaming down her cheeks she greeted me with the words: 'Albert, we lost our baby.' She had pictured to herself how Delores [their other child] and Norma Jean could play together and grow up together. Now one was gone." At nearly the same time, Albert's father had two strokes and was now "practically helpless. Never before have I known or realized just what that means!" *[February 1937]*. From back in Hildreth a few weeks later, Albert wrote his mother: "Another Sunday is passed. I thought about you this morning before church and wondered how you were getting along. Even though I'm not there, I think of how dad lies there and you and the others take care of him. I hope that everything will turn out well sometime" *[8 March 1937]*.

Against this backdrop of family suffering, Albert heard the call he had been waiting for at a pastors' conference in Kansas:

> A person should pray about his work, and I prayed quite regularly for about a year. . . . The morning session began, and the chairman, who was also a member of the Foreign Mission Board, said, "I have very sad news for you. This morning, we just had a cable from Papua New Guinea that Missionary Daniel Spier died on Karkar Island of an intestinal obstruction." When I heard that, *my whole being was filled with the desire to take his place, and I was really riding high* [emphasis mine]. As soon as the morning session was over, I went up to the chairman and said to him, "God has called me to take the place of my friend who died." I knew Daniel, I had been with him in school. He looked at me, and his jaw dropped, and he said, "Well, if that's the case, wonderful!"
>
> Then I went home to my congregation, and I preached my Sunday sermon, and after the service was over, I said to them, "The Lord has called me to Papua New Guinea, and I'd like you to give me a release from this congregation."

Most of them, except one or two, said, "Well, if God has called you, we can't hold you back." And that was the beginning of coming here [Papua New Guinea].

We heard this story many times when we were growing up. This particular version is from an interview recorded with Albert's son Jonathan, 44 years later. Once Albert had received the call and accepted it, there were no obstacles to his desire to serve as a missionary. Even though that desire contended with his strong connection to his family, the call was ordained by God. Everything fell into place. Our parents taught us that they were called by God. This was the primary reason why, for so long, we accepted their decisions about our lives.

Albert, the rational, dispassionate commentator on other people's lives, the wise virgin, was at his most passionate in his relationship with a being infinitely larger than himself. He could act intuitively, out of his heart, when he was inviting a little boy to Sunday School. Here, without a moment of reflection as to whether Spier's death was the sign for which he had been waiting, he made the single most important decision of his life, from which he never wavered. Equally striking in his account are the reactions of other people: the chairman of the meeting and his own congregation accept his decision without questioning him. He simply told them that he had received the sign he had been asking for.

When describing his decision to Jonathan during the interview, Albert agreed that his situation was unlike an approach in which one prays, weighs the options, discusses them with others, and then makes a considered decision. He compared himself un-selfconsciously to the Apostle Paul, who actively persecuted Christians until he was struck down and temporarily blinded. When he recovered, Paul converted to Christianity and committed himself to winning converts. Albert remembered the process of leaving his family and country as having been easy, a sure sign that he was doing God's will: "I had no problem in giving up my congregation, no problem in selling my property, and doing everything possible to get going. Everything worked out beautifully." When Jonathan asked about leaving Sylvia behind, Albert said he told her that he hoped that she would join him on the mission field someday. As always, his relationship with God took precedence over his relationships with people. Those who loved him came to understand that they were never first in his life.

Not surprisingly, the letters from that time tell a different story that shows the human cost a call from God can incur. They display my father's feelings for his family and for others close to him, but those feelings were subordinate to the biblical principle of "the one thing needful," as Jesus said. He saw his call to replace Daniel Spier as God's will. When Albert returned to Hildreth, he wrote first to his parents, placing his desire in a broader context, hoping they would understand and accept it. He was deliberately low-key and, I must admit, deceptive:

> During the last week at our Conference in Kansas, I heard a lot about mission work in New Guinea. The more I think about it, the more I'd like to be a missionary to New Guinea. They need three men there. This is a question that a person cannot answer by saying "yes" or "no," but it is a question one must pray about, asking God <u>what His will is</u>. . . .The work among the heathen is to be done—someone must do it. *[29 March 1937]*

By going to New Guinea, Albert would be part of the imperative that Jesus gave his disciples to spread the Gospel everywhere. How could one argue with that? His parents would indeed be giving "one of their own," in the words of the mission festival hymn. Here was a cause big enough and worthy enough for anyone.

LESS THAN A MONTH LATER, Fred died, aged 84, having given his approval for Albert to go to New Guinea. Those weeks between the call and the aftermath of Fred's death must have been among the most intense in Albert's life, emotionally and spiritually. They show me the best and the worst in him. They show me his strong faith as well as the callousness with which he treated his mother, a new widow, when she stood in the way of his living out his faith as he believed God wanted him to.

In a momentous letter to Sylvia, Albert began by telling her about his father's dying:

> You addressed your card "Mon. Eve." And wrote of the joy of living! About that time, my mother, my brothers and sisters and I were sitting at the deathbed of my father. One feels very insignificant at a time like that. There was nothing we could do, but watch death draw nearer and nearer. Father's breathing became short and very unsteady after midnight. He became quieter with each passing hour—and at about three thirty on Tuesday morning he departed from this life. I read the liturgy for the "Commendation of the Dead" just as he was dying, which added a certain solemnity to the occasion. It was the first time that I saw a person depart from this life—I need not add that it moved me deeply. Sorrow was mingled with joy. There was joy because I believed that father's soul was going to Paradise. I'm convinced that he was a believer. Now it seems a little different when I pray the Lord's Prayer. I must say, it is good to be of that faith. Death has lost its sting.

Albert responded to the death of his father out of the faith that was already fully a part of him: yes, he was sad, but he could also feel joy. To someone not "of that faith," Albert's words might seem artificial: he moved too quickly to distance himself from grief. But Albert was simply drawing on the reserves that his faith had given him. And then, for the first time,

Albert told Sylvia of his call:

> When I heard the sad news [of Spier's death], the urge
> to take his place became very strong within me. You know
> that I have been interested in missions for a long time. I've
> prayed that the Lord should open the way if He desire
> that I should go into the work. I waited three or four days,
> but the urge remained. In fact it is just as strong today (if
> not stronger) as it was then.

Curiously, he had not written her during those three or four days. By
the time he did write, he had made most of the necessary arrangements
for leaving:

> I've written to the Secretary of the New Guinea Mission
> and have received a reply. He writes that there is a crying
> need for men and enclosed a copy of the constitution of
> the Lutheran Church of New Guinea and a copy for a
> physical examination. I passed the physical examination
> and now the decision rests in the hands of the Board of
> Foreign Missions. The President of the Central District
> has given them a good recommendation. If I am called,
> it will mean that I'll leave for New Guinea sometime this
> summer and remain there for seven years.

Albert went on to consider the human side of his decision, particularly
his mother's opposition and what going to New Guinea might mean for his
relationship with Sylvia:

> A few things trouble me however, my mother is very
> much opposed to my going, but my father as much as
> gave his consent before he died. I dread to think of asking
> my congregation for a release if and when the "call" comes.
> I've thought of you also. I don't think that I shall ever
> forget you, Sylvia. I know too that we are not engaged.

> The Mission Board advises this—that a young missionary
> go "unmarried," work on the field for a few years and then
> if it is desired, his "better half" will be sent to him. . . . I
> have the "inner call" to go to New Guinea, which call and
> desire I shall not try to smother and explain away, but
> shall follow. God knows what I think about you, also how
> I feel toward you. What your feeling toward me is, He also
> knows. *[April 1937]*

How did my mother feel when she learned of Albert's call, including
how much he had already done to arrange going to New Guinea before
even telling her? Albert said clearly, as he would for the rest of his life, that
his relationship with God came before his relationship with her. Whatever
misgivings Sylvia might have felt, her response was generous and open—
"Don't count me as a hindrance"; of course Albert should do what he felt
called to do. Somehow, the Lord would take care of their relationship.

But Anna could not let go. George wrote later that Anna "liked to
keep all her children with her"; others in the family spoke of Albert as her
favorite son. She ascribed Albert's going half-way around the world to help
black people he didn't know to be "the work of the devil." Albert never gave
Anna an inch, although to Sylvia, he admitted that perhaps he was violating
the Fourth Commandment by going without his mother's approval. He
could not simultaneously acknowledge his mother's feelings and believe in
the validity of his call. I still wonder why he couldn't have waited another
six months or a year, when the worst of Anna's grief over the death of
her husband might be waning. In his 26-year-old self-centeredness, Albert
seems never to have considered alternatives. Three weeks after his father
died, Albert wrote Anna his coldest letter:

> Mother, you write me a lot of things that you don't
> mean. You have not given me one good reason why I
> shouldn't do foreign mission work. Your reasons for not

wanting me to go are selfish—you want to keep me near. I'm glad that you love me, but you could always love me regardless of where I am. . . .

Try to spend the rest of your days working at something to keep your mind occupied and do a little, a little more good in the world before you too must go. I'll also try to do God's will! I want him to lead me! *[13 May 1937]*

The conflict between mother and son heightened when Albert learned that Anna had written a letter protesting Albert's decision to Johannes Lehmann, President of the Central District of the American Lutheran Church. Even more intensely than Albert, Lehmann dismissed Anna, judging her because she did not have his own mother's sacrificial attitude. He presented Albert's decision as completely God's decision, removing any responsibility from Albert and trying to silence her into accepting it. He even sent Albert a copy of his letter to her, an act of collusion, ridiculing a mother to her own son.

How different mothers are. My mother was a poor widow, whose husband was so shot up by the 1870-71 [Franco-Prussian] war that her entire young happiness sank into the grave and she had to raise her four children alone and with great troubles. And this mother promised at my birth: if God would bring me, presumably stillborn, into life and keep me alive, then she would save and work in order to make it possible for this, her youngest son, to serve God in his church. . . .

My dear Mrs. Frerichs, you say that you don't want to let your son leave, so you mean you cannot do that? When God calls him and when God wants to have him? If it is only your son's will and not the will of God, then God will arrange things so that nothing comes of the matter, and that he remains in this country. If God wants him, however, then Mother Frerichs will follow God's will and not only allow her son to go where God calls him, but she will lay her hand on his head in blessing, and even amid tears but with quiet humility say: then go in God's name, my dear son, and carry the seeds of the Word—You are a child of God and as such you don't know any NO to the YES of Our Father. *[14 May 1937]*

Anna, a farmer's wife with a third-grade education, could not have had much to say in response to this educated man in a high position. And yet, she never relented in opposing Albert's decision.

I didn't meet my grandmother until 1954, when we returned from New Guinea on our first furlough. She was 81 and I was nine. She lived in a small house behind the original farm house, too small for the clutter of old pictures and furniture. It smelled of the medicine for the chronic sores on her legs and the bandages they made necessary. I don't remember ever speaking to her, although we must, at least, have greeted each other. I was repelled by the odors in her home, and I pitied her for not having good health. I, after all, had left home to go to boarding school when I was six and prided myself on my independence. It was too late for Anna, and I was too young and too sure of myself to benefit from the strength of the one person who spoke fearlessly from her heart against the power of men and of the church.

When Lehmann sent Albert the copy of his letter to Anna, he gave more ground to Anna's wishes than in the letter itself: "I hope your mother will not object to your going when the time comes to make the final decision. But you must be firm and certain that you follow the call of God, if you should not be certain about this all important question, you have no right to go against the will and wish of your mother. And I hold no doubt, that you are convinced it is God calling you." *[14 May 1937]*

To Anna, Albert then wrote:

President Lehmann wrote me that you wrote him. He wrote that he wrote you that if it was not God's will that I should go, then nothing would come of it. But if it was God's will that I should go, then you could not say "no." You must believe what he says, Mother. He is the President of the Central District. Please do not write any more letters. Other preachers will say the same thing. . . . *Won't you let me follow the desire of my heart?* [emphasis mine]. I am praying that you will. *[16 May 1937]*

Anna was to accept, unquestioningly, the male authority of the church. Was Albert responding selfishly, or out of the pure conviction of his call? As a child, I never would have said that he was being selfish. Now, I think that probably both motives were present, and I don't feel a need to separate them.

In the middle of his exchange with Anna, Albert received his formal "Letter of Missionary Call." The Mission Board was as single-minded as Albert:

The urgent call from the field for missionaries presses our board for undelayed action. After your medical papers proved you to be sound in health and fit for the tropics, and all other matters being equal, the New Guinea Section, not able to meet in regular meeting before some time in June, voted on your call by mail. . . . May God grant you readiness to accept the call. . . . Will it be possible for you to leave for New Guinea at an early date, perhaps in the middle of July? . . . . We do not wish to crowd you, but know that the field needs you urgently as early as possible. *[12 May 1937]*

Albert told Sylvia, "Utterly incapable of grasping the far-reaching consequences of all this, I sit here somewhat in a daze. Next Sunday, the matter will be presented to the congregation. The Lord will have to give me courage to tell people whom I love, that I feel that I have been called to another field of activity." He was still troubled by his mother's opposition. She had not given up, phoning him the morning he received the notification, asking him not to go. Of the struggle, he said, "It's the hardest battle I've ever had, but who can say 'no' when he feels that the Lord says 'go'" *[24 May 1937]*. On June 7, one day before his 27th birthday, Albert received the release he hoped for from his congregation.

What about Sylvia? They had not seen each other since the previous August, although they had written regularly. A Lutheran youth conference in Minneapolis created a perfect occasion to meet, and then Sylvia would travel to Nebraska with Albert to meet his family. They spent two weeks together, a time Albert later referred to as "glorious." The day after he installed her on the train back to Minnesota, he wrote that he couldn't be sad because "the thought of a happy future gives me a light heart. Then too, why should one feel depressed after two weeks of real happiness!" *[6 July 1937]*. They both felt it was too soon for a formal commitment: Sylvia still had a year of college, and then she wanted some teaching experience. For his part, Albert knew that he needed to test himself in the mission field.

Albert left San Francisco on July 23, 1937, to cross the Pacific. That December, Anna wrote Sylvia to say, "I want I want [*sic*] Albert back" *[11 December 1937]*. Neither she nor Sylvia would see him again for six years.

THE CIRCUMSTANCES OF ALBERT'S CALL encapsulate the central dilemma that Albert's life posed for those around him. His mother, his wife, and his children were irrevocably affected by the way he lived out his call. On the one hand, for Albert, the nature of his call required his absolute submission to it. Yes, he loved his family, but his work came first. We were perfectly clear about his order of things, which was also God's order: God, our mother, and then us. How could any of us argue with the will of God? And yet, others, not Albert, paid prices for Albert's call. Three mothers—his, Sylvia's, and ours—were separated from their children for exceedingly long periods of time. Sylvia's and Albert's relationship with their families of origin could not develop for them as adults as it would have if they had been able to see them regularly. One of Sylvia's sisters remembers their mother crying in church because she missed Sylvia so much. Sent away each year to boarding schools, first in New Guinea, then in Australia, we sometimes felt as though we had raised ourselves.

"Vocation" comes from *vocare,* Latin for "to call." In religious contexts, there is always the implication that someone other than the individual, whether God or other people led by God, has marked this person for service. Responses to the call vary. In the New Testament, the fishermen to whom Jesus talks simply lay down their nets and follow him. Paul, to whom Albert compares himself, is first struck blind and then accepts the call. Albert describes another experience: passion. The call came to him as his deepest expression of himself, the "desire of his heart." The other side of the passion was his coldness toward anybody who stood in his way. If you lived with the person who had this passion, but did not share its intensity, the only way you could make a place for yourself in his life was not to question it.

I began with the question of why Albert became a missionary. I can answer partially: his faith was strong, he wanted adventure, and he had prepared himself to respond to an event such as Spier's death. He was well-prepared, to a degree that he probably could not have realized at the time. The skills and values deriving from his life on the farm in his German Frisian family would later make it possible for him and his family to live successfully on isolated mission stations. For all his love of the farm and of the family into which he was born, there was also his adventurous spirit, angling, as in his letters to Mabel Ranum, for a way off the farm. Albert's open and direct way of approaching people, including strangers, allowed him to talk easily about the Gospel to anyone who would listen. He had a solid foundation in

Christianity, gained through Sunday School and then through his education at Wartburg College, Wartburg Seminary, and St. Olaf. Years of prayer, other reflection, study, and action had made his faith an indivisible part of his identity. He lived as a wise virgin with "pure and utter confidence," as Sylvia said in one of her early letters to him. He knew what he believed in, was ready to act on it, and did so when the time arose.

In so many ways, then, Albert seemed an excellent candidate for mission work. Noticeably absent from his preparation was any significant knowledge of the cultures of New Guinea. Nowhere in the correspondence of that time does he ever acknowledge this absence, or that its omission could have serious consequences for anyone working intimately with indigenous people. The Mission Board must eventually have recognized that such preparation was an essential part of one's call. Seven years later, missionary candidates spent seven months at "Mission School" at Wartburg Seminary, taking classes from four experienced missionaries in such subjects as "ethnology, anthropology, geography of New Guinea, Graged language [one of 700 native languages], history of the mission, practical matters of how to live there, and, most importantly, the mission method." A mission doctor also instructed them in tropical medicine. In contrast, Albert simply went into the field.

I believe in calls in the Christian sense. I believe in God's presence in our lives even though he doesn't control them. I believe that Albert experienced a genuine call when he responded to Spier's death. The nature of his response reminds me that he remained fundamentally human with all the contradictions that that implies. The call became an excuse to elevate his actions to a point where they were beyond reproach. For those around him, it was difficult to acknowledge both the call and his single-mindedness and stubbornness. One can appreciate the virtue with which Albert tried to live, but not the self-righteousness that his letters of advice to his sisters and mother exhibit or his comments about people who don't go to church.

These very qualities can intrude when one is in situations where one would benefit from openness to world views and practices that are fundamentally different from one's own.

For me, as Albert's daughter, the basic question of his vocation is its cost in human pain, seen thus far in his mother's anguish at his departure and at his refusal to acknowledge her feelings, and later in its effects on his wife and children. I cannot wholeheartedly accept this verse that I grew up knowing by heart: "He that loveth father or mother more than me is not worthy of me; and he that loveth son or daughter more than me is not worthy of me." (Matthew 10:37). For my father, verses such as this provided justification for going forward that he did not, would not, question. For me, whatever peace I possess about Albert's life comes from looking at it as a whole—the results of his work—and not at the way in which he made his initial decision to be a missionary.

Chapter Three
I want to live in as beautiful a way
as I have vision for and am able.

As a child, I adored my mother: I couldn't get enough of her. When I was in my mid-20s, wanting to be myself but also not quite sure I measured up, I told her that I had wanted to be exactly like her when I grew up: beautiful, smart, stylish, a good cook and seamstress, and an excellent musician. As her warmth drew people to her, so would people be drawn to me. My voice would be clear and musical as was hers. My wishes were no accident, Mother said. She had wanted the same qualities for me and had tried to pass them on. We never finished the conversation. Did we both agree that she had been successful in shaping me?

As I write about my mother now, she seems more elusive than these aspects of her that I wanted to match. It has been years since I wanted to dissolve into her because I was sure of who we both were. Even so, I would like to be on firmer footing now when I write about her. I might have known more of her if the last 15 years of her life had not been clouded by Alzheimer's. I might also have known more if her family had not moved so often when she was growing up: there are no records of the kind that are available for my father—high school grades, letters home from college, her first teaching contracts, or daily diaries. How to explain something that she did the day after Dad died, February 8, 1984. Four of us had spent the week of Dad's death in their home. We followed the custom we had grown up with, of having family devotions after breakfast and dinner. But after

Dad died, Mother never again suggested devotions, either immediately after his death or later, when I was visiting.

For me, growing up, family devotions showed that we were a family who took its Christianity seriously. More than anything else we did, more even than going to church, devotions sustained that seriousness. Didn't Mother really care about devotions? Or was it that family devotions had come to represent Dad's sometimes heavy-handed and always pious domination of our lives? More likely the latter, since she also rearranged the living room furniture within a week after his death. A pecan-wood hutch, which she had recently bought and which was one of the few pieces of attractive furniture she owned, had been placed to the left of the front entrance, not easily seen by someone entering the house. But the hutch held her collection of porcelain tea cups and saucers, and the vases for the flowers she loved to arrange—her most beautiful possessions. She moved the hutch so that it would catch a visitor's eye immediately, especially at night when lit up from the inside. First impressions of visitors mattered, as did her own pleasure in looking at what she loved. Undoubtedly Dad had wanted a chair placed in that spot, and undoubtedly, there had been some practical reason why. Perhaps Mother had given in, although she wouldn't always have done that.

Mother died in 1999, at the age of 83. It wasn't until she was in her 70s that I knew she had any German forebears. She used to explain her maiden name, Fritz, by saying that her grandfather had changed his name from "Johnson" to "Fritz" because there were so many Johnsons in Minnesota and Wisconsin. She always described herself as Norwegian. I never asked her what that meant to her, but I grew up associating it with being tall, strong, smart, and refined. As with everything else about her, I too wished that I was 100 percent Norwegian. Mother made no secret of the fact that being Norwegian was better than being German: Norwegians were more cultured. Of course, we knew as children that Dad was German and therefore we were half-German. There must have been so many ways in which Dad's views prevailed; here was a way for Mother to make a statement. Did we also feel put down? I don't remember that feeling. For one thing, I liked most of what I knew about Germany and Germans, regardless of what Mother said. They were among my best friends at Wau. My favorite folk songs and Christmas cookies were German.

I know now from an essay that Mother wrote as a college freshman ("How I Happen To Be an American") that she had known her entire adult life that a paternal great-grandfather, John Fritz, was German. Perhaps she thought the connection was too attenuated to be worth mentioning, and she liked being able to say that she had a single, strong ethnic heritage. Perhaps she just forgot. I can also believe that she did not want her children to know that this particular German great-great-grandfather had had an affair with his wife's sister, divorced his wife, and married his sister-in-law.

No one is completely frank about everything, and I do not expect that of my mother either. But I always wanted to be the center of her life, as close to being one with someone else as was possible, or at least second after Dad. With Dad, we always knew where we stood—third, after God and Mother. The New Guineans were in there too, with God. Dad's work with them was the primary way in which he expressed his faith. Although beloved, Mother was second. That left no place for us but third. I never heard Mother express her hierarchy as clearly as Dad did. She acted as if it was the same as Dad's. There is a certain comfort in knowing one's place, and we had at least that. On the other hand, if I could win Mother's attention away from her many tasks as a missionary's wife and mother of six other children, nothing made me happier.

So the letters she wrote to me in boarding school never came often enough or, when they came, were long enough. I was sure of who my mother was, sure that it was she I wanted. In my middle age, when the devotions stopped and when I learned that Mother was part-German and may have purposely tried to hide that fact, I had the unsettling feeling that there were probably other things about her that I did not know or understand. To what extent were Dad's choices her choices? As a young woman coming from a traditional home, she would have expected to follow Dad's lead, but she was also independent. Therefore, the hard choices that Dad had made must also have been her choices, even though I'm sure they caused her more pain than they did him. It was easy to forget her part in the choices that shaped our lives. Dad simply was who he was, living out his call, which no one ever questioned, except for his mother. Mother's letters rarely hinted at the complexity I now see in her. She was almost always captivating, even when she was only a sophomore in college.

SYLVIA WAS BORN into a devout Norwegian Lutheran household on October 16, 1916, in Ray, North Dakota, a speck of a town on Highway 2 on the plains of the northwest part of the state. She was the eldest of eight children of Charles Arnold Fritz, the local Norwegian Lutheran pastor, and Pauline Peterson Fritz, who had met Charles the day after she moved to Ray to teach school.

Getting an education was paramount for Charles. He attended three colleges before he felt called to become a minister, which meant attending Luther Seminary in St. Paul. At this time, Charles also changed his name back to "Fritz," having met an unsavory character at Luther by the name of Charles Johnson.

Sylvia's mother, Pauline Peterson Fritz, also grew up in a Norwegian immigrant family that valued education and hard work. Her parents, Lars Pederson and Regine Andras, settled near St. Peter, Minnesota, in about 1867, when they were both 17 years old. Pauline's parents were instrumental in founding a Norwegian Lutheran church in Renville and then in building another in the 1890s when a tornado destroyed the first. They had 11 children, of whom only five grew to adulthood.

The children of Charles and Pauline Fritz were more ambivalent about being Norwegian than Sylvia conveyed to us as we were growing up in the New Guinea bush. Two of her younger sisters remember their parents being proud of their heritage but also not making a special point of it. None of the children learned Norwegian: that was the "gossip" language, which their parents used when they wanted to talk about their parishioners. The children were to speak English without a Norwegian accent. One sister remembers a sense of superiority in the home that stemmed from her mother and her mother's sister, Clara, who was living with them. Pauline and Clara may have encouraged the sense of superiority that Sylvia showed later in New Guinea through their "we are right" attitude—we are right (and therefore superior) because of our values, our education, and our ability to use our intellects.

Faithfulness to the church, a commitment to education, and a love for classical music were all hallmarks of the Fritz household, Sylvia's counterparts to the German values of God, community, and family with which Albert grew up. She took these ideals with her to New Guinea. Her seven siblings lived them out as well. All but one had some education beyond high school in spite of the Depression and World War II. All had musical training. Two became artists. As adults, they have taught, run businesses, worked in the medical field, served with distinction in the armed forces, and been active in their churches and communities. Most had five or more children, and no one is divorced. It seems fair to say of them that they have made the most of their abilities and opportunities.

Both my parents wanted us to know our aunts and uncles. Growing up, I felt I did, including what they stood for. Even though they were half way around the world, they helped to shape me. From my father's family, I learned steadfastness: several cousins still live within a few miles of the original farm. From my mother's family, living as they do around the country and in various modes, I learned how to go out into the world with assurance.

As the eldest of Charles and Pauline's eight children, Sylvia grew up with the expectation that she would make something of herself. Her father was especially important in Sylvia's nurturing. In her baptismal photograph, he is holding her up and away from himself so that he can easily look straight into her face, gazing at her with a smile that says there's no one else in the world. Anyone would feel special if she, if he, were looked at and held in this way. When Sylvia was four years old, she sat on the fence around their yard, waiting for Charles to come home from work. Music was an intimate part of Sylvia's life, indivisible from her very self. She often told us that she learned to read music before she could read words. By age twelve, she played the organ well enough to play for church services.

In spite of all that Charles gave her, she must also have been aware of his frailties. Sometimes he was in poor health and could not work. Supporting a large family during the Depression was an additional burden. For four years, in the mid-1930s, he had no regular employment because small country churches could not afford pastors. Sylvia's sister Nancy remembers a time when there was only 25 cents in the house.

Sylvia graduated as salutatorian of her high-school class in Albert Lea. Her grades averaged two-tenths of a percent less than those of the valedictorian, she often told us as children. In autumn 1934, she matriculated as a freshman at St. Olaf College, then a college of the Norwegian Lutheran Church in Northfield. Although Albert had chosen St. Olaf somewhat haphazardly, Sylvia had never wanted to attend any other college. Her grandfather had studied there, but the college's emphasis on music mattered the most. Like me 30 years later, she was unable to win a spot in the First Choir, but she took every opportunity to immerse herself in singing and playing the piano.

SYLVIA AND ALBERT met in November 1934, her first year at St. Olaf, when both of them were visiting the local Oddfellows' Home with other students. Albert always said he noticed her because she played the piano so strikingly well. He didn't want us to think it was just her good looks. They became close that year, the only year Albert spent at St. Olaf, having arrived as a senior. Their correspondence began the following summer. Sylvia's letters reveal a bright, earnest, exuberant, and independent young woman, intent on defining who she is and what kind of relationship she wants with the quiet, serious farmer's son from Nebraska, six years her senior. Her letters could not be more different from Albert's plodding letters to his family at the same age. Sylvia emerges as more mature, as better prepared for college. Yet, Albert was writing to his parents and siblings, and he must not have wanted to seem too different from them, even as he realized that he was daily becoming more different. Sylvia was writing to an older man, a pastor whom she wanted to impress. Because Sylvia's college letters were so strongly affected by the fact that she was writing to a man she came to love, and because they are my only source for her life in college, I can write best about these four years if I intertwine these two loves of hers—Albert and St. Olaf—as they are in her letters.

When Sylvia was a sophomore, Albert, soon to become pastor of his first church, wanted some kind of commitment from her. She, however, was unwilling even to commit to writing on a weekly basis, although she clearly wanted the relationship to continue.

> Have you heard of people's getting into ruts? Well, that's what would happen if we agreed to your plan of weekly dispatches. I guess I'm a person of whimsy or something and if I write a letter when I'm not in a certain mood, why, it gets to be a dumber letter than I usually write. Savez-vous? I know perfectly well that that is not a particularly healthy way of looking at things—I mean not wanting to do something if you don't feel like it—but I seem to be made that way. *[18 July 1935]*

Albert made decisions based on what he thought was right and wrong. Sylvia was much more conscious of how she felt, regardless of the principle that might apply in a certain situation.

Albert visited her later that summer in Hayward and met Sylvia's family for the first time. Sylvia later wrote that her family "quite approved" of Albert; her mother thought him "almost an ideal guest" *[4 September 1935].*

Sylvia had left St. Olaf in the spring, not knowing whether she would return, because of her family's finances. That summer, a loan came through, and she was ecstatic about being able to continue her education at her beloved college:

> I am completely under the spell of this place again—
> there is no other way I can describe it. I doubt if the campus
> has ever been more beautiful in the fall. There is that bed
> of canna lilies, down below the Ad [building] in the little
> boulevard, that is simply flaming in its gorgeousness now
> and the trees all over are nipped with touches of color here
> and there (if trees all over can be nipped here and there!).
> Then you know that spirit of peace and remoteness that
> pervades the atmosphere of the whole campus: well, it is
> still here. I love it all. *[24 September 1935]*

She talked about the courses she was taking, "terribly enthusiastic" about them. Sylvia was unreservedly passionate about St. Olaf and her studies.

But she was less clear how to continue the relationship with Albert, who, less than a year after their first meeting, again wanted more than she was ready to give:

> I've been thinking a lot since you were here about
> what you said concerning the final result of our friendship.
> Please, for your own sake as well as mine, don't keep on
> thinking too seriously in that same line of thought. I
> admire you greatly as a friend and I'm exceeding grateful

to you for many things you've done for me (many of
which I'm sure you don't realize) and I want still to be
your friend—may I?—but I am young and infinitely
ignorant of my own real self. You understand, don't you?
I have often wished I had not allowed you to say even as
much as you did. *[24 September 1935]*

By the "many things you've done for me," I think Sylvia meant the
way Albert's faith inspired her. They had seen each other only once that
summer; it's unlikely that she meant something he had done or given
her. Sylvia's next letter stated as clearly as she could what she wanted
from life:

Thank you for saying we are still friends. . . . You
mentioned a career—or the possibility of there being
someone else. Thank you again for your kind attitude, but
I had better make myself clear. A career is not the ultimate
goal in my life. I think I want to do something on my own
for a little while, but I'm afraid I wouldn't be entirely happy
or satisfied with that alone. I want to be married and have
children and *live in as beautiful a way as I have vision for
and am able* [emphasis mine]. As for the possibility of there
being that well-known someone—I can honestly say there
is no one. *[21 October 1935]*

Living in as beautiful a way as possible is living aesthetically and with
a design. It is a sensual approach to life, one that recognizes natural beauty
and pays attention to detail, whether it is the crust on a loaf of bread or
the phrasing in a Chopin étude. The attitude also assumes a reliable level of
financial support, not necessarily from her. Her idealism carries with it the
energy of someone who has decided that her life is going to count.

The focus in her subsequent letters was almost completely on her life
at St. Olaf:

I am slowly finding myself in all the chaos in me
and accordingly seeing things in what I hope is a truer
perspective. . . . I was home [over Thanksgiving for]
four whole nights and days and during those days I did
a good deal of honest-to-goodness living. I discovered
some books of Daddy's that are going to keep me plenty
busy when I'm at home—books on psychology, science,
religion (naturally!), music (of course!). et cetera. I'm
going to learn Greek and read Ibsen in the original. I'd
like to read the Bible in French—the only French book
we have in the house, I believe. In chapel this morning,
Prexy [President Boe] talked on the preciousness of time
and how we should fill it with the best we can and how
we have to slave along on the technique and mechanics of
life in its various phases before we can enjoy the thing in
its ultimate beauty and freedom, whether it be music or
history or English or Christianity. *[4 December 1935]*

As was often the case, Sylvia could most clearly see whatever truth she
was trying to express in music; in the same letter, she writes,

Last night, a girl who graduated from here four years
ago and who has been studying piano in Berlin since gave
a recital; she was or is a brilliant example of one who has
superseded simple mechanics. Her power and scope are
tremendous and nothing seems impossible for her to
accomplish on the keyboard. *[4 December 1935]*

And yet, the self-doubt under all this exuberance is also profound. Just
two weeks later, responding to something in Albert's letter, she wrote.

I feel so small. And you talk about your two-by-four-
mind. Sometimes I doubt the expediency of my spending
so much money on college and think I should settle down,

marry a farmer, and raise a brood of young 'uns—which would, of course, be not such an inglorious life, but for some reason or other not the kind I have planned and hoped for for myself. *[22 December 1935]*

Sylvia did much more in her letters than reflect on the meaning of life. Albert's interest in her and her attraction to him forced her to think about who she was and what she wanted earlier than she might otherwise have done. Most of the time, however, Sylvia wrote about her family, her classes, and the people with whom she boarded while she attended St. Olaf. Often, she was playful, sometimes silly. In January 1936, she began a letter by saying that her mind was a blank. Then:

Oh yes, last Sunday I had a lovely time simply fooling away time. There are two sisters, Sadie and Evelyn, who live across the street from me and those two, and a Ruth Mannes and Margaret Jacobson and I all ate dinner down town, acting perfectly silly. We took all the bread and butter that we didn't eat, wrapping it up in several bundles and sticking them in our purses. (After all, we had paid for it!) Then to salve our consciences a bit we each left a penny tip for the waitress. Home to Sadie's and Ev's where we proceeded to give each other facials and manicures. I got the urge to try on a dress that they have—a formal made from silver metal cloth ($25 a yard!). It was made beautifully simple with a high neck in front and no back at all down to the waist. Then there was a bouquet of artificial violets at the waist in back. I put that on, braided my hair around my head, put on the requisite cosmetics for an outfit like that, also put on a beautiful brown velvet wrap. Then I got the brilliant idea of running across the street to Paulsons' to show them so I put on Sadie's new black seal coat and took Ruth with me

and sallied forth—looking as tho I was to be presented to
the new King Edward VIII. *[30 January 1936]*

Sylvia looked so striking that Mr. Paulson's nephew, who was visiting, photographed her: "[H]e arranged me on the davenport with all the lamps on me and I'm anxious to see the result."

Albert, not exactly a stand-up comedian himself, thought she should be more lighthearted. Sylvia construed his remark as a criticism. Her last letter to him before he arrived to visit Sylvia and her family again in August 1936 began this way:

> So, Mr. Frerichs, I'm sedate, huh? Hvad taenker du om
> dette [What do you think of this]: Wednesday evening I
> played Wink'em, Farmer in the Dell, etc., with the Junior
> Leaguers—just went down and played with them and
> had heaps of fun. Thursday night I played kittenball as a
> sub on a Glenville girls team against the Albert Lea team
> under lights and with a paid admission, and we won with
> our nine players as against their full ten with a score of 8-5.
> Friday afternoon I played in a foot-and-a-half of water up
> at the beach with John, Mae, and Harriet [three of her
> siblings] all afternoon long, and Friday evening when it
> rained—for the second time in over a month, Margaret,
> Paul, John, Harriet, Colly [more siblings and a sister's
> boyfriend], several neighbor kids and I all played leap frog,
> ten step, touchback and so on in the rain and barefooted.
> And I promise you, my dear sir, that when you come, if
> the time we have and the things we do are sedate, why, I'll
> do something really wild. *[18 May 1936]*

Their time together was unexpectedly gratifying. Before Albert's visit, she had called their relationship "a big question mark." In her first letter after Albert returned home, she wrote that the day after he left, "I was practically a minus quantity to things of this world. I was sleepy, but sleep held no attractions. I looked with scorn on dishes and sweeping and such homely duties. . . . You said something about 'four perfect days.' From my end I say, yea, yea, Amen, with a full heart. They are days that will not easily be forgotten no matter what happens" *[14 August 1936].*

Their "dates" that fall consisted of listening to the same radio program at the same time, usually concerts of classical music. In October, Albert sent her a dozen roses for her 20th birthday, the first flowers anyone had sent her: "Oh, Albert, dear, they are lovely. I wish you could see them—a delicate shade of rosy pink against their green ferns and a whole dozen of them, when a single one holds enough beauty in its heart to speak a million words and then to have twelve times that much! It's unspeakable" *[23 October 1936].* Her uncertainty of the year before had evaporated.

Sylvia's Christian faith is one other thread on her path toward marrying Albert and to missionary work in New Guinea. She seems to have taken her faith for granted, as much a part of her identity as being Norwegian-American, a musician, and a student. Yet, it had not figured in her letters to Albert until the summer of 1936, after she spent several days at a Bible camp that St. Olaf sponsored. One of her professors had been opposed to her going, saying that Bible camps "use religion as an excuse for a glorified vacation; that the experience is apt to be artificial and therefore not lasting" *[24 August 1936].* She went anyway. Within four days, any skepticism she might have had had melted away. The letter she wrote Albert about it conveyed the intensity of the experience. She immediately felt connected to the faculty and students who were there:

> [W]e haven't had the slightest trouble in getting ac-
> quainted because (as you would put it) we're all brethern
> and sisterns [*sic*] in Christ and when two things are equal
> to the same things they're equal to each other. Just by shak-
> ing hands with them [the students] and smiling into their

faces and receiving their smiles I was under their spell completely. They're all so sincerely Christian and Christ-like.
The faculty are the same way only in a deeper, richer, more
experienced way.

The dean of the camp gave talks at vespers "that dig and dig and churn
around inside until they hit the spot where I at least need it most." She
couldn't rest there, as she wrote to Albert: "I'm arriving closer and closer
and realizing more and more how far I yet have to go before I can feel that
pure and utter confidence that you show" *[28 August 1936].*

Sylvia returned to St. Olaf that fall on borrowed money. Her situation
was precarious: she paid for half her voice lessons by washing dishes at a faculty home, thus freeing up money that she would otherwise have had to spend
on dinners. She could hardly contain her joy at being back at St. Olaf:

> Again I'm all enthusiastic about school. The campus
> is in perfect condition yet—no frosts to even start the
> leaves to changing. It almost looks spring-like, only there
> is that full, mature richness about the air and trees and
> grass that belies their fresh greenness. My teachers and
> subjects are pulling me hard into lots of thrilling things.
> Friendships seem happier and deeper. Work doesn't seem
> like the irksome stuff I remember it as—not even washing
> dishes twice a day *[23 September 1936].*

That fall, Sylvia joined the Young Democrats and walked into the family
home wearing a Roosevelt pin. She did not clearly explain her reason to
Albert. In fact, she seemed not to have fully understood it herself: there
were still "many many points where I am as ignorant as a backwoods
housewife" *[undated, fall 1936].* Her focus remained on the personal, her
faith, her studies, and her music. Two women she met that fall gave her a
vision of what she might become:

> The first was a missionary to China, who spoke at a

candlelight service, standing between candelabra of candles
talking about light and how easy it is really to forget about
the usual necessities of life when your mind and life are
taken up with greater things. Simple and beautiful are the
only two words I can think of in describing her. She is
Trudie Roe's aunt [Trudie was a good friend of Sylvia's]
and has the same rich, vibrant personality only tuned just
a bit finer by her experience than Trudie's is now.

With almost no transition, Sylvia moved on to music and the second
woman:

> Days that I have my voice lesson or my piano lesson
> are especially high days in my young life. I take voice from
> Miss Hjertaas (some more vibrating personality) and even
> tho my voice sounds awful in practice something in her
> just draws out the best that is in me—so that my voice
> (the way I'm used to hearing it) is almost unrecognizable.
> *[undated, fall 1936]*

In another way, Sylvia was developing a more public voice. She already
had the confidence one derives from performing as a musician. Her sense of
self radiates out in a full-length photograph in the 1938 St. Olaf yearbook.
She is standing straight and tall, in a cape and beret, looking out into
the distance. In March 1937, when she was a junior, she was invited to
deliver a five-minute speech at the National Young People's Luther League
convention on "how one may give to the Luther League of his time, talents,
and means." She also gave a 20-minute talk over St. Olaf's radio station on
"Religious Influences at College" *[31 March 1937]*. Speaking publicly about
her faith must have sharpened her sense of its definition in her life, thus
strengthening her for the decisions she would soon have to make.

Events that spring brought her up short. She had known from the
previous fall that Albert's father had had a stroke. The letter in which Albert

told her of his father's death told her at the same time that he would go to New Guinea. Of his father's death, she wrote, perhaps thinking of how close she was to her father: "But one's father is so definitely a part of one's idea, one's whole plan of life that there must be an empty, blank spot in your heart. Yet all the more reason 'it is good to be of that faith' as you put it. . . ." Of Albert's going to New Guinea, she wrote:

> I am trying to write in the way that seems to be what God would have me write. I am intensely happy that your prayers and that inner urge that you speak of seem almost to be satisfied. I hope that you will be able to go. And if something should hinder you this time, I agree with you—do not squelch that driving force and desire in you. . . . I am scared to write the rest. If I seem too bold, please forgive me and put it down to my desire for frankness and understanding between us. Tersely, this is it: don't count me as a hindrance. I am wholeheartedly in favor of your going. . . .You say you will not forget me—I'll have to say that God only knows how I feel toward you, I don't know—at least not yet. But I do know this positively that no matter where the man I love goes, I will follow. If you should ever find it in your heart to ask me to marry you and if I could say yes knowing that it is with yours [that] my destiny lay—I say if all that, I would love to come out to New Guinea after a few years and work beside you, make a home with you and raise a family with you.

Taken aback by her own forthrightness—she has, after all, said she would marry him before he has asked—she wrote later in the same letter, "[P]erhaps it should not be my place to talk as I have. But after all this is the 20th century when looking at life honestly, seriously, and frankly is the thing to do" *[3 May 1937]*.

IF SYLVIA were riding solely on the shirt-tails of Albert's faith, she could not have spent 30 years in New Guinea, giving up close relationships with her family and her children. Like him, Sylvia knew all the Biblical stories of people, usually men, who were called to serve. She would have compared her situation to theirs, as did Albert, but what was in her heart, independent of what she thought she "should" do, was more important. Sylvia's call never caused the conflict with her parents that Albert's did with his mother. Her father Charles had had his own call, and her mother Pauline understood her subservient role, even though she had her own feelings.

For Sylvia, the questions arose much later, when she struggled to accept the reality that she was sending her children away to school when they were too young. As a college junior, she could write easily that she looked forward to raising a family with Albert. During her time in New Guinea, I wonder when she acknowledged to herself that this dream could not be realized as she had imagined it.

Chapter Four
New Guinea or Bust

Albert, bursting to go to New Guinea in 1937, sailed from Los Angeles on July 21, with several other young men also bound for New Guinea mission work. In about five weeks he reached Madang, on the north coast of New Guinea and the headquarters of the Lutheran Mission. He left full of confidence, finally able to pursue the purpose for which he had been casting about while a pastor in the tiny Nebraska town of Hildreth. His letter to Sylvia on his last day in the United States ended with a drawing of an ocean liner and "New Guinea or Bust" written on its hull.

His mother had never softened her position about his decision to be a missionary, but he had every other sign that he was doing God's will. His future with Sylvia seemed sure, as well. He had just spent two glorious weeks with her. She would finish college in a year, teach for one or two years, and then come to him in New Guinea where they would be married. He could not have understood how something that he wanted so much—to live out his calling to be a missionary in New Guinea—would challenge every part of his being.

Albert wrote wide-eyed letters to Sylvia from the ship. The young man who had spent most of his 27 years on the plains of Nebraska and who had never traveled outside the Midwest was now trying to comprehend the immensity of the Pacific Ocean:

Thursday morning dawned rather gloomy, but it was

not so in my heart! It's a great sight to look east, west, north, and south and see nothing but the dark blue expanse of the Pacific and a few stray sea birds with a gray sky overhead! All the time, morning, noon or midnight, the ship going steadily forward in a southwesterly direction. *[26 July 1937]*

And then, from near the Fiji Islands:

The stars in the tropical heavens seem so low that one could almost touch them. The moon casts a spell over a lover of night. The phosphorus in the water makes the ocean glow as though it were lighted by some brilliant light. Never before did I so fully realize that we are living in a truly wonderful world. *[2 August 1937]*

In another letter, he described ten Mormon missionaries on board ship, "young men not very well prepared for that kind of work, but I admire their courage. . . . The Mormon church is a menace to Christianity." Seemingly unaware of his own lack of preparation, he yet saw theirs. The Australians and New Zealanders on board "make themselves conspicuous because of their broken English, or perhaps I should say their accent!" *[26 July 1937]*.

Albert felt immediately at home on the day that he spent in Pago Pago, Samoa. Being among brown people who were welcoming, Christian, and unaffected by American materialism no doubt gave him an idea of the South Pacific paradise he might help to create in New Guinea:

The native boys and girls acted as self-appointed guides to conduct us about their village. They were so kind and congenial. The boy who first escorted me, told me that he loved the Lord and that he too was going to be a missionary when he grew up. After a walk around the city, he found another boy and together they rowed me across the lagoon to the ship dock. I gave the assistant a dime (which he put into his mouth) and my guide fifty cents. We saw little brown boys running about without a stitch of clothing on. Nearly every one on the island goes to church. One of the boys said: "American movie men say money is God. Money is not God. Money not help one to go to Heaven. Only the Lord help one to go to Heaven." Another boy said: "Samoan people no steal, no murder—they love each other too much." They are called the friendliest people of the South Seas—a people unspoiled by civilization.

Albert's letter to his mother describing the visit ended by saying, "I hope that the people in New Guinea are as likeable as those in Samoa were" *[2 August 1937]*.

When Albert landed in Sydney, two weeks of travel still lay ahead of him. Apparently, there was no direct way to Madang. His hosts in Sydney, the Smith family, served him a dinner that could not have been more different from the solid farm meals of two meats, several vegetables, and desserts so familiar to him:

The maid brought in the first course in covered dishes. Mrs. Smith, assisted by her daughter served! First a piece of bread came down the line on a fork. I took off the piece of bread and passed the fork back. Then came the plate and finally the dessert. Australians use the knife very freely in eating. There was no tea or coffee served, but at 10 o'clock when we were ready to go back to the hotel, crackers, tea and cake were served. It was fun! *[10 August 1937]*

Albert and his colleagues set sail from Sydney on August 12th on a much smaller ship that still had much to fascinate him. First, a "small" herd of cattle was on board and "Sometimes the smell comes into the dining room." Then, the passengers ate seven times a day, on a schedule worthy of a luxury liner: "In the morning at 6:30, our room steward brings a cup of tea, a cracker, and an apple to us in bed. After that he shines our shoes. We have breakfast at 8 o'clock. Just a few minutes ago, ice-cream and cookies were served. It is 11 o'clock. Dinner will be served at 1 o'clock. At 3:30 we have afternoon tea; at 6 o'clock supper and at 9:30 tea again" *[18 August 1937]*. Their journey to Madang was as circuitous as their on-board schedule was languorous. They stopped in Townsville in northern Queensland, and then went north to Rabaul, then the capital of New Guinea even though on the island of New Britain, and finally south again, down to Madang on August 29.

THE PART OF THE ISLAND of New Guinea at which Albert arrived had been a German colony for barely 30 years. Germany had claimed northeast New Guinea in 1884 and named it "Kaiser Wilhelmsland." After Germany's defeat in World War I, Australia administered it for the League of Nations. That New Guinea as a whole was colonized so late is a mark of its geographic isolation as is the fact that the Melanesians of New Guinea possess distinctive physical features, cultures, and languages. One learns nothing about them by studying the Australian Aborigines, who are right next door, or the Southeast Asians who live not much farther away in what is now Indonesia. The island's geography also makes isolation within it inevitable. Western-style travel even now is difficult. New Guinea indeed has large, open, grassy valleys, but there are many more jungle-covered mountains, the highest being 14,900 feet. Fast-flowing rivers, dropping down from such heights, are typically not navigable. Even today, with towns and villages quite numerous on the coast, the overwhelming impression of the land from on board ship a mile out to sea is that it is impenetrable. Beautiful, yes, but what place is there for an outsider? The more than 700 languages spoken by the peoples of New Guinea, many of which have no linguistic relationship to one another, reinforce the geographic isolation.

For Albert, a sense of New Guinea's isolation would have arisen from the length of his journey. Not that it bothered him: going far away from home and family was part of what he had signed up for. The cost of the isolation would be living in an alien culture, being able to communicate with the inhabitants in only perfunctory ways, going for weeks without seeing another white person or receiving any mail, and having no radio contact. He would have to live all this before he could grasp it.

Nor could Albert have known much about the people whom he had traveled so far to work with and to know. True, he had left Nebraska in considerable haste, leaving little time for specific preparation in any such matters. More basically, however, the field of anthropology was still in its infancy. Margaret Mead and her second husband, Reo Fortune, an anthropologist from New Zealand, had done the first fieldwork in New Guinea in the early 1930s, in an area to the north of where Albert was to go. (Interestingly, when Fortune returned on his own in 1935, it was to work with the Kamanos in the Central Highlands, just a few miles from Albert's second posting in 1940. Fortune remained only a few months because of the inter-village fighting that erupted and published nothing from his notes.)

Contemporary scholars of Papua New Guinea, historians of Lutheran Mission work in New Guinea, and anthropologists agree on the broad outlines of the traditional Melanesian world view. It is the antithesis of Western individualism and trust in the rational. We Westerners fall easily into dichotomies: reason contrasts with emotion, the physical with the spiritual, the Third World with ourselves. Melanesians view themselves as integral with their world. Spirits pervade every aspect of life. To explain an illness, one points not only to physical causes but to the complete environment, even to the cosmos, within which one lives. The New Guineans that the early missionaries met were on intimate terms with magic and sorcery in their daily lives. Magic could help them grow good crops; sorcery was a way to be rid of an enemy. While daily life was hard, ceremonial dances and festivals celebrated living. There was also an abiding sense that knowing a particular secret might unlock the mysteries of life. When New Guineans encountered the wealth of white men, they were sure that the white men had a secret that, if told to them, would reward them with the same goods. Men and women lived separate lives, as white observers often noted, with women doing much more physical labor than men. And while neighboring tribes sometimes traded with one another, conflict between them was equally likely to be present.

For Melanesians, relationships are key. They live out their relationships so differently from Westerners that a Christian American such as Albert would have had to devote considerable effort to be able to connect the gift he was offering the New Guineans with the world views they already possessed. At the heart of Christianity is the belief that humans require divine intervention if they are to live out their fullest potential. Jesus died on the cross so that all of humanity could be saved. We need only to accept that and then show the fruits of that belief through the way we live our lives. Usually, we make the decision to re-orient our lives as individuals and we place a premium on expressing our commitment verbally. Christians believe that we are forgiven when we ask for forgiveness, or when a pastor, acting on God's authority, says that we are forgiven.

No such intervention is needed in the traditional Melanesian world view because one lives as a part of the entire whole. People do not see themselves as individuals or in isolation. They belong to a group—a family, a clan, and a tribe. Their ancestors define them as much as does any living person. One is simply to be in the right relationship with those who matter, whether living or dead. And, for a Melanesian, words are much less important than deeds in establishing or correcting a relationship. Melanesian languages are said to lack the phrase "thank you." But a contemporary Papua New Guinean emphasizes that, "Mothers here do not teach their children to say 'thank you' but to do 'thank you.'"

Traditional Melanesian cultures are self-regulating in ways that Western cultures are not. They do not have a word for our word "law," seeing instead their entire way of life as that which guides them. There were no prisons in New Guinea until white people arrived. Having no laws or prisons did not make New Guinea a tropical Eden, however. The Melanesians felt free to murder or steal and then to seek vengeance when the same was done to them.

The challenge that Albert and all missionaries face is embodied in a story that a Papua New Guinean told recently while discussing cross-cultural work:

> There is the story of the monkey which felt sorry for the fish and pulled it out of the water so that it would not drown. Unfortunately, the fish did not appreciate the good heart of the monkey and, after threshing around wildly, died in safety.

What connects the worlds of the monkey and the fish so that each can benefit from the other? If the monkey believes that he or she has something essential that the fish lacks but would be glad to have, how can the monkey offer the fish this gift while still allowing the fish to be a fish?

THE MISSION that Albert joined, its shape and its approach to working among the New Guineans, was a direct product of German colonialism, with later influences from Australian and American churches. Johannes Flierl, the first Lutheran missionary, and one of the first from any Christian denomination, had landed near Finschhafen, on the northeast coast of New Guinea, in 1886, two years after Germany had claimed it. When Germany was defeated in World War I and Kaiser Wilhelmsland became a Mandated Territory of the League of Nations, the Australians, its new administrators, intended to remove all German missionaries from their posts and to give their stations to other Protestant missions in New Guinea. After lively intercession from the Lutheran church in Australia and the Iowa Synod in the United States, which also had strong German roots, the missionaries were allowed to stay. German, Australian, and American Lutheran churches eventually shared control over the work in New Guinea. The first American missionary, F. Edward Pietz, went to New Guinea in 1921, and it was the Pietz family with whom Albert lived during his first few months there.

Albert had a great deal of freedom about how he could spend his time, being expected to observe and ask questions on his own. His only regularly scheduled activity was to study what he called the Ragetta language (more commonly known as Graged). He seems to have known from the beginning that he would soon go to Karkar to replace the missionary who had temporarily fulfilled Daniel Spier's duties after Spier died.

The day after he arrived, Albert wrote Anna that he was on an island in a South Seas paradise:

> Madang is a beautiful place! I am staying with the Super-
> intendent of the Mission in the guest house which is hardly
> as good as our wash houses [where the laundry was done],
> but it is very clean and cool. There are two screened open-
> ings to allow the breeze to pass through. In this country one
> wants to get all the breeze he possibly can. Toward morning
> it was so cool that I had to cover up. The ocean is only about
> one hundred yards from the house. The singing of the birds
> in the palm trees which surround the place awakened me
> this morning at daylight. Rev. Pietz has chickens, cows,
> and ducks. A hen with little chicks walked past the door a
> few moments ago. The cows supply them with milk and
> chickens supply them with eggs. *[30 August 1937]*

Albert did not describe the Madang harbor as a whole: well-protected, dotted with small islands thick with palm trees. There would have been few power boats in 1938. As they did then, New Guineans still stand as they gracefully paddle their dugout canoes, perhaps going out to sea to fish or traveling to a relative's home to visit. An observer feels peaceful and serene.

Albert first encountered New Guineans in the three young men who did the laundry and cooking in the home of his host. Within his first 24 hours in New Guinea, he had heard a story about "native boys," a story that I too heard many times while I was growing up:

> This story is told about a certain native boy. The woman for whom he was working wanted to serve her guests a very fashionable meal, so she told her native cook-boy to roast a small pig after the pig had been cleaned! Before he brought the pig in to serve it, he was to put a lemon in the pig's mouth and some parsley back of the pig's ears! He did not understand correctly so he put the parsley back of his own ears and the lemon in his mouth and then brought in the pig. Of course everyone laughed.
> *[30 August 1937]*

Stories such as this one must have shaped Albert's early attitudes towards New Guineans. I know they did mine. Europeans customarily referred to New Guinean adults as "boys" and "girls." The boy in this story misunderstood, as did many New Guineans trying to function in an alien culture in which they did not set the rules. The boy felt ridiculous. He thought he was following the woman's directions, yet he comes across as slow. Did Albert then think the same of the three young men who worked in his host's home?

Two weeks later, Albert and Pietz travelled to Amele, one of the outlying mission stations, 16 miles from Madang. They walked and rode horses, Albert's favorite ways to travel. A young man named Tagwrap carried Albert's luggage on his back—Albert's introduction to another role that New Guinean men commonly fulfilled for white people from the government, as well as for businessmen and missionaries. At Amele, Albert witnessed his first group baptism of 40 New Guineans, attended a wedding, and sat through a church service with a sermon lasting 45 minutes, not a single word of which he could understand *[10 September 1937]*.

Albert's first letter to his sister Elizabeth and her husband Louis conveyed his optimistic interest in everything around him. First came a report on the weather and learning to live with the constant presence of insects:

> Yesterday and today, New Guinea has showed me that it can rain. It rained most of Saturday night, much of last night and will probably rain some tonight. We had a shower this evening. It isn't very disagreeable, however. The ground doesn't get very muddy and in the day time the sun generally shines. . . .
>
> New Guinea is also a land of bugs and insects. It is almost impossible to keep ants out of the food. Anyway, one doesn't mind an ant or two in the gravy, oatmeal or whatever it may be.

Liking the food eased his early days there. Another theme recurred in his letters—the necessity of a good loaf of bread—which in turn led to his first attempt at a job description for missionaries:

> The food here is excellent—all the bananas one can eat. They are not only eaten raw, but they are also baked and sometimes boiled. . . . I have been trying to learn to bake bread before I go out to Karker Island. Here, one makes his own yeast. It is made somewhat like this: one cup sugar, one cup flour, and two lemons, one cup warm water. This mixture is poured into a bottle in which there is a little yeast left from the previous baking. This yeast acts as a starter. Thus far, I've only watched how everything is done. As soon as possible, I'll teach a boy on Karkar to do it for me because a missionary has a lot of other work. He must treat the wounds of the sick; he must run the native

stores and a hundred other things. He hasn't too much to do—just enough to keep him out of mischief. Oh yes, he must learn the native language. I have a start! "O nea ite?" means "What is your name?"

The letter closed with a description of the first church service Albert attended in Madang, an experience similar to the one he had just had in Amele. There was much to take in. He wanted to be sure his readers knew that the New Guineans, especially the women, were appropriately dressed. They were also liberated in a way he had not expected: they smoked. Albert began with the service itself:

First, we sang a song, then prayer and Scripture reading followed by a sermon. But when the time came for the sermon, the native who was to preach wasn't there. (The natives conduct many of their own services.) After waiting a few minutes, a man from the audience arose, went to the front and talked ten minutes. Then Missionary Fliehler spoke, followed by another native who preached about twenty minutes. The natives are very good speakers. Then another song, and a prayer and we went home. I forgot to say that all the women wore dresses, but the men wore only loin cloths. During the week, the women wear just a short skirt. By the way, the women smoke here in New Guinea. Several of them put their cigarette stubs under the church pews. Some of the men sat on the floor—I believe they were more comfortable than those on the benches. Anyway, it's all very interesting! *[13 September 1937]*

In early October, Albert received his first letter from Sylvia and responded by telling her his ideas about the role of a missionary wife:

It seems to me that a missionary should eventually seek marriage. The missionary wife may have a very important position in the mission. Mrs. Walsh has a school for some of the girls on their station. Ah, there is so much that the girls should learn, cleanliness etc. A few days ago, Mrs. Pietz had to make a trip to the native village because of a confinement case and this morning at 6:30, she was again called—a mother has pneumonia. There is so much that a lady missionary can do for the natives. She has time to do that work outside of her home because she may have plenty of servants to do the work there (in her house). *[4 October 1937]*

A month later his letter explained why a missionary needed a long engagement:

I agree wholeheartedly with you on your idea of short engagements, but in our case it will have to be a little longer than would ordinarily be the case because of the fact that I'm on the one side of the world and you are on the other—and when a missionary is married, he must obtain permission from the board here. That is they must have time to arrange a home for him and his wife. Then too, the Mission Board in the United States must know about it in order to arrange for transportation funds etc. One year is almost necessary! This by way of explanation! Sometime within the next twelve months, I hope to ask you that all important question. *[5 November 1937]*

He had just attended the wedding of a fellow missionary, once again walking the 16 miles to Amele and back. He didn't mind that three families had flown in from Madang in ten minutes, whereas he had hiked for six hours:

[It] was a lovely walk—birds calling to you from the tall trees and thick bush—natives greeting you with a warm

"Fale" when you met them—overhead a few large white clouds floating beneath a blue sky. If a person doesn't have to go too fast, these long hikes are a pleasure even in a tropical country. Immediately upon arrival, one gets under a cool shower and the results are one feels like a new person. *[5 November 1937]*

The bride, whose homeland was Canada, had arranged to arrive shortly before her wedding. The ceremony itself had typical New Guinea touches, both in the decorations and the informality. No doubt Albert hoped his description would show Sylvia how lovely a New Guinea wedding could be, what she too could look forward to:

> The wedding was beautiful. Natives had built an arcade of palm branches which led from the missionary's home to the church. The church also was decorated—leaves from the banana trees covered the aisle which led to the altar. During the ceremony many natives surrounded the church and watched the proceedings through the open windows. Some also came in. After the ceremony Mrs. Welsh's native girls served a three course wedding dinner. It was gratifying to see how efficiently they worked. It goes to show that something can be accomplished with these so-called ignorant, stupid, dirty natives. Each girl appeared in a clean dress, barefooted and with her hair cut short (like that of a boy). During the course of the evening these girls sang "God will take care of you" in Pidgin English for the bridal couple. *[5 November 1937]*

Early on, Albert's often ambivalent ideas about New Guineans and what could be accomplished in working with them allowed him to consider whether there might not be another way to look at them. They did not need to remain the "other," perpetually regarded as both different and inferior.

These girls were up to European standards, unlike the boy with the parsley behind his ears and the lemon in his mouth. Although Albert doesn't say so explicitly here, the longer he was in New Guinea, the clearer it was to him that Christianity made the difference in enabling New Guineans to act in appropriate ways. It hadn't yet occurred to him that he might have something of value to learn from the New Guineans.

Soon after the wedding at Amele, Albert moved into his new home at Narer on Karkar Island, only 55 miles in circumference. Mt. Kanigioi, a 7,000-foot, still active volcano with three peaks, dominates the island. Lutheran Mission work had begun there in 1890, when Georg Kunze, a German missionary, and four other missionaries established a station near the village of Kulubob (now Kavailo), on the north coast. Kunze detailed his experiences in *In the Service of the Cross*, its themes characteristic of the pitfalls as well as the satisfactions awaiting early missionaries. Many of Albert's experiences were similar, although less bruising simply because he arrived 50 years later.

Although the Lutherans had had a relatively long presence on Karkar, Narer itself was new, having been established just two years earlier, in 1935. Albert was the third missionary assigned there. He was on his own in seeking to put the station on firmer footing. Narer's location must have emphasized that for him: from the station, one can see the ocean, perhaps 2,000 feet below, but nothing else suggesting human habitation. When Sylvia visited for the first time in 1949, she called it "the most isolated spot I've ever been at" *[4 November 1949]*. Fifty years after my first trip to Karkar as a child, I found the sight of the ocean a comfort, knowing that Albert was not completely hemmed in by the jungle. He said little about his house in his letters to his family and Sylvia, perhaps because of how primitive it was. He didn't want to alarm them. Many years later, Daniel Spier's widow described the house as a "shed." The Japanese bombed it during World War II when they overran the island.

Albert's letters to his family and to Sylvia during his 13 months on Karkar do not give a reader much sense of the larger picture of life on the island with its many villages and the large coconut plantations owned by Australians. Not too far from Narer, there was a Lutheran plantation, Kurum, and a Catholic mission had been established on the other side of the island. The state of Christianity in Albert's part of the island would have dismayed even someone much more experienced than he. In an early report, Albert listed "poor church attendance, much fear of sorcery, much dancing [seen as a problem because of the promiscuity and sorcery it encouraged], especially on the many plantations on all sides of Karkar, and few new volunteers for mission work," although he was impressed by the helpers and teachers with whom he worked.

Another missionary, writing the following year, gave additional reasons for the problems on Karkar: there had been too many different missionaries in too short a time, the white managers of the Karkar plantations were opposed to religion, and the indigenous Christians who were elders and teachers were not well prepared. Albert served with another handicap. Because of the laxity of church members, the mission headquarters had placed a ban on the sacraments, which was in effect for the entire time that Albert was on Karkar. There could be no baptisms and no celebration of Holy Communion, the ritual in which bread and wine are consecrated and then eaten and drunk to re-enact Christ's sacrifice for all. As a junior missionary, Albert would not have challenged the ban from mission headquarters. Even so, I can imagine him agreeing with his mentor, F. Henkelman, who visited in 1938 and questioned its value, since it deprived faithful Christians of their most important means of support in their worship and had no effect on weaker Christians.

Basic communication was another difficulty for Albert. Graged, the language that Albert was studying, was one of three official church languages. Educated Christians on Karkar would have spoken it, but everyone else spoke

Waskia or Takia, the island's two languages. Even if his language study had been directly useful, he had little time for it. The house had to be repaired and the chickens tended to. The poor health of the New Guineans demanded daily medical care, and the small trade store that he ran was so popular that it required his nearly constant presence. He was also responsible for supervising the 43 mission schools in each village on his side of the island, elementary schools run by New Guineans who themselves had a few years of schooling and then had been trained as teachers on the New Guinea mainland.

Some of the irritations he felt were personal: the cockroaches were eating his rayon underwear, and he asked his mother to send "some cotton undershirts and broadcloth shorts" *[31 December 1937]*. Keeping malaria at bay was a never-ending challenge. In my brother Jonathan's 1979 talk with our father, Albert described how thoroughly malaria dominated his life. He took quinine once a week, which made him sick for two days. Then he worked unencumbered for four days, but his dread of the quinine he had to take the following day diminished whatever he tried to accomplish on the fifth day.

Even for someone as self-reliant as Albert, the isolation must have made him desperate. He was still only 27. Although he had been away at college and seminary and then lived by himself in Hildreth for two years, his primary experience had been a Midwestern farming community where families were large and close. The mission boat from Madang was scheduled to arrive once a month, his only means of receiving and sending mail. Once, the boat didn't appear for nearly two months. He had no radio for most of the time he was on the island, learning about Hitler's increasing aggression in Europe only by word of mouth and by reading magazines that reached the island months after they were printed. Weeks would go by before he saw another white man—a white woman even less frequently.

Albert developed relationships with the New Guineans, but he must also have been told during his orientation in Madang that he should maintain some distance from them. He most likely also discussed the approach advocated by Christian Keysser, an early, influential German missionary. Keysser stressed living among the New Guineans and understanding their culture from within. At least in Albert's first few months on Karkar, he was conscious primarily of the distance he felt he needed. After six weeks on Karkar, he wrote to Sylvia that "I am beginning to love these brown chaps more and more—but I'm told that one should not become too familiar" *[30 January 1938]*. Maintaining distance meant eating and sleeping separately and spending free time alone—the little he had. He may also have been grateful for these small separations. They helped him to replenish his reserves. He could show an emotion such as anger at a task poorly done by a New Guinean, an emotion that he felt appropriate for his position as a white man. But there was no one with whom he could have an easy, informal conversation over a cup of tea.

Albert's letters reflect his contrary feelings. In his New Year's letter to Sylvia, he wrote: "Well dear, life here isn't as dark as you may think—there is joy in working in the Lord's vineyard here—and there is so much to do before the Day of Grace ends [the time before Christ's Second Coming]" *[1 January 1938]*. A month later, during which he had seen only one white man "for a few minutes," his mood was quite different: "These last two months have been the most difficult ones in my lifetime—never before so close to Satan, nor so close to God!" Questioning whether he was doing the right thing, feeling his loneliness gnaw at him, losing his temper, struggling with malaria: all of these experiences made him feel that Satan was tempting him. When he saw the difference his medications made, when he knew the language well enough to have a meaningful conversation with one of the work boys, when one of Sylvia's animated letters was on the mail boat: yes, then he knew he was doing God's will.

For the first time in this letter to Sylvia, he acknowledged some sympathy for his mother: "I am beginning to realize more fully now what it meant to her to lose dad and then my going shortly after!" *[6 February 1938]*. The isolation must have been intense for him to show this degree of feeling for her.

IN SPITE OF ALL OF THESE OBSTACLES, Albert was always trying to solve problems and be responsive to those he had come to serve. By March 1938, he could speak Graged well enough to give short talks during the Sunday services. Whenever he made a mistake, one of the teachers would immediately correct him, and he accepted the revision good naturedly. A letter to his mother detailed a typical week:

> It is a cool rainy Sunday afternoon. It has rained much of the last three days and nights! Friday, I wanted to go to a conference, but the water in one of the creeks made me turn back. One has to learn to like a lot of rain here. No doubt all this rain will make the bananas bigger, the pawpaws juicier and the pineapples sweeter. Here's hoping that it does! But it isn't helping my chickens very much. I have about fifteen hens and one rooster—ten chicks a few months old. As yet I haven't eaten an egg. Tomorrow, I think I'll have the boys go to the beach and get some sand for them. They are being fed bananas and wheat! Probably because they haven't had much care for about six months, they aren't laying. . . .

The jumble of the letter reflected Albert's own sense of how much there was to do and learn, along with his wish that his mother understand the details of his daily life. The days were not long enough to fit everything in:

> The last week was a very busy week. There was much repair work that had to be done on the station, shelves to make, screens to mend and what not! There is yet much to be done. Then too many natives come to the store to buy

kerosene, lamps, hoes, axes, loin cloths and other things. I
have sold about thirty dollars worth of goods last week! Later
sick people will be coming to the station for treatment, but
when everything is in order, things will go more smoothly
and I'll have more time to study the language.

The letter also mentions Kambar, the young man who cooked for him
and did his laundry. Albert spent more time with him than with anyone,
even so, always aware of the boundaries between them. Kambar's wife had
died less than a year before, but that's of no more importance than what
he'll cook for Albert's supper. He couldn't acknowledge that Kambar might
still be mourning the loss of his wife:

> Kambar, a native boy, does all my cooking. I tell him
> what to cook and he does the work. He also washes my
> clothes by hand then irons them. We have large irons here
> in which the coals of burnt cocoanut shells are placed. This
> will keep the iron hot for about three hours. This boy does
> a good job, but he forgot to starch the shirts. Well, it doesn't
> make so much difference because one hardly ever gets to see
> a white person. The reason this boy knows how to do things
> is because he was trained by another missionary's wife. This
> native boy has been married. He told me the other day that
> his wife died last summer in July, if I'm not mistaken. He is
> coming to make supper. I'll have cauliflower, potato soup,
> bread, butter and cheese for supper. That's enough, isn't it?
> If I get time, I'm going to plant a garden this week, at least
> radishes and tomatoes! If one had the time, one could have
> a very good garden. I'm also going to plant some beans. It
> gets tiresome to eat from tins. *[8 January 1938]*

Later that year, Albert again wrote about Kambar, this time to his
mother, who said she was making an apron for him. He felt free to slap

Kambar (and to tell his mother about it) when he considered him to be disrespectful on a trip they took together on the New Guinea mainland:

> That is very good of you [making the apron]! But sometimes I think that he doesn't deserve it. One day on the trip [that they had made recently with another missionary] when we were high up in the mountains, he became angry and said that he wanted to go home. He said too that he didn't like sweet potatoes and that was about all they were getting for food. Even though the climbing was hard and it was cold, his attitude was not a good one. I slapped his face and told him to keep still. After that he was a much better boy and said nothing more about his desire to go home and his dislike for sweet potatoes. *[26 November 1938]*

Daily life must often have seemed overwhelming. Karkar was nothing like the paradise of Samoa in which he had spent one day. Albert did his best to present his experiences in a positive light, as in this letter to his brother George:

> Things have been going quite well here on the whole. During the past weeks, I've had a little difficulty with my stomach. It seems that I ate some spoiled pawpaws. Consequently, there were a few dark days. But I'm trying hard to learn how to live here—took 15 grams of quinine for five consecutive days which should kill the malaria for a time. Living here is not as simple as it may seem. It's very difficult to bake good bread and you know what poor bread can do to a person.

He continued with examples of medical work he had done in one day, surely an example of his indomitable persistence:

> Here's an idea of some of the work—last Monday morning I gave Neo-salvarsan injections [for yaws, a

disease similar to leprosy] from 9 to 2 O'clock in the afternoon. The needle broke, some were rusty, one man got angry, one went home before he was injected, etc., etc. Thirty-six injections were given and you should see the results. Babies that had five and six sores and even more found that their sores were healing after a few days. This medicine works wonders. A little boy with a tropical ulcer several inches wide surrounding his anus is almost completely cured. This morning a little baby (perhaps 3 yrs.) came up with two big ulcers on one leg. The native boy and I treat it, but the child should also have an injection. A girl, age 10, came up with an ulcer about three inches long on the upper part of her arm—another one on her leg. One could write pages about the diseases and physical troubles of the natives. *[6 February 1938]*

Although Albert still had to be conscious of his own health, he could see that, at least in medical terms, he was making a difference in the lives of others. What he knew about health matters he would have learned from Dr. Theodore Braun, the person who, more than anyone else, helped establish the Lutheran Mission's medical presence in New Guinea.

Albert's letter to his brother continued, with frank comments about his state of mind. He took some satisfaction from his medical work, but keeping a perspective on the mission work as a whole was a constant vexation, particularly when he could see that so much was beyond his control:

There are problems aplenty—the church blew down three weeks ago. Today I heard that they were going to rebuild. I've asked them several times when they are going to build, but they don't seem to know.

There are things here that are pleasing to God, but also very much that is not so. When I feel well, which

is most of the time, and when the Devil lets me alone, I
enjoy the work immensely. I can't afford to worry, nor
can you! I've written this only to give you the other side
of a missionary's life. If you were to come up the path
from the beach this afternoon, I could greet you with a
smile—but at times the work is trying.

By referring here to the Devil, Albert probably meant the temptation to
doubt his effectiveness ("I can't afford to worry") and to dwell on questions
that still troubled him about leaving his mother and Sylvia. Although he
was writing to his trusted brother George, he saw no need to name his
temptations. That would give them more power than they merited. Albert
ended this letter by connecting himself to his family and his life on the
farm. There were at least some areas in which he had the necessary skills for
a missionary: "When it comes to fixing fences and repairing things around
here, I feel grateful for the training I had under a good old dad and two big
brothers!" *[6 February 1938]*.

IF ALBERT OFTEN FELT LONELY and ambivalent about his work and its
effectiveness, exploring his new home was an unambiguous pleasure. In May
1938, he and Henkelman made a three-hour trip by motorboat to Bagabag
Island, southeast of Karkar. Bagabag is smaller than Karkar—325 people lived
there at that time. Albert was impressed by the shelter that he and Henkelman
were given: "Our dwelling was of the native type—the roof of palm branches
and the sides of cane. A layer of sand covered the ground floor. There was not
a nail used in making the structure. It was quite comfortable—the roof did
not leak." For Albert, the four-day visit was an opportunity to observe village
life and talk with the islanders, who had had contact with missionaries for 40
years. They left on a Tuesday afternoon in a rowboat carrying "twenty-three
natives, a pig, and material for a new house" *[22 May 1938]*. After nine hours
of rowing on a calm sea, they arrived safely back at Karkar.

Later that year, he explored the volcano that so definitively marks Karkar, relying on New Guineans to carry his luggage and supplies. The beauty and strangeness were intoxicating. At the same time, he was forced to confront the dangers of this sort of travel—even though doing so would not deter him from taking extreme chances in the future. He and his companion barely made it out of the volcano's crater in the pitch black of the tropical night:

> On Friday morning, two native boys and I left for a trip up the mountain. On the way up, the boys' wives joined us. Later this proved convenient even though I at first disapproved. They gathered wood for the fires, found water for cooking, helped to build a house while the one boy and I explored the upper regions. It took approximately nine hours (not counting rest periods) to climb from Kurum [the Lutheran plantation] to the rim of the volcano. A strange sight awaited us, a great cavern 15 miles in circumference, at the bottom there were two craters, one of which is very small—also huge lumps of lava and a few bushes.

> Steam and smoke were continually arising from the mouth of the crater. On Saturday, we climbed to the summit of Konigioi, which is two hours from the rim of the crater. This locality is indescribable, very cold and invigorating. The view of the Pacific, the mainland and other islands is worth the effort alone. It was like living in another world, in the realms above! The boy and I made a wooden cross on the very highest point to signify that Karkar Island is for Christ.

> By noon we were back to our camp on the edge of the crater. After an hour's visit, the boy and I began the descent into the crater. It was most difficult, sliding on

our seats, swinging from tree to tree like monkeys and clinging to roots! We explored the crater bed and then tried to climb out. It was almost impossible. We could not get out where we came down. It was too steep. We tried another place—to no avail. Finally after walking a long distance we found a place where the wall sloped a little and we climbed out—but it was dangerous! Many times I felt that we should not have gone down into the crater. Night overtook us before we reached camp and that meant walking in the jungle without a path. How many times I bumped against trees, and how many times I became tangled in vines, I cannot say. It also began to rain which made matters worse. From time to time we called, but those at camp could not hear us. Finally they heard and a boy came with a lantern. Ten minutes later, we reached camp! We were cold and wet to the skin, but happy that we arrived safely. *[26 September 1938]*

THE NEW GUINEANS' HABIT OF STEALING infuriated Albert as it had Kunze. A 20th-century Papua New Guinean comments that theft from a missionary could be a straightforward Melanesian way of saying "You don't belong here." That interpretation or a simpler one—they saw something they needed and took it—seemed never to have occurred to Albert. Instead, he reacted from within the Christian framework he knew best: "Thou shalt not steal." To maintain his authority and to teach by example, he felt he had to uphold the basis for Biblical morality.

Most often, the New Guineans stole food from Albert—two eggs, some rice, or maybe some fruit. He did not think to compare the relative luxury of his diet with that of the New Guineans. When Kambar was eating only sweet potatoes and tiring of them on the trip to the mountains, Albert had a more varied diet of canned food. For Albert, only the principle of the thing mattered: if he could track down the thieves and punish them, he always did. When one man stole some rice from the food intended for all the workers, Albert "went after him and took the rice away from him. Then with loud words, I scolded him until he shivered (trembled). He should have been beaten! But I didn't think that it was the thing to do" *[6 February 1938].* When another man stole some fruit, Albert responded the same way, even though, "the fruit is a native fruit which I do not relish" *[18 April 1938].*

The most disturbing incident occurred shortly before Albert left Karkar. He described it in a letter to Sylvia written the day after Christmas:

> I too had an enjoyable Christmas except for an incident with one of my work boys. On Christmas Eve he carried my rooksack [*sic*] to Bangame where the Christmas program for the northern half of the island was held. When the program was finished and I wanted to go back to Narer, I couldn't find him. Finally I left the rooksack. On Christmas Day he did not attend the service. I sent word to his village at noon, but he did not come. Consequently I went to the village and brought him here into my house [evidently, with the rucksack]. I asked him to explain his conduct. He replied that he did not understand—a lot of poor excuses. I then put on my boxing gloves and let him have a round. He resented it—perhaps it was not the right thing to do. I know that it spoiled the day for me. We had a second day Christmas service this morning. I noted that he was present.
> *[26 December 1938]*

The first time I read this letter, I didn't see how I could use it. It was *useful* because it illustrated this part of Albert's experience in a dramatic way, but the missionary who boxed a defenseless New Guinean was also my father. Here was colonialism at its worst, I thought, exactly the sort of behavior that some people think of right away when they think of missionaries. What was the use of saving someone's soul for eternity if you could not treat him with respect on earth? Was I seeing the true core of my father, the part I remembered lashing out at us, especially my brothers, when we didn't measure up?

There are ways to explain Albert's actions from his perspective. He strove for consistency in applying rules of law such as the Ten Commandments. He felt he needed to show who was boss. I feel some empathy for him when I remind myself of his youth, inexperience, and isolation. Further, losing his rucksack would have significantly interfered with his ability to do his work. How would he carry what he needed on his frequent trips around the island? There was no place to buy another rucksack in New Guinea. He would have had to ask his brother George to send one from the States. At the earliest, it would arrive three months after he made the request. Even so, if Albert were here now, he would be quick to condemn the boxing. Already in his letter, he says it "spoiled the day for me."

ALBERT'S ACCOUNTS OF HIS TRAVELS around Karkar show that he took many occasions to reflect on what was right and wrong in the behavior of his new neighbors. Heathen practices were anathema to him. They were so far outside of what was acceptable that he felt free to judge them. His sense of authority, the distance he felt he was expected to maintain, and his bias against much of the local culture meant that he often dismissed local practices as simply heathen. "Heathen" described anything that implied a belief in a power other than God, using magic or sorcery to call on that power, and committing actions such as stealing, adultery, and killing that were forbidden in Christian morality. He must also have been afraid of heathen practices because he did not understand them, although he could sense their hold on people's lives. The power of Christ was supposed to be stronger, but could it actually win out? The New Guineans often did not share his belief that one should become completely Christian and leave the old ways behind. He, however, could not tolerate the mix, even though he could do nothing about it.

During Henkelman's visit in mid-1938, Albert and he toured the island. In the village of Wadan, Albert approvingly observed the behavior of a teacher who, although his youngest child had just died, "carried on nobly and conducted his school as though this sorrow had not come to him." Then Albert and Henkelman were asked by an elder to go to the men's house, to see a man who was dying:

> Upon entering we found a middle-aged man breathing very heavily. His forehead was already cold. He lay on a long platform, which is the men's resting place. To his right near his head, his wife sat. Other women, also men and children and several of the native dogs were in the hut. The dying man was a member of the congregation. After Bro. Henkelmann offered prayer, asking the Lord to receive his soul, we repaired to a shady spot near the village square and waited for some one to carry one of our bags to the next village. Our other carriers had gone on.
>
> We sat there about a half hour when a man stepped out of the hut, walked to the big wooden drum and began beating it slowly and deliberately. He was sounding the death knell. The man had died. Within a few moments more women came, carrying little children. All went into the hut where the corpse lay. Then followed the singing of hymns intermingled with heathenish wailing. We spent another half hour waiting for a boy to carry some of our outfit. The wailing and singing continued—enough to drive a man to insanity. It seemed as though a battle between Christianity and heathenism had taken place. *[8 June 1938]*

From Albert's perspective, if the man's family had been truly Christian, they would have accepted his death, just as he had his father's: they would have known that the man was going to be with God. They did not need their "heathenish wailing."

Ceremonial dances undermined the Christian life. About six weeks after the experience with Henkelman, Albert learned about a large dance that had drawn villagers away from a church service he was offering. He took the dancing personally as an affront to what he represented as a Christian missionary, concluding that he had the license to disrupt the ceremony by separating the Christians from the "heathens." Without question, the Devil was present for him in the dancing. The elders and teachers who went with him appeared not to have any second thoughts about what they were doing:

> On Sunday I went to Bangame (1 hour and 10 minutes from here) to conduct service. The attendance was small due to the fact that a number of the surrounding villages were participating in a dance in one of the secluded villages high on the side of the mountain. The dance began Saturday night, continued all night and also Sunday (heathenism). At times one could hear the beating of the drums quite distinctly. It made me angry, so after the service I told some of the elders and teachers that if they had any Christianity about them, they would go with me in the afternoon to the place where they were having the dance and we would admonish their brethren. They consented. After eating a bit, I got on my horse, and we went.
>
> Before I reached the place, I had to dismount and walk because of the ruggedness of the land! What a sight to behold after climbing the last hill: about 150 men, women and children, but only about twenty men were dancing. The dancers were decorated from head to foot,

beads, shells, red paint, blue paint, feathers in their hair etc. Each carried his little drum! Of course there was a little excitement when we came upon them. One old heathen dancer looked very angry! We lined the Christian dancers (among them were an elder and an ex-teacher) in one row and the heathen in another. Then I told them in the best way I knew what they were doing! There is much adultery and sorcery connected with the dances. The teachers and elders also addressed them telling them that they were on the way to Hell! And that they should repent! After we left, they finished their dance—but in the evening all became quiet. Just what effect it will have is hard to determine, but we tried. Believe me Sylvia, the Devil has a grip on these people! One needs wisdom to work in the Lord's kingdom. *[late July 1938]*

Although Albert feared heathen beliefs because he could see no simple way to eradicate them, he seems never to have feared for his physical safety on Karkar, apart from his hike down into the volcano. But in August 1938 he and several other missionaries and wives traveled by boat to Bunabun, up the coast of the New Guinea mainland from Karkar, to pick up Henkelman, Mager, and Thogersen, other missionaries who had made a trip inland. When Albert and his party arrived at Bunabun, only Henkelman was there, telling them the story that Albert related to Sylvia about the attack on the three missionaries and the New Guineans accompanying them:

When [the three missionaries and their carriers] were far inland, their guides deserted them. Upon reaching the outskirts of a certain village, they found a savage native guarding the path. He wanted to spear the first carrier, but when he saw the three white men he fled. The missionary party hurried on. After they traveled for a time, all of a sudden they found themselves surrounded by hostile natives. Spears and arrows began to fly before they realized the seriousness of the situation. One arrow grazed Mager's hat, he dodged a few others and then one struck his side. During this time, Thogersen shot four times, wounding at least three natives. This frightened the wild cannibals and they fled.

Some of the missionary party carried Mager (who was suffering) throughout the night as the party hurried from that locality. Henkelmann who had to carry two rooksacks fell into a pool of water. Later when it appeared that they were being surrounded again, four of the natives of the missionary party deserted the group, which made matters even worse. But by the grace of God, a week and a half later, they reached Bunabun, three ghost-like men. Thogersen nervous and fever-ridden, Henkelmann emaciated and Mager pale and sore! Mager told me that he could not lie down. All three went to Madang, Mager for medical treatment and the others to report the incident to authorities.

You can imagine how Mrs. Mager felt when she arrived at Bunabun and was told that her husband was wounded and was being carried out on a stretcher. They had been married only a few years. While they were gone, the plantation boys and I prayed for them in our daily devotions. It gave me a good feeling when I heard that they had been rescued from the jaws of death. . . . The station boys who went along are also weak and sickly. Many of them have sores. One stepped on some sharp wooden pegs, a trap which the heathen set. One of the pegs pierced his foot. But in spite of that he went on three days until he wasn't able to walk. Now the swelling is down and he is able to walk with a cane. One must admire the courage and perseverance of such a native. *[30 August 1938]*

Only at the end of his account did Albert tell Sylvia that, had he gone along instead of declining the invitation to accompany them, he might have "received an arrow. Now I am beginning to realize more and more what mission work is." The letter must have frightened Sylvia, perhaps feeding her indecision about committing to travel to New Guinea.

FOR ALBERT THAT FIRST YEAR, New Guineans were almost always inexplicable, alien, and sometimes threatening. Yet, he was also beginning to see them on their own terms. In a June letter to Sylvia, he was thinking aloud about what it could be that had such "a lasting effect on these natives. It seems that they live in an unreal world—a dream palace—a fairyland. The native is not a shining light intellectually, but in the mystic world he is a radiant star" *[26 June 1938]*. Another time, he was willing to attribute intelligence to them in Western terms. A young man named Miley had acquired a typewriter. Albert taught him how to touch-type and was amazed at how quickly he learned. Albert was also grateful to Miley for telling him about the "inner life" of the congregation, "things I would not otherwise find out" *[7 August 1938]*. A few weeks later, when Albert led a poorly attended service for the white congregation in Madang, he wrote Anna that "I would sooner preach to the brown natives on Karkar" *[23 August 1938]*.

In another letter, he concluded that New Guineans were destructive in the same ways as anyone else. An elder in a Karkar village told him of a time when another missionary informed the head men of his village that they should attend church more regularly. They became angry and tore down the church. The government punished them, and the men retaliated by reintroducing heathen dances. Albert ended by saying, "It goes to show that the human heart is everywhere the same" *[8 June 1938]*. As Albert was preparing to leave Karkar in January 1939, he told Sylvia that "Even though I had a few difficulties with the boys, I learned to love them" *[12 January 1939]*.

If Albert rarely praised those with whom he worked, he was just as hard on himself. On the occasion of dedicating a new hospital, several missionaries journeyed to Karkar, among them Rev. Welch from Amele, whose 25 years of experience made him the senior person in the mission. Albert reflected with him on his work thus far: "He and I had a lot of arguments—sometimes I felt that I was disrespectful. However when he left he told me that what I was doing here made him happy. Ah, dear, I could do a lot more if I dedicated myself body and soul to the work. I'm ashamed of myself and hope that someday I'll really work" *[30 August 1938]*.

At a mission conference in Madang in the middle of July, Albert learned that he was to be sent inland in about six months when the "regular" Karkar missionary returned from furlough. First, however, he would have to study Kotte, the language that the Lutheran Mission had designated for use in the Highlands. There he would "work among people who have hardly been touched by civilization—many of whom have never seen a white man—another language and new experiences. It will take the best that I have" *[11 July 1938]*.

THE COMPLICATIONS IN ALBERT'S RELATIONSHIP with the New Guineans, for whom he had turned his life upside down and to whom he would devote himself for 40 years, arose mainly from himself: his strong-minded sense of mission, his devotion to God, and his values of hard work and determination. He felt responsible for and empathetic with the people on whose behalf he worked, but his way was often patronizing and sometimes inhuman. Anyone looking for stereotypes of the overbearing missionary can find them in Albert's early letters from New Guinea.

His role as a missionary was made more complex by his youth and inexperience, along with his personality. His letters display his occasional vulnerability, but they also show his considerable power, which often expressed itself as superiority. He liked the fact that he was taller than any New Guinean. In many matters, physical and spiritual, he was in control. While wishing that he had a better medical background, he could see that his simple medications often healed people. In the mission trade store, he sold highly coveted items that the islanders could not easily otherwise obtain: matches, salt, axes, newspaper, tobacco, loin cloths and dresses, rice, and other basic foodstuffs. He was the superintendent of their schools as well as the keeper of their souls.

Twentieth-first century readers may be most disturbed by his physically disciplining those for whom he was responsible. Yet that was a prerogative that white men of that time and place felt was theirs when they worked with "natives." He saw New Guineans as lazy, unable to make up their minds. He met only one New Guinean on Karkar who had "that which it takes" to run a plantation. The rest, he said, "would rather sit in their little huts to chew betel nut and smoke" *[9 January 1938]*. Albert's focus, discipline, commitment, and German Lutheran values—positive as they are in a receptive context—also made it more difficult for him to accept the New Guineans as people during his first year.

With experience and maturity, Albert came to appreciate the complex humanity of the New Guinea people. Being a wise virgin was a good thing but it was also not enough. In a rational way, one could be ready without yet having opened one's heart to what was to be received. The monkey could not save the fish without seeing the world from the fish's point of view. Albert had begun the painful and disorienting process of seeing himself as never before and of seeing those around him as human, no matter how different they were from himself.

Chapter Five
A Similarity of Soul Pattern

Albert's path after leaving Karkar was circuitous. He must have felt that he was marking time by spending all of 1939 waiting to learn where the Mission Board would send him for a permanent placement. He knew it would be in the Highlands, but that was all. Did he ever question the urgency with which the Board insisted that he go to New Guinea? He lived in three different places with missionary families while he was studying Kotte, the church language for the Highlands, after he had passed the language examination in Graged, the first church language he learned. Sylvia's sporadic letters (only six that year, and all of them in the first six months) did not help his frame of mind, particularly when he was trying to persuade her to commit to traveling.

Albert's first place of study was Boana, an inland station 100 miles southeast of Madang. He felt fortunate to be at Boana, "by far the best place in New Guinea where I have been." Fresh fruit, vegetables, and meat were abundant, and he had an escape from the constant threat of malaria and the humidity of the coast. The Boana climate was "eternal spring."

Trying to explain to Sylvia why Kotte was more complex than Graged, Albert wrote: "It has [a] near and remote past, also a near and remote future, a regular present and then one that expresses continued action, also three dual forms and an exclusive and inclusive first person plural" *[26 March 1939]*. To practice the new language, Albert talked with young boys, giving them sticks of tobacco to encourage them to return. Language study was never a burden for Albert, but rather like climbing another mountain: who knew what was on the other side? Over time he wrote sermons in five languages: English and German yes, but also, Graged, Kotte, and Jabim, the third official church language.

The new year was less demanding and more relaxing than 1938 had been. Without the responsibilities of a mission station, Albert was free to do the exploring that he loved so much. A three-week trip to the Sarawaged mountains with Rev. Gustav Bergmann, the missionary at Boana, was "the most interesting tour I have made to date." From the window of his room, Albert could see the peaks of the Sarawaged range early on clear mornings— unknown, mysterious, and challenging.

On the Sarawaged trip, he and Rev. Bergmann stopped along the way to visit villages that were among the missionary's responsibilities. Years later, Albert told his son Jonathan that he made the trip just to make the climb. Christian Keysser had climbed Sarawaged, and so would he. A photograph shows him standing beside Keysser's umbrella, still in a cairn on top of Mt. Sarawaged, the highest peak. Jonathan hiked the same trail in 1980; for those five days, he saw no one.

The hike was Albert's kind of challenge. Mr. Raabe, the mission airplane mechanic, was also going on the trip, and the young women who worked for Mrs. Bergmann made mattresses stuffed with kapok for all of them. The kapok, a cotton-like substance that grows on trees, would help them stay warm during their nights high in the mountains. Fifteen young men would carry the mattresses in large bags, along with the "butter, jam, sausages, condensed milk, coffee, etc."

Albert described highlights of the trip for Sylvia, delighted that somehow the botanist he met unexpectedly up on the mountain sensed there was someone special in his life:

> We slept at an altitude of 12,500 ft. for four nights
> which was one hour from the peak of Mt. Sarawaged, which

is 14,000 ft. above sea level. It was very cold up there—about 40 degrees F every morning—our butter hard and the water ice cold! Two times Brother Bergmann and I climbed to the top of Mt. Sarawaged. It was thrilling so high above the world! . . . Part of the time we hunted kangaroos [actually, wallabies]. Mechanic Raabe shot one small one and wounded several others. We met Mrs. Clemens, a botanist, who is collecting specimens for the Berlin Museum. She has been in the Sarawaged territory about five months. Her husband was chaplain in the US Army. Mrs. Clemens is young at 67 and a very interesting person. Without a word from me, she gave me a few flowers and told me to send them to "The Lady Friend" . . . Then she also handed me a forget-me-not and said to send it to you.

Their trip ended at the coastal mission stations of Ulap and Sio, northeast of Boana. They reached Sio one day before the local missionary, Rev. Wagner, arrived by boat with his bride. The bride and groom received a typically exuberant New Guinea greeting that let Albert imagine how he and Sylvia might be welcomed. The bride reminded him of Sylvia, even the particulars of her hairstyle:

Just before the small boat reached the shore, an elder offered prayer. Then a few of the young men rushed out and sprayed salt water over the bridal couple. Then they were carried to shore and led to the mission house. A dozen native dancers in festive costumes danced, sang, and beat their drums while they led the procession. There were several thousand natives on the beach to welcome the new bride. He and she were much thrilled—especially she! You may well imagine what thoughts I had! Mrs. Wagner

reminded me a little of you—pleasingly plump—hair parted
in the middle—a small roll in the back! *[30 April 1939]*

Albert's attitudes toward the New Guineans continued to be interwoven
with what he thought Christianity could bring them. One April day, he
and Rev. Bergmann walked for seven hours up and over a mountain ridge
to the mission station of Gabmatzung. The local people there were the
Laewumbas, "the fiercest warriors in the area," before the missionary arrived
16 years earlier. One Laewumba man confessed to having killed 40 people.
If a man wanted a wife, he had to first present her with the skull of a man
he had killed. Albert wrote Sylvia that, "Now they divert their strength into
other channels, such as making big gardens and handling heavy goods at
port [Lae, now capitol of Morobe Province]."

Albert continued to see customs that required changing. Because
Laewumbas were expected to marry people to whom they were related, the
unions often resulted in physically deformed or mentally retarded children.
A woman who wanted to marry outside the tribe would be beaten until she
consented to the husband chosen for her. Albert concluded, "Christianity
is helping to raise the standard of women, but it is a slow process." That
Sunday in church, Albert heard the Laewumbas sing, 600 of them. A
phrase would begin in unison, and the singing would be a chord by the
time it ended. At times the women and men sang different words, but the
combination was beautiful: "When that congregation of 600 people sang,
I thought of the singing in Heaven, of the St. Olaf Choir and the like.
And then to think that these were only natives, murderers, adulterers etc.
singing their native tunes to the praise of God" *[23 April 1939]*.

Albert didn't know what to make of what he had heard. As a colonial,
he saw "only" primitive natives. As a Christian, he saw evidence for the
transforming power of God's grace. He didn't take the time to reconcile
these contradictions for himself and Sylvia.

AFTER THE SARAWAGED TRIP, Albert continued his language study at Heldsbach, a Lutheran school near Finschhafen that trained teachers. Although Albert didn't swim well, he loved the natural swimming pool near Heldsbach, created by a waterfall of cool mountain water. He felt privileged to be living in the last home that Rev. Flierl, the mission's founder, had occupied before he returned to Germany. Of the half-dozen other Germans at Heldsbach, a Miss Kepler impressed Albert most forcefully. At 71, she was the oldest person in the mission and had also served the longest: 40 years *[7 June 1939]*. She must have moved him to hope that he too would be capable of similar dedication.

Albert was also gratified to be working with Rev. Georg Pilhofer, the head of the school. He had translated the New Testament into Kotte. Every evening, Pilhofer would walk out into the night with him, pointing out the stars of the Southern Hemisphere. Like Keysser, Pilhofer believed that New Guineans had to be approached on their own terms. The music of the New Guineans had yet to be studied, he told Albert. No one knew the "rules" governing its structure or performance. Albert immediately saw that Sylvia would relish such a task *[8 August 1939]*.

Albert and Pilhofer undoubtedly talked a great deal about how to approach mission work, the older man from his perspective of 35 years in New Guinea. Pilhofer's approach was similar to that advocated by Christian Keysser. In the *Gospel for the Heathen*, Pilhofer's manual for New Guinean evangelists written in Kotte in 1931, he declares that learning the local language and the values and customs of the people should take precedence over teaching stories from the Bible to the natives. Even the word Pilhofer used for "heathen" in Kotte, *qapuc*, does not carry the negative connotation of "heathen." It means simply, "not knowing."

Freed from the responsibility of running a station, perhaps Albert felt relaxed enough to reflect on his experiences at Narer and to conclude there must be a better way than trying to force people to become Christian.

Pilhofer's approach now appealed to Albert. It allowed him to build on his awareness of New Guineans as spiritual beings, which he had already noticed after just six months at Narer: "The native . . . in the mystic world is a radiant star." Now, at Heldsbach, he observed a "similarity of soul pattern" between the New Guineans and himself. He sensed in them the same yearnings that Christianity fulfilled in him: recognizing a power larger than one's self at work in one's life, believing that one needed a sounder basis for action than serving one's self, and valuing the coming together of like-minded people into a community. The Gospel was indeed able to transcend time and place and culture.

Heldsbach itself impressed Albert as an example of what dedicated mission work could accomplish. He called it "an educational center," notable simply for being in New Guinea, "where ignorance and dark heathendom still reign in many areas." The 114 students, all men, were studying to be teachers or evangelists. They spoke 20 languages. No wonder that the church had confined the doing of its business to only a few "official" languages.

Days were full. At dawn, a drum summoned everyone to the creek to wash, and then they assembled for morning devotions. Classes in arithmetic, reading, penmanship, dictation, Bible history, and church history filled the rest of the morning. The students' questions surprised Albert, and he wrote some of them out for study so that he could better answer them. "Can a Pope be saved?", "Why did God allow Satan to bring about the fall of Adam and Eve?", "Who made Hell?", "How can those who have been eaten be resurrected?" (The tribes to which some of the students belonged had a tradition of cannibalism.)

One student found it impossible to believe that the earth was larger than the moon. Albert felt, "The colossal works of the white man and his superior wisdom leaves the Papuan dumbfounded." At the same time, they saw more (wealth, power) was not necessarily better. European culture, including the persisting presence of Christianity, had not necessarily improved white people: "Why are there still so many unbelievers and so much war in countries like Europe where they have so many schools, churches and teachers?" (Albert would have agreed. Why haven't we Europeans done better, given all our advantages?) Even so, they were eager to learn more about Christianity, finding it difficult, after a Bible class, to concentrate on arithmetic ("How much are five net bags of taro worth @ one shilling and six pence per bag?"). Once, when Rev. Pilhofer could not teach for several days, students gathered on their own to study their notes.

Classes were taught only until noon. Afternoons, students worked in their gardens to provide food for their families, if they had brought them from their home villages. They grew sweet potatoes, bananas, and corn, and they raised cattle, hogs, and goats. Between harvests, they had barely enough to eat. Other unusual difficulties had to be dealt with. Students from the mountains suffered attacks of malaria. One student was so nervous that he kept his pen steady while writing only by holding it with both hands. Work on plantations or in gold mines tempted the younger men to leave school. A student who committed adultery was expelled, and three elders walked for three days from his village to take him home *[June 1939]*.

While Albert was impressed by the students' willingness to sacrifice so that they could learn, the lack of work ethic he saw in New Guineans bothered him, just as it had on Karkar. Working hard was a European (not only Christian) quality that he felt he must pass on. Albert wrote his brother George that he had used him as a model to teach industriousness to the students:

> Rev. Pilhofer asked me how many livestock my brother had. I told him and the class that he had 50 hogs, 8 horses, 30 cattle, and 600 chickens. . . . He then asked how many servants you had? I said one boy. He then asked if your hogs broke out of the pen and destroyed the crops like the native pigs? I answered 'alicine' (no). He then asked if you, like the natives, starved your pigs and chickens?

I answered that you feed them 'jacgon' (corn). He then asked if you had a dog and if that dog was a 'good-for nothing' like most of the native dogs. I answered that you have one dog and that he gets the cows. *[7 August 1939]*

The comparison had at least some of the desired effect: all the students decided to raise more pigs and chickens when they returned to their villages.

WORLD WAR II INTRUDED DIRECTLY into mission work and Albert's life within a month after Britain and France declared war on Germany in September 1939. Since Australia was a member of the British Commonwealth, it too was at war. As the government responsible for the Territory of New Guinea, Australia immediately interned most German missionaries, and the mission placed Americans on their stations in their stead. Albert never wrote directly about seeing his friends and colleagues removed so harshly. For Sylvia, he placed the matter in the only perspective that mattered to him: "In these days when the hearts of so many are filled with fear, we are especially grateful that our lives center around Him who is not of this world—our Lord Jesus Christ" *[29 September 1939]*. Albert was to go to Ogelbeng, to replace Rev. Hermann Strauss, who was deported to Australia. He returned to Madang to await the government permit to travel inland. Never one to sit idle, Albert taught in the Chinese school there. It had just seven students: "Chun Ming, Ameng, Foiseng (girl), Chun Miou, Chun Lung, Afong, and Mei Young" *[2 November 1939]*.

The mission conference held in Madang in December 1939 lifted the three-year ban on the sacraments that had been in effect during Albert's entire time on Karkar. One station reported 390 baptisms on the first Sunday in Advent. Albert's conference report noted the challenges the young mission faced, both within itself and as a group concerned with the larger society of which the missionaries were a part. Without German missionaries, how were stations to be staffed? How were buildings to be maintained, given their rapid deterioration in the tropics? Young men were leaving their villages for years at a time to work on plantations far away. How could they marry and establish families under these conditions? New Guineans who were first-generation Christians were fervent in their faith, but what about their children?

The conference also decided that Albert would go to Raipinka rather than to Ogelbeng. Another station in the Highlands, it too had lost its German missionary. The change probably did not bother Albert. What mattered was to be on the frontier of mission work.

"UNEXPLORED." THE WORD IS WRITTEN in red across a 1930 map of the New Guinea Highlands. There are rivers, mountains, and a few settlements up to about 100 miles inland, and then nothing. Though the scale was different, I imagine the prospect of exploring the New Guinea Highlands to have been not so different from the feelings had by members of the Lewis and Clark expedition in 1804 as they were about to set out on their exploration of the American Northwest.

German Lutheran missionaries, together with New Guinean evangelists, had scouted part of the area in the early 1920s, but it was a group led by Michael Leahy, an Australian explorer and prospector, who made the first systematic explorations, between 1930 and 1934. He was looking for gold; in *The Land That Time Forgot*, his account of his travels, it's also clear that the journeys themselves were enormously exciting and demanding.

The New Guinea interior was thought to be a continuation of what one saw from the coastal settlements: rugged mountains covered with impenetrable jungle, probably with very few people living there. Who could live in such inhospitable surroundings? What Leahy and his men found, instead, were many villages, grassy, open spaces, and well-cultivated gardens of sweet potatoes, beans, and sugar cane, irrigated with drainage ditches. The only tools in evidence for this impressive work were stone axes and sharpened sticks.

No doubt, the first missionaries saw the large indigenous population and temperate climate as signs that here was a good place in which to win souls. In 1931 the Lutherans established a station not far from what became Raipinka, part of a larger area called the Upper Ramu—so named because it includes the headwaters of one of New Guinea's major rivers. The predominant tribe was the Kamanos. The missionaries could not have had much sense of the alien Kamano culture. As a child living at Raipinka, I knew that fights between villages were common, that cannibalism occurred, and that women were treated badly. Anthropologists' studies from that time period provide an idea of the extent of these practices.

In 1935, the anthropologist Reo Fortune received a permit for field work with the Kamanos from the *kiap* (government official) at Kainantu, the government outpost in the Upper Ramu. Fortune concentrated on a group of villages to the north. The *kiap* ordered him out after just five months because of the escalating levels of violence between villages, but he was able to complete a preliminary grammar of the language before he left. World War II and a lack of funds prevented Fortune from returning until 1951. When he finally made it back, he met Albert in Lae, where we had moved from Raipinka. That same year, Albert picked up the Australian anthropologists Ronald and Catherine Berndt at the Lae airport, as they were on their way to begin work south of Raipinka and Kainantu. He also wrote them a letter of introduction to the missionary then serving in Raipinka.

Once at their field sites, both Fortune and the Berndts were unnerved by the ways in which the Kamanos and nearby tribes greeted each other. Fortune noted that a man greeting another man would touch the other man's penis and say, "thy penis greeting." A woman greeting a man would say the same or "thy scrotum greeting" but not touch the man. A father greeting his daughter would say, "thy vulva greeting" and touch her. The Berndts, entering their first village, were greeted by excited crowds calling out, "I eat you!" Even in 1951, in that area south of Raipinka, many had not yet seen white people and regarded the Berndts as ghosts, returned ancestors, and thus to be treated with reverence. Because the Berndts were ancestors and therefore kin, the villagers at first assumed they would not have to teach the Berndts their language. They would need to be there only a little while before they remembered it.

Fortune and the Berndts describe the same general patterns of village life that Albert saw and that I remember from my childhood. Men and women led separate lives. There was no class structure; governing decisions were made informally, by one or a few "big men." The men lived communally in a single large house, built with flattened woven bamboo walls and a thatched grass roof. The house had a dirt floor with a fireplace in the middle. There was no chimney: the smoke worked its way out through the thatch. There was only one door, the more easily to protect those inside, and no windows. The women and children lived in smaller houses, one for each wife.

The roles of men and women were clearly defined, with women responsible for most of the day-to-day tasks. The men's main occupation was to fight with neighboring hostile tribes. They would clear land for gardens, but the women did the actual gardening, carried the water, reared the children, and tended the pigs. Wealth was carefully distributed and redistributed within the tribe as couples married. Other than trading with outsiders, villagers had little reason to go beyond the immediate vicinity of their villages. Everything they needed was there. Besides, enemies were close by, and the terrain was rough.

Ronald Berndt describes a creation myth, prevalent among the tribes he and his wife studied. Jugumishanta and Morufonu emerged from sacred ground in a swampy area. At first, they did not look like humans. Jugumishanta made herself human and did the same thing to Morufonu, giving them both genitals. They had intercourse, and then there were children. The two gods went from place to place, creating gardens and putting people to live in the gardens. They told them the ceremonies they should perform.

Gardens continued to be important in contemporary tribal culture. Often, the dead were buried there to continue to fertilize the ground.

Both Fortune and the Berndts noted the ways in which women were subjugated and hypothesized about why the gender that grew the food and bore the children—essential aspects of any culture—was so frequently mistreated. The root cause, they concluded, was male fear. The Kamanos recognized women's power but refused to honor it. Women were to be completely subservient to men, illustrated by what was expected when a husband died: they were to cut off a finger joint. Since they married in from other villages, they were fundamentally outsiders, never to be fully trusted. Sorcery was available to anyone, even women. If the crops failed or a child died, perhaps a woman did it on purpose. Certain rituals, forbidden to women, were said to increase men's strength. The men played sacred flutes. If women saw the flutes, men would lose their strength, and the ritual would be meaningless. Another ritual dramatized men's control of their bodies. They swallowed lengths of thin cane, thus inducing vomiting. By protecting themselves from overeating, they were guarding against the weakening influence of women. This ritual had to take place in running water so that the vomit would be washed away and thus could not be used for sorcery.

The abuse of women was also reflected in the informal "courts" which dealt with wrongdoers. Only men sat in judgment. Although both men and women could have extramarital intercourse, for women, it became adultery at some point not clearly specified. In the 30 cases of adultery that Ronald Berndt recorded, all the perpetrators were women. Their punishments were horrific. Berndt described one of them in detail. First, the woman's grass skirt was cut off, leaving her naked. Then several men raped her, an elder beat her in her pubic area with a hot cane, and another man shoved a piece of wood into her vagina. The woman was left to be cared for by other women when she was almost unconscious.

Violence was a regular part of daily life. A young man had to kill at least one person, but preferably as many as five, before he could marry. War was the primary basis for interaction between the various "districts" the Berndts studied, the "breath of life," the men told Ronald Berndt. A man must always have his weapons and always be prepared. The frequent fighting reinforced male domination and the distrust of one's neighbors. Fortune estimated that 50% of the deaths of men, women, and children were due to violence.

Government officials and the few missionaries in the area had no tolerance for the fighting and the mistreatment of women. And then there was cannibalism. I first read Ronald Berndt's description of this practice on a Friday, as I was working on this chapter. I spent the weekend in a daze, trying to take in what I had read. According to Berndt, Fortune said of the Kamanos, "Their bellies are their cemeteries." Berndt claims that the last public act of cannibalism occurred among the Kamanos in 1951, although it continued secretly after that.

As both Fortune and Berndt explain, the Kamanos were not headhunters, killing people to eat them. They simply regarded dead human flesh as food, supplementing their diet that was otherwise low in protein. Men and women, enemies and relatives—all were eaten and, if they knew they were going to die, would often request to be eaten after they died. There were only a few restrictions: parents were not to eat children and vice versa, as with an incest taboo. Some tribesmen preferred decomposed human meat and would bury a body for several days and then dig it up. They scraped the maggots off the body and cooked them separately in a banana leaf, considering them a delicacy. Special parts of a body would be given to particular people—a man's penis to his wife, for example.

I know Albert was skeptical about anthropologists. I remember him saying that the New Guineans told anthropologists what they thought they wanted to hear. Since he knew both Fortune and the Berndts, it seems likely that he was referring to them and perhaps especially to their claims about cannibalism and the Kamanos. My experience as a reader is different, however: the detail, the accuracy of what I know to be true, and the matter-of-fact way in which the anthropologists' accounts are written—all of this persuades me to trust them.

Now, when I think about our living among the Kamanos, I remind myself most of all that whatever revulsion Albert must at times have felt, he never gave up working with them. During the years at Raipinka he came to see them as human in the same way he was. For him, it was the Gospel that allowed one's true humanity to shine through.

ALBERT WOULD HAVE KNOWN LITTLE of Kamano culture when he learned that he was to be sent to Raipinka. Surely, what would have been most on his mind was the history of fighting among villages and tribes and the times when white men were caught up in it, which then affected the government's willingness to allow missionaries to continue working. The way the government responded also sometimes affected relationships between the mission groups, although I doubt that was the government's intent.

For example, in 1934, a large Lutheran mission party had completed a promising exploratory expedition. Soon after, two Roman Catholic missionaries were killed a month apart by Chimbus, who lived west of Raipinka. The colonial government immediately curtailed any mission work. No new missionaries would be allowed into the Highlands. In 1936, the government took an additional step. Since all of the New Guinean evangelists were from the coast, they could now live only on mission stations where a European missionary also lived. The Lutherans objected: they relied on evangelists more than did the Catholics and Seventh Day Adventists, the other church groups working in the Highlands. With evangelists now restricted to mission stations, the Lutherans felt their work as a whole was being stymied.

Albert's German predecessor at Raipinka had been caught up in several different tensions. Martin Zimmerman, who had begun the station in 1937, had left after only two years. He did not get along with the Australian government officials in nearby Kainantu, who saw his formal manner as too "Prussian." What's more, he kept a picture of Hitler in his living room. They wondered why he had to do his target practice by shooting at moving tennis balls.

Australian officials were also displeased by the Lutheran policy of teaching Kotte in their schools rather than Tok Pisin, the *lingua franca* increasingly in use in the Territory. The missionaries did not take Tok Pisin seriously as a language—a policy that was to change later. Because the villagers were learning Kotte, the missionaries and evangelists could talk to them more easily than could the government officials, a situation the officials regarded as inappropriate. Zimmerman was among the first German missionaries to be interned in Australia in September 1939.

Before Albert arrived, tensions between the Lutherans and the Seventh-Day Adventists had increased, particularly since the primary Adventist missionary in the area was more aggressive than Zimmerman. The Adventists and Lutherans approached mission work in contrasting ways, with sometimes contradictory messages for New Guineans who might listen to both. The Adventists worked from a centralized post, whereas the Lutherans relied on evangelists who spread out into the villages. Adventists worshipped on Saturday, and Lutherans on Sunday. Adventists forbade the eating of pork, thus introducing a prohibition that directly affected economic and ceremonial aspects of village life. They also placed a high premium on cleanliness, making Adventist villages easy to identify—even easier, in later years, as their goats replaced pigs. For anyone accustomed to the central position that pigs occupy in New Guinea cultures, it is still startling today to be traveling in the Central Highlands and to see goats running freely rather than pigs.

The confusion and dissension that competing missions created have always plagued mission work in New Guinea. I see the competition for souls as one of the areas in which missionaries are most vulnerable to criticism, and I understand why skeptics ridicule them. The New Guineans become commodities, not so different from the gold and, later, the oil and the lumber for which other Europeans were competing. Missions' competitiveness undermined much of the good they did in education, health care, and in improving the status of women.

ALBERT KNEW ABOUT THE CONFLICTS between missions and the need to be concerned about his own safety. But what was most important to him at the time was that, after a year of language study and frequent moves, he was now to have his own station. At the end of 1939, when he finally received permission from the government to travel to Raipinka, he may have felt that he was now a real missionary. He was to fly in by chartered plane, and he could hardly wait:

> [Raipinka] is delightfully cool and has good soil for growing all kinds of vegetables. There are about 20,000 natives in the circuit with approximately 20 helper (native evangelist) stations. This will mean that I'll get plenty of exercise traveling around to visit them. I wish tomorrow were Wednesday that I might go already tomorrow. *[31 December 1939]*

After a 40-minute flight over the Finisterre Mountains and along the broad and grass-covered Ramu River Valley, the plane landed at Kainantu. Albert was met by two Australians—the local *kiap*, and a medical assistant—who offered him a cup of tea. Albert rode the three miles up the long hill to Raipinka, and students from the mission school carried his belongings and supplies. During the entire time, a large group of New Guineans of all ages crowded in on him, watching everything he did.

Although Albert had previously witnessed New Guineans living as they had for centuries, he would now be living among them for the first time. His initial description of them was harsh, a classic instance of "first contact" responses reported by Europeans of that time. For Albert, however, their deplorable condition was less to be attributed to their not being European than to their not being Christian, a matter that affected one's entire being, not just one's invisible soul:

> Being in the midst of a group of heathen natives, reminds me somewhat of *a trip thru an asylum for lunatics at home* [emphasis mine]. Some stare, some laugh and most of them act distrustful and shy. That in addition to their filth and squalor makes a very unpleasant sight. At first one thinks that they hardly belong to the human race, but later one's opinion changes and one realizes more fully to what extent man without the Gospel may sink into the mire of degradation.

Approvingly, Albert described the New Guinean mission teacher and his students who carried Albert's belongings. They "looked clean and much more human than the others" *[January 1940]*.

Rarely, if ever, do Westerners encounter the degree of difference that Albert encountered on that three-mile ride to Raipinka. Even if other Europeans had been present, he must have felt completely alone. Sitting above the crowd, on horseback, intensified his separation from the New Guineans. They could touch his pantlegs, but his hands and face were out of reach. The smell of rancid pig grease on their skins was not as strong as if he had been walking among them, but it filled the surrounding air. Highlanders at that time bathed infrequently; neither did they swim. Both sexes clothed their genitals and not much else. The headdresses that some of the men wore appeared to be growing out of their heads. Boar tusks and pointed shells protruded from their noses. Whatever "similarity of soul pattern" in New

Guineans that Albert had seen at Heldsbach was obviously not apparent in these people. Nevertheless, although at "first one thinks that they hardly belong to the human race . . . later one's opinion changes."

To understand the Highlanders' reaction to Albert, one must understand two facts about them. The less important fact is that they had seen Europeans for only a few years. The far more important fact is that the Highlanders were always aware of their dead, hearing them whistle or sing, particularly when someone was dying. It was necessary to retain a good relationship with the dead. Suddenly seeing Albert and people like him who must be dead because they were so pale, they were confused about how to react.

Seeing Albert that first day, the Kamanos probably believed that they were seeing someone superhuman even if they had previously seen white men. The men in the photographs that Michael Leahy took while searching for gold look startled. They turn aside; sometimes they're running away, perhaps "recognizing" a dead relative. One of the European men accompanying Leahy had false teeth that he occasionally removed, which confirmed that he could not be alive and therefore must be a spirit. If you were with a spirit, you would, if possible, take on some of their qualities. The easiest way to do this was to scoop up their excrement and eat it. Leahy and his men witnessed this practice as did early missionaries, including Albert, much to his disgust.

ALBERT WAS ALL BUSINESS as soon as he arrived at Raipinka. There was work to be done, and there were souls to be saved. He liked his house with its six rooms and running water (I remember only one faucet in the kitchen). The climate was also pleasant. Nights at an elevation of 5000 feet were cool enough to require several blankets for good sleeping. His baby chicks remained inside their crate until nine in the morning for warmth. The young men who worked for him were not so lucky: they were shivering when they arrived for work early each morning, wearing only a lap-lap, a rectangular piece of fabric tied around their lower torsos, and wrapping their arms around themselves to make a bony sweater. By noon the air had warmed significantly, and Albert had to guard against sunburn *[14 January and 28 January 1940]*.

As at Karkar, Albert made sure as soon as possible that he had good bread to eat. Again, the flour was a challenge, as he told his sister and brother-in-law: "There were two tins of whole wheat flour here that were very much alive with black insects. I don't know where or how they get into the flour. I put it into the sun and had two boys pick out insects for almost a half day. Now there are only a few left in it. This flour mixed with a little white flour makes excellent bread." *[28 January 1940]*. Four months later, he had decided that the bread his houseboy baked at Raipinka was better than what he had eaten at Karkar *[3 April 1940]*. By and large, Albert was pleased with the conditions under which he lived. In New Guinea, he told Sylvia, "dirt isn't as dirty as it is in America" *[14 February 1940]*.

Having animals both as pets and as a source of food was important to Albert. When he arrived in January, the mission pastured 20 cattle and six horses. Chickens, three ducks, a cat, and two dogs rounded out the household. By September, he had acquired pigs, goats, and sheep, along with a bull that was continually running away to visit the cows of a nearby miner *[12 August and 25 September 1940]*. One of the few times he ever admitted to being unhappy was at the death of his German shepherd puppy in early April. The flea bath that Albert had given him had poisoned him *[3 April 1940]*. A second German shepherd was so beloved by him that we children grew up knowing his name: Panther. A talking parrot, Kraecherlein (German diminutive for "loud talker I'm fond of"), would answer back when Albert scolded him for interrupting a conversation.

Being in the company of other white people was infrequent and difficult to arrange, as it had been on Karkar. Rev. Gustav Bergmann left the station soon after Albert arrived, making the six-day trek back to his family and his own station at Boana. (Why Bergmann, a German, remained in New Guinea after the other German missionaries were ordered out was never explained.) Albert invited the few gold miners in the valley to dinner on occasion. Other guests were the government officers at Kainantu, Seventh-Day Adventist missionaries, and people who lived on an agricultural station about ten miles away. Albert spoke about his faith to anyone he met, including Europeans who were not Christians—who probably sensed that he did not entirely approve of them. Within a few weeks after he arrived, he debated a miner over the existence of God, a discussion that helped him "grow mentally" *[29 February 1940]*. Contact with the outside world was much more frequent and reliable than at Karkar. A plane flew into the airstrip at Kainantu once a week, bringing mail and essential supplies for anyone who could pay the freight, and the government officials there had two-way radio contact with stations on the coast.

Albert's annual report for 1940 records a count of about 26,000 New Guineans in his circuit, and yet he could not immediately begin his evangelizing work. Either he had been ordered to wait or he decided himself that he should wait before visiting the villages in his circuit: the villagers were "rather wild" *[28 January 1940]*. There had not yet been any baptisms in the area. Even so, there was no shortage of work for himself and the 63 evangelists and teachers at the 19 schools he supervised. He never complained.

When Albert was finally allowed to travel, the faithfulness and persistence of the lay evangelists invariably impressed him. After these young Christian men from coastal areas had been trained, they volunteered to live in a village with their families. They'd learn the language and become familiar with a village's customs. Only when the lay evangelists felt that the villagers were ready did they approach them indirectly with something of the Bible. When Tok Pisin became a common language in the Highlands, many years later, this method would be called *tok bokis*, literally, "talk in a box." Instead of preaching outright, missionaries and evangelists told stories, often parables, and let the people themselves "open the box," do their own interpreting.

The evangelists' work required great courage: they were hundreds of miles from home, in alien territory, the equivalent for us of being in a hostile foreign country with little support. The garden of an evangelist in an outlying area that Albert visited had been destroyed while he was away; even the banana plants had been speared so that they could not bear fruit. The evangelist chose to stay, although he moved his wife and children to a safer area. Albert saw the lives of these evangelists as examples of strong and uncomplicated faith. Helupe was an evangelist of 20 years' experience, both on the coast and in the Highlands. Many years earlier, his first son had died, and now, his third son had just died. Albert applauded Helupe's perspective: he was convinced that God had taken his son, not the sorcery that some villagers suggested. The night of the funeral, Helupe's wife gave birth prematurely, and the infant boy died a few minutes later. Helupe remained steadfast in his faith, Albert noted *[12 February 1941]*.

The Berndts, observing evangelists at work in the early 1950s, would have acknowledged the difficulty of their work, but the Berndts also saw them in their fervor exacerbating tensions between the villagers' traditional beliefs and the Christianity they were being taught. Ronald Berndt concludes that the evangelists were not well enough trained. He observed them to be quick to condemn most native beliefs and practices—more so than a European missionary might have who was a more mature believer. I'm sure that Albert was aware of these shortcomings. Part of his ministry was to support these evangelists, many of whom were young. It was unreasonable to expect that they had a faith as developed as his.

ALBERT'S LETTERS WERE FULL of his nurturing of the congregation at Raipinka. In June 1940, he baptized six babies of "mission helpers" (as Albert referred to evangelists), his first baptisms in New Guinea; he was thrilled *[20 June 1940]*. A little over a year later, he persuaded the Kamano people who worshipped at Raipinka to build a church. He pointed out that they built houses for ceremonies in which only men could participate. Those were houses "in which you often speak evil and conceive evil plans. Why not now build a house for both women and men in which you will hear the 'good talk' of our heavenly Father?" *[26 August 1941]*.

Representatives from six villages soon gathered to level a building site on a hillside, using only hand tools. Men, women, and children carried poles, bush rope, and grass for the roof. One man carried a 20-foot green pole, six inches in diameter, staggering under its weight. Women carried bundles of grass on their heads, some loads weighing 100 pounds, Albert estimated. When the workers from a particular village did not show up one morning, Albert learned that "a village that is outside our influence" had told them that if they built a church they would have to die. In his letter describing the construction, Albert says simply that he overcame the villagers' fears, and the work proceeded. Albert's influence and the power of traditional beliefs were at loggerheads here. What made the difference in the outcome? Albert would have credited the Holy Spirit. He had already persuaded six villages to come together to build the church. Perhaps it was not so difficult for them to carry through with their promise. Chief Menteno, one of the Kamano leaders, was also a strong supporter. When it was time to set the poles into the ground, Menteno decided to dig one of the holes. Albert was grateful for his support even though he knew Menteno would not consent to baptism anytime soon: mission policy would require him to give up four of his five wives.

After three weeks, the 20-foot by 40-foot church had a grass roof, pine-bark walls, slabs of timber for pews, and a few planks for the altar and lectern. Its dedication was a major event, attended by people from six language groups. Men traveled for several days with their pigs, which would be roasted in an oven in the ground over hot stones. Women brought sweet potatoes, yams, and other vegetables, also to be cooked in the in-ground oven.

The actual dedication began with dancing and singing at dawn on Sunday. To dramatize the new life the people had accepted, a group of men showed how they would lure women from a neighboring village away from their husbands and children. They decorated a pole set on a small hill and sang the songs that, in the past, would have attracted the women. Then they uprooted the pole and flung it away at the same time that a group of mission helpers on the roof of the church raised a white cross and nailed it above the entry to the church. Talks followed in four languages saying that, just as women in the past deserted their families when they saw the decorated pole, so everyone should now leave their work and their villages on Sundays to worship at the church *[26 August 1941]*. In drawing this comparison, the Kamanos were making a connection between what to them was an immoral act (women deserting their families) with a moral act (going to church). What may seem an illogical comparison was not the point, however. The passion in both actions was what mattered. Everyone present knew the power of the decorated pole. The cross was now to have the same power to attract people.

Later that year, Albert performed his first confirmations, the ceremony that, in the Lutheran church, marks a teenager's commitment to follow Christ. Some of the teachers and evangelists had worked for 14 years in the Raipinka area and had children of confirmation age. Again making a connection to traditional practices, the evangelists asked the parents to tell the young people what tribal initiations had been like. Boys were taken to a hut built in the jungle for that purpose and they were circumcised there. Next, they had to fast for several days. They were then immersed in a deep pool and released only when they could no longer hold their breaths. When they came out, they were herded into a great fire. If they passed all these tests, they were given ornamental shells. Among other tests, the girls were required to stand above a smoldering fire and inhale the smoke and fumes without collapsing. In the week preceding the Lutheran confirmation ceremony, the young people were told these things. They were then told that they no longer had to pass the physical tests of initiation, but they had to show their spiritual strength by confessing their sins in public. Theft was the main sin, with disobedience and lying also common. For the confirmation itself, the six young people gathered with Albert far from the church. Singing, they walked toward the church, which was closed. A voice inside asked if they wanted to accept Jesus and give up stealing and lying. They said yes, the doors opened, and they were invited in for the service *[27 October 1941].*

Efforts such as these allowed Albert to catch up with the Adventists. In a history of the Upper Ramu, Robin Radford notes that Albert improved relations with officials and set out to regain ground lost to the Adventists. By 1941, the Lutherans occupied 17 of the 22 villages allocated to them, and the Adventists, 19 out of a possible 25. Through appeals to the local *kiap* and, eventually, to the District Officer in Madang, Albert strengthened the Lutherans' position to the point that the Lutherans occupied as many villages as the Adventists by the time that World War II ended the civil administration in 1942.

As in Albert's first two years in New Guinea, contact with other missionaries was critical, both for him personally and for his continuing to feel part of the larger mission enterprise. He most deeply looked forward to the annual mission conferences, during which all the mission families met at Madang for a week of worship, fellowship, and meetings on mission policy. Not learning about the 1941 meeting until one week before it was scheduled, Albert began walking with 20 of his evangelists the following Monday, arriving in Madang just in time for the conference on Saturday.

Always for Albert, the journey was as important as the destination. The infant daughter of an evangelist in one village had died since their last visit. The wife of an evangelist in another village had died, leaving him with three young children. Albert gave injections, bandaged ulcers and, having forgotten to carry a net under which to sleep, spent the nights fighting off mosquitoes. The travelers had obeyed government regulations for travel in "uncontrolled" areas by carrying four guns. A teacher used one of the guns to shoot a wild pig weighing 225 pounds. They butchered it on the spot, roasting some of its parts on hot stones, but cutting up other parts, placing them in hollow lengths of bamboo, and roasting them over a fire. Each of the men in the group carried ten pounds of pork in bamboo as they made their way to their next stopping point *[January 1941]*. When Albert made the same trip for an elders' conference in July 1941, he noted especially the reactions of the Kamanos traveling with him when they reached the coast: they had never seen the ocean and did not know what to make of the waves crashing on the beach *[23 July 1941]*.

WHEN NEW GUINEANS BECAME CHRISTIAN, Albert could more fully relate to them as people. The foreman who had been in charge of building the church was also one of the teachers. Albert and the man didn't always agree on what should be done, but they could compromise, Albert wrote. He was moving away from strictly separating himself from New Guineans, as he thought he had to do on Karkar, although he still saw himself and would have been seen as the final authority. He hired Basengkec, a young man, to work in his house, and the relationship lasted for 25 years. As the threat of war with the Japanese increased, his isolation from other white people increased as well. Any companionship he may have wanted would have to be found with New Guineans. Wanting them to convert to Christianity, he realized that flexibility would be required. The Kamanos could not set aside their deeply held traditional beliefs overnight. Either Albert would allow Christian beliefs and practices to coexist with traditional ones, or he would have no converts. So he welcomed Chief Menteno to come to church even though the chief might not ever be baptized.

The villagers who persisted in their traditional beliefs and practices were a different matter, however. Albert could see them only as people living in darkness and depravity who blamed their condition on the power of sorcery. Early in 1941, a young man died in a nearby village. Because he was young, the only explanation that satisfied the villagers was sorcery from one of the other villages. Albert guessed at which of several methods they were using to determine which village was responsible. They might place a cowrie shell on the dead man's chest, tucking feathers into the shell's opening. If the feathers quivered in response to a particular name on the list of suspected villages being named, that village had done the sorcery. The bereft family allowed Albert to speak at the funeral, but they also observed their own burial practices. They dressed the dead man as a warrior, then propped up the body in a sitting position and carried it to a grave outside the village. The deceased's two wives shook his hands, turned his head, and rubbed his body, chanting all the while.

The effects of sorcery were never far away. In the same village where the evangelists' gardens had been destroyed, the residents had recently made peace with a neighboring village. Walking home from the ceremony, these villagers began to fight among themselves, accusing one another of sorcery. One man was wounded and left on the path, helpless. Later that day, three men of his own village returned to kill him. On the following day, Albert and his men found blood-stained arrows and a shallow grave off to the side. The men who committed the murder had themselves been wounded. When Albert offered to dress their wounds, his helpers objected, saying that they had told the villagers many times to stop fighting. Albert acquiesced in not treating the wounded men, although he didn't fully agree with his helpers' reasoning *[May 1941]*.

For the villagers, when mission practices interfered with the effectiveness of the sorcery they called on, they found ways to circumvent its teachings. The son of a *luluai* (village leader) died, and the mission teacher wanted to honor the school boy by burying him in a wooden box rather than burying his body directly in the earth as tradition demanded. The *luluai* decided that his sorcery was not working because the boy's body was nailed in a box: his spirit could not help the *luluai* in his sorcery. The *luluai* therefore went secretly to the grave and removed the bones from the box *[25 December 1941]*.

Sometimes the problem was not sorcery but simple immorality, as Albert saw it. The Kamanos occasionally tried to cheat Albert out of produce he bought. On one trip, a woman did not empty out the full bag of vegetables that Albert had paid for. She left, and he insisted that she be brought back:

> With cat-like eyes, ornamented ears, a necklace of sea
> shells around her neck and a light colored grass skirt, she
> was the picture of another Jezebel. She could give no valid
> reason for her conduct. I then had the interpreter tell her
> that she was a thief and a bad character. After emptying
> the rest of the sweet potatoes, I threw the bag into her face
> and went into my house. In loud terms, the head men of
> the village and the teacher continued to reprimand and
> admonish her. *[4 April 1940]*

On the surface, only a few sweet potatoes were at stake. Still, maintaining face was also at stake, as well as following the letter of the law. The men around Albert agreed. This incident reminds me of Albert's actions on Karkar when New Guineans stole some rice or fruit or his rucksack. Here, the culprit is a woman. His harsh characterization (she's "another Jezebel") is not so different from Albert's treatment of his mother.

WHY DID SO MANY HIGHLANDERS, Kamanos among them, convert to Christianity? No single answer can account for why thousands of people so dramatically changed their world view. Albert would have answered by stressing above all the work of the Holy Spirit in opening up the Kamanos' hearts to a more hopeful, less fearful, way of living. If one believed in a God of love, then a sorcerer's power need not be feared.

Albert also built on spiritual beliefs the Highlanders already had or that he thought might be fairly easily modified. He may have known of the work of Georg Vicedom, a Lutheran missionary and perhaps the first European to study systematically the Hagen people in the Western Highlands. Vicedom saw the traditional beliefs as quite fragile. When the first Hagen people visited the coast, they came back with news that undermined their basic cosmology. There was no land of the dead, no place where the legs of the sky met the earth. At the same time, Albert could connect with their strong spiritual sense. They already believed in a power larger than themselves, that they were affected by forces for good and evil that they could not control, that humans had "souls" or some quality that transcended the physical body, and in life after death. So it was not so difficult to accept another expression of spirituality.

When it came time to decide about baptism, Albert followed the lead of the mission method developed by the early missionary, Christian Keysser, who thought it essential to build on the communal nature of New Guinean cultures. He would not baptize anyone in a village until everyone, led by the chief, was ready. The intrinsic value of Christianity was difficult to make explicit: in one village, the locals explained to Albert that if God gave them axes and knives, they would become Christians *[May 1941]*.

Yet, Albert would have been willing to acknowledge the practical reasons for converting to Christianity. The Kamanos, like the rest of us, had mixed motives for their actions. The greater power of the Europeans was undeniable. The Kamanos could see the advantages of the white man's way of life over theirs: a steel axe instead of one made of stone, or striking a match to make a fire instead of rubbing sticks together. A corrugated iron roof never leaked, but a roof of thatched grass did, and it also caught fire in an instant. The young man who told Albert in late 1939 that the mission had brought "a good road, plenty of food, and a peaceful sleep" spoke for many. Life seemed easier with the mission around. If you could get what the missionaries had more easily by agreeing to believe what they were teaching, why not?

Albert would also defend the missionaries' reliance on material well-being. He and his colleagues saw themselves as bringing an entire way of life that they wanted local cultures to enter into and adapt to their physical circumstances. Medical assistance was to be offered before spiritual guidance, and education would follow soon after. Once the appropriate context was established, economic help could be given. Because missionaries usually remained in their posts for long periods of time, the villagers had time to come to trust them as they learned how to deal with the attractions of European ways. Albert and other missionaries wanted to guide and advise the New Guineans as they moved so rapidly out of the Stone Age.

*David and Catherine leave for boarding
school for the first time in 1952.*

*Catherine and her friends at a Girl Guides
meeting at boarding school, mid-1950s.*

Eighth Grade class photograph,
St. Peter's Lutheran College, 1959.
Catherine is standing behind the teacher.

David and Catherine on
Catherine's confirmation day,
St. Peter's, November 1960

*The Frerichs family, on furlough in 1963. Back row, l. to r.:
Jonathan, Angela, Catherine, David; front row, l. to r.: Sylvia, Ruth,
Paul, Albert, Peter. This may be the last photo taken with the entire
family present.*

*Anna Frerichs, Albert
Frerichs's mother, in her
kitchen, late 1950s*

Albert Frerichs in his early 20s

Sylvia Fritz in her early 20s

Kamano men,
Central Highlands, early 1940s

Hagefino, a chief of the
Kamanos, exhorting his men,
late 1940s

*Kamano woman gardening
with a stick, 1940s*

*Albert Frerichs with Kamano
men, late 1940s*

*Sylvia Frerichs teaching Kamano women
at a baby clinic, late 1940s*

Albert Frerichs the year of his retirement, 1975

Sylvia Frerichs the year of her retirement, 1975

*University students with whom Catherine met
on her return to Papua New Guinea in 1999*

Chapter Six

Half a world and a war between us whichever way you go.

Albert was committed to being a successful missionary. Building a life
with Sylvia was a close second. Neither of them could have predicted the
difficulty of achieving this second goal. They had a semester together at St.
Olaf after they met in late 1935, saw each other once in the summer of 1936,
and then in 1937 before Albert went off to New Guinea. Now, there were
new obstacles, trying even their idealism and commitment. They didn't know
exactly when they would see each other again. Even without that uncertainty,
maintaining a connection was a challenge. They wrote, knowing that there
wouldn't be a response for six weeks, at the earliest. Sylvia's letter writing
habits hadn't improved either. Because she moved three times in three years
and wrote infrequently, Albert often didn't know where she was. He sent her
letters to her father, who forwarded them to her.

There was another factor neither of them had considered when they were
making promises to each other before Albert left. World politics, with both
Germany and Japan interested in expanding beyond their borders, became
increasingly unstable. As best they could, Albert and Sylvia continued to
plan for their lives together. As late as January 1942, after five-and-one-half
years of separation, Sylvia could acknowledge the difficulties they faced—
"Half a world and a war between us whichever way you go"—while still
insisting on the strength of their love. She felt they had "a deeper affinity, a
truer one" than during their last time together in the summer of 1938.

Albert wrote regularly, usually two letters each month. Sometimes, months would go by before he received anything from Sylvia. Those she wrote between the fall of 1937 and 1942 no longer exist. When Albert was forced to leave Raipinka in early 1943 because of the encroaching Japanese army, he put the letters in a tin can and gave them to a teacher for safekeeping. They had disappeared by the time he returned in 1946. My inferences about Sylvia's actions and feelings come from Albert's letters, relevant minutes of meetings of the Board of Foreign Missions, and stories she told me. I feel an enormous loss, not having those letters. With them, her voice in these pages would be so much stronger and clearer. As her daughter, I would then have a more complete picture of the mother from whom I always wanted more.

After her graduation from St. Olaf in 1938, Sylvia was most immediately concerned with how to pay off her college debt. Albert understood her wish to pay off her debt, even though that conflicted directly with his strong desire that she join him in New Guinea as soon as possible. He left, not having proposed marriage, but they both assumed they would be together.

During Albert's first year in New Guinea, he floated the idea that his family might help Sylvia pay off her debts, doubting how much she could set aside from her teacher's salary:

> I think you'll find that in teaching, money does not pile up very rapidly—there is board and room to pay, clothes, institutes, fees here and there. At least I found it so. During my two years, drawing $75 the first and $85 the second year, and no board and room bill, and by working three summers at about $45 per month, I was able to save only enough for two years of college, a trombone, and $300 share in a Chevrolet.

Albert ended his discussion as he did whenever there were possible differences between them: gently and with respect for her viewpoint. "For the present teach with all your might, and may God bless your efforts and give you joy in doing it!" *[26 June 1938]*.

Another issue that troubled them both in the first few years of their separation was whether Sylvia could date other men. Responding to her January 1, 1938, letter that he had just received in March, Albert wrote,

> You write about your dates—you know dear that I have
> no objection to an occasional date. But as you yourself write,
> one must be careful. Boys and girls often misunderstand
> and misconstrue actions and motives. Young men and
> young women are human after all! You may not see any
> danger in dating frequently, but one never knows! If you
> find it hard to enjoy social life without dates, just imagine
> yourself out on an island, where you see a white man only
> once every six months perhaps! Ah, dear, just continually
> tell yourself, I want to do God's will! *[March 1938]*

As a way to remind Sylvia of his complete devotion to her, Albert referred to her coming to join him whenever he could. In one letter, he translated a conversation he had had in Graged with some young New Guinean men, who had asked when his wife was coming. He said he didn't know ("Later perhaps. The road is long.") and went on to tell Sylvia of a missionary, wifeless for a long time, who had been brought a New Guinean girl for his wife *[18 April 1938]*. Albert never seemed to have considered this possibility for himself.

Albert clearly missed Sylvia's physical presence and the daily details of her life. He wanted to know everything about her family and her teaching. He knew she liked to sew and wondered what she had made or bought lately: "You must tell me about the color, the style etc! We men are interested in girl's hats, dresses and general attire. When one sees grass skirts and loin cloths so much, one sometimes wonders just how a well dressed charming girl would appear in contrast. I'll be looking for all these things in a ten page letter. Is that an agreement?" *[4 October 1938].* Sometimes, he and the other single missionaries expressed their longing in humorous ways. When he was at a mission conference, people started calling the single men by the names of their girlfriends. (Albert hastened to add that this happened only during social hour.) Albert, of course, was "Sylvia," someone else was "Esther," and someone else was "Eleanor." Earlier, a fellow missionary had sent a letter to Albert addressed simply, "Sylvia, Narer" *[7 August 1938],* and it was delivered.

In mid-December, 1938, more than a year after Albert had arrived in New Guinea, he finally wrote Sylvia to ask her to marry him. The letter could not have been a surprise: they had often discussed their future together, and Sylvia had said she would marry him if asked. Still, it was important to both of them that Albert ask directly. I am always moved by the letter's formality and sincerity. Behind its rational tone lay Albert's deepest feelings about the only person he felt could carry out his vocation with him:

> After much deliberation and meditation, a deep inner urge gives me the courage and the desire to write this missive.
>
> Much happiness and a better understanding of life have been mine because of knowing you. And more and more it seems to me that we should not be apart, but that we should share life with its joys and sorrows in the most intimate of all human relationships.
>
> I know of your present circumstances, that you are teaching, that you love your work, that some of your friends may urge you to teach longer, and that you have a debt. But if you desire that teaching shall not be your life work, then why teach much longer? Your education and cultural advantages will be a help to you also in this remote part

of the world. Several girls' schools are already conducted here. I feel that you too will find this new world with all its possibilities very fascinating.

If you decide to come later, that is if you teach another year, it will mean that you would not be able to come before the last of 1940. Whereas if you decide to come after this school term is closed, you may be able to do so in the fall of '39. . . .

You wrote about Nurses' Training. That such a training is an advantage, there is no doubt. But one can get along without it. Much can be learned from experience. Read books on First Aid etc. Have conferences with your family doctor. He could give you much advice about living. Your mother too could be helpful!

I know that you do not favor long engagements. But because of the approval of boards, a medical examination and much preparation, an engagement must extend over a certain length of time. Then too the Mission Board does not consider it wise for a young lady to make the voyage alone. . . . Because of world conditions, it might be wise not to wait too long.

Dear, if you choose to come, do not choose for my sake alone, but also because you love the Lord and would like to serve Him in His work here in New Guinea. I am asking you to come because I feel that you are one whom the Lord can use in this work and because I love you!

Pray about it! Ask God to help you decide and then answer, my dear! *[14 December 1938]*

Later in December, Albert wrote that he was not quite sure what he would have said had he been there in person: "Perhaps only a whisper:

'Sylvia, will you be mine?' And then silence! But dear even writing the letter was thrilling!" *[26 December 1938].* Two months later, Albert received Sylvia's letter saying "yes." He wrote back right away, while on board the mission boat:

> Well, my dear lady, a thrill ran down my spine when
> I received your airmail letter a few days ago, before I left
> Madang. I understood those pages just the way you wanted
> me to understand them. What I like most is the fact that
> you really want to come sometime, that you feel that God
> wants you to work on a foreign mission field.

And then came the first notes of a theme to be sounded throughout the year: why Sylvia should come sooner rather than later:

> When to come was the question which confronted you
> when you wrote the letter. I suggested the last part of 1939
> for several reasons. First, because I feel that together we can
> do more than I alone. After spending six months studying
> the Kotte language, I'll be stationed somewhere, God willing,
> perhaps in the far inland. But regardless of where it may be,
> I feel I'd like to be with you. Of course, there are two sides
> to the question. We might have to do a little pioneering with
> regard to housing etc. . . . . I feel that you and I could adjust
> ourselves to any situation that may arise—and that makes for
> the building of characters. . . . Secondly, I thought of your
> coming in '39 because of the uncertainty of world peace.
> That a war will not come is uncertain.

> What you wrote about teaching is certainly true. It
> does not seem fair to a school to teach only one year. . . .
> If you decide to teach another term, you could probably
> come in the summer of 1940. But as I have written before,
> one cannot say tomorrow I'll go to New Guinea and be

able to carry it out. There is the home board to consult, a medical examination, preparations, clothing, a few small items of furniture (sewing machine) etc., passport and traveling arrangements to be made. . . .

And now <u>dearest</u>, everyone else is gone to bed. The boat still rocks gently while waves break on yonder reef. On the shore there are a few torches and a dim fire in the native village. Within a short time, the moon will rise and enhance the beauty of this night. What would it be, if you were here too? *[8 March 1939]*

THE SPRING OF 1939 must have been a complicated time for Sylvia. For anyone contemplating overseas travel to a remote destination, the world situation was not encouraging. Hitler had not yet invaded the Sudetenland, but he obviously had interests beyond Germany. Japan had occupied parts of China and probably would not stop there.

In April, Sylvia knew that Albert had received her acceptance letter because her engagement ring arrived from Albert's brother George, not from Albert himself. Even if there had been a place to buy an engagement ring in New Guinea, it would have been stolen en route to America. In later years, Sylvia was quite open with us about not liking her engagement and wedding rings—not because the diamonds were only chips, but because she and Albert had not selected the rings. They chose an opal ring for her during a stopover in Australia in 1954. Sylvia always said this was her real wedding ring.

Sylvia accepted Albert's ring but not his idea of when she should travel. Instead, in April, probably before she received his March letter explaining why she should come sooner rather than later, she accepted a new teaching position in Kanawha, Iowa. There, she would earn more money and thus could pay off more of her debt.

Could there have been other reasons why Sylvia delayed her travel? I know she loved to teach and, after just one year, she could see that she was a gifted teacher. She had had a taste of herself as a professional person. Surely, she didn't have to give it up so quickly. She still disliked being pinned down, just as she had been unwilling to promise to write Albert weekly when she was in college. But it did seem to be beyond her understanding that others, not she, would control whether and when she would go to New Guinea. I would not have been as patient and calm as Albert was when he learned she would not be traveling in 1939. She had said all the right things to him, but her actions spoke otherwise. He began carefully, perhaps trying not to show the desperation he felt:

> In regard to your letter let me say first of all that I was
> not greatly surprised. Knowing that you considered the
> matter prayerfully, I can only agree with your decision,
> which I take to be that you wish to teach another term.
> You will use that money and a part of what you earn this
> summer to pay your obligations. I feel that this will not
> suffice and that the balance will remain after the spring
> of '40. But here's a solution of that! If that balance is not
> too large, I am certain that my mother and my sisters and
> brothers will alleviate that and make that contribution to
> mission. If you come in the summer of 1940, it will mean
> that you and I may spend four years here before furlough.
> If you would not wish to come before the summer of '41,
> I would have my difficulties to persuade the board to
> send you. They would not send any one for three years of
> service. Instead they would tell me to wait with marriage
> until I returned to America. Please don't put the wrong
> interpretation into these remarks, but they are the facts
> as I see them! There are psychological reasons also why

our marriage should not be delayed too long. . . . Brother
Bergmann [the missionary he was living with] told me
that his wife said that it was unwise for a woman to come
to the mission field a long time after her fiancé.

For Albert, her decision should be obvious:

You have often written that you love me. I have no
doubt! You also want to do foreign mission work! Then
surely the summer of '40 will be the year when you sail
the seas for New Guinea. Those are your thoughts too, as
I'm sure. But you will write about your reaction to this
letter in your next one, will you not?

Albert then commented on her parents' reactions, comparing them
with his mother's:

I admire your parents! The thought of parting with a
daughter who is loved must be depressing, but they look
further! My mother begged me with tears in her eyes to stay.
She is still somewhat heart-broken, but I'm confident that
I did God's will in going. Your parents will not keep you in
America, but a school board may try to do so with money.
Would-be-friends and well-meaning ones may also try to
dissuade you. Someone who hasn't been in a mission field,
doesn't know what a mission field has to offer! With God's
help you can solve all problems. *[3 May 1939]*

In accepting Albert's marriage proposal, Sylvia knew she was taking
on a far more complicated life than that lived by any of her family or her
friends. I'm sure her acceptance letter was beautiful and convincing. Later,
she probably also wrote beautifully about why she couldn't come just yet.
She was used to having her way, and somehow this too would work out.

Sylvia's dating continued to be an issue even after she accepted Albert's
proposal. They were half a world apart, and Sylvia was young and beautiful.

Could she have relationships with other men? The question arose when she was at her first job in Canton. She had written to Albert about Joe, who had begun to drive her home after choir practice at her church. They also went hiking together and, in general, confided in each other. Albert waited until the end of his letter to admit being jealous: the drive home was permissible, but the hike was going too far. At first, he seemed mainly to be concerned about what others would think: "I could not go on a long hike with one of the nurses—and get away with it. I couldn't have done it at home and 'gotten by.'" It wasn't just a question of appearances; for Albert, their relationship was "sacred." He was sure that his loneliness was greater than hers: "Put yourself in the position of an unmarried person on the mission" [7 June 1939].

Sylvia wrote back to say that she and Joe were still friends, although they no longer hiked together. Joe was recovering from a broken engagement and was wondering whether he could ever again trust a woman. To help him see that trust was possible, Sylvia told him about the two weeks she and Albert had spent together in 1937 before he left for New Guinea. That time had continued to sustain them. Sylvia wrote all this to Albert, hoping it would show him that it was indeed possible for Christian men and women to have a meaningful, although still platonic, relationship.

Three months later, after Sylvia had moved to Kanawha, presumably leaving Joe behind, Albert's response arrived. She must have seen how hurt he was, although she may also have been offended because his answer implied she was no better than anyone else: "I agree that the theory of friendship with Christians of the opposite sex is good, but it generally doesn't work out in practice. . . . One never knows exactly how the other party is reacting—one can be deceived. The human heart even in the best of sinners is sinful." Sylvia, he implies, is "the best of sinners." Albert would have hastened to add that he too was a sinner. How would Albert have come to this pessimistic conclusion about relationships between men and women?

Then came the part of the letter that would have been the most difficult for Sylvia to read. Albert obviously felt betrayed, and she may have felt humiliated: "To tell him your innermost thoughts—about our last weeks together—I couldn't have done it. . . . I think those thoughts are too intimate, too sacred! I want to tell only two persons about them—with the One I speak to daily concerning our relationships. The other I want to tell during the days, months and years, when 'we' grow in knowledge of each other, in love, and in our relation to our maker and Savior, if He be willing" *[31 August 1939]*. There are no more references to Sylvia's male friends in Albert's letters.

Instead, Sylvia threw herself into her teaching in Kanawha. She was hired to teach English, History, and Choir. She was appalled that the high school did not have a library and decided to start one with the help of a librarian in Mason City. The high school had no band either. With the self-confidence that stood her in good stead throughout her life, Sylvia decided she knew enough to organize one: her preparation consisted of beginning brass and woodwind classes at St. Olaf.

That fall, Albert applied to the Board of Foreign Missions for permission for Sylvia to travel to New Guinea. In October and then again in December, he sent her the same list of things to bring once the Board had given its permission:

SOME THINGS YOU MAY WANT TO BRING WITH YOU TO NEW GUINEA

1. Sewing machine (not too large).
2. Metal traveling cases (like the ones I had—don't lose the keys)
3. Heavy shoes for yourself that can be used on hikes.
4. An inexpensive camera (Cameras don't last here—mine is getting bad!)

5. A new dictionary (a good one that is not too large)

6. A rain coat!

7. Kitchen=dishes, utensils, a small scale for weighing ingredients in cakes, medicines etc.

8. Tablecloths

9. A reed organ [a portable, four-octave organ which he hoped his mother would buy for them] and phonograph?

10. A few good books (I have not yet unpacked all my books.) (I am sending for a book on medicines.)

11. A few vocal duets for "us."

12. A lot of summer dresses! And riding clothes! (Occasionally the ladies ride horses here. The riding clothes should also be light.)

13. Tinted glasses because of the glare of the water in traveling.

14. A tropical helmet can be bought on the way!

DO NOT BRING

1. Too many photos (I've sent most of mine home because they were becoming brown)

2. Very many hand towels (There are hundreds of them to be had here.)

3. I get the following magazines: "Lutheran Standard," "A.L.C. Magazine," "The Bible Banner," "The Lutheran Missionary," "The Christian Herald." You will keep that in mind when you order magazines or periodicals for yourself before you leave.

4. A typewriter (I have a good one) *[19 October 1939]*

The vividness of the list must have been part of what convinced Sylvia that she should travel in the summer of 1940. She and Albert agreed on what else she was to bring: their wedding rings, her dress, and fabric for the bridesmaids' dresses, which she would sew out there. I'm sure she was sorry her family couldn't be there for the wedding. That regret was dwarfed by her excitement at the adventure she was about to undertake.

Albert's eagerness in response is touching. Almost every letter in the first half of 1940 contains a reference to her arrival. On Valentine's Day, he wrote her a heart-shaped letter that filled an entire page, assuring her that he looked the same as he had in 1937, and that he still had good table manners. Another missionary had seen Sylvia in the United States during the past year, and Albert wanted to talk with the man. But visiting him would have meant a two-day walk each way, and he could not justify the time away from Raipinka. When he did go trekking, he sang "Sylvia, Oh Sylvia" to the tune of "Delia, Oh Delia" from Franz Lehar's *Merry Widow*, or so he told us. He dreamed about her continually. He kept pictures of her out where visitors could see them, and then he would tell her their always complimentary reactions. He noticed any change in her hair style or clothing. A missionary friend joked to Albert that he would have to serve seven years for Sylvia, just as Jacob earned Rachel. The joke was off by a single year.

As dearly as Albert wanted Sylvia to travel to New Guinea, he also tried to be realistic. In June, he wrote that the worsening world situation might delay her coming. If he anticipated her decision, it would be easier for her to break the news. In May 1940, Hitler's army had overrun Holland; Belgium surrendered at the end of the month. In early June, Italy entered the war on Germany's side. Hitler's grip on Europe continued to tighten. France under Marshal Petain signed an armistice with Germany and then with Italy. Britain, the only country that now stood between the United States and Germany, withdrew its forces at Dunkirk. The United States, under Franklin Roosevelt, began frantically to rearm. Sylvia's letter confirming that she would not be traveling reached Albert in August. He responded by assuring her he wasn't shocked: "You are no doubt in a better place than in New Guinea." She assured him she was "engaged and faithful." "Great words," he said *[12 August 1940]*. If Sylvia could not travel to New Guinea, she could still work on her debt by increasing her salary. She did so by moving for the third time in three years, this time to teach high school in Willmar, Minnesota, west of Minneapolis.

By October 1940, Albert had seen the minutes of the Board meeting in which Sylvia was listed as one of four women to be traveling to New Guinea. "That paragraph of the minutes reads like 'I love you truly,'" he wrote *[16 October 1940]*. Three days later, on her birthday, he wrote about everything he did that day to show how it was organized around thoughts of her, even though he couldn't remember how old she was.

The day began at 6:00 a.m., when three blasts of a conch shell awakened him and the boys who worked for him. They soon gathered for morning devotions (a discussion of Acts 12: 6-17 and then the Lord's Prayer). After breakfast, he met with the man who was to preach on Sunday to discuss the text for the day. Next, he aired his bedding on the porch and nailed another board onto the door of the pig pen so that the pig could not jump over it. He had a little time to study Kamano, and then, at 11, he and Basengkec made Sylvia's birthday cake, a one-egg cake into which they put another egg, for good measure. While the cake baked, he gave Neo-Salvarsan shots to three people who needed his medicine for yaws—the same disease that had taken so much of his time on Karkar. The cake burned a little around the edges, but Albert decided to see the darkened part as rich chocolate frosting.

After lunch, he read, then cut the cake, which he pronounced good. The rest of the afternoon was spent butchering a pig. The boys boiled water for singeing the hair off the skin, after Albert had shot it. He even had the lard rendered before dinner that evening. The pig already dead and butchered, Albert haggled about the price: the pig did not have enough fat to make it worth what the owner was asking. They agreed on 22 shillings.

Albert ended the day in Sylvia's honor by listening to Grieg's *Peer Gynt Suite* and a Rachmaninoff prelude on the radio.

It was difficult for Albert to sustain the optimism of his birthday letter to Sylvia. He did his best by saying that whatever happened was God's will. Even so, he admitted to Sylvia that he felt "a bit despondent." He was fighting off malaria, contracted in early January 1941 while he attended the annual conference in Madang. A course of quinine had brought him back to normal, but he felt "melancholic and unstable. Satan uses those opportunities also to distort one's thinking" *[26 January 1941]*. Perhaps his loneliness made him feel particularly vulnerable to his perception of how Satan worked on Christians to muddle their sense of purpose.

Choosing to ignore the uncertainties of darkening world politics, he tried to think of how he could control all the obstacles that might prevent Sylvia from coming. He was willing to stay in New Guinea for eight years without returning home if that would make the Mission Board more willing to send her because she would be there for a longer time. It would be difficult to get word to him about exactly when she was coming, but if he knew far enough in advance he would walk to Madang to meet her if necessary. Sylvia also tried to remain optimistic. In spite of the uncertain world situation, she didn't give up on joining Albert, writing the Mission Board in January 1941 that she hoped to travel that summer.

SYLVIA'S LETTERS WERE MORE PRECIOUS to Albert than anything else. In May, he picked up the mail in Kainantu as he began a tour of his circuit. Reading Sylvia's letter, he saw again that she was planning to come. It started to rain, and he put the letter away. He and the young man with him continued their journey, he on horseback, soon reaching a river in flood. In the pouring rain and the flooding waters, Albert's main concern was protecting the letter:

The horse plunged into the water up to his head and the water came up to my pocket where your letter was. I thought to myself, I'll read the whole of the letter before I cross another stream. When I reached the next stream, I found the bridge gone, so I read the whole of your letter while the boy went to the nearby village to get help to make a bridge. In crossing, the horse almost fell through the improvised bridge. About an hour later, it began to rain, but I was able to shield the letter under the rain coat. *[11 May 1941]*

Sylvia and two other brides-to-be planned to travel together. Then a new problem arose: the two other women were refused permits to enter New Guinea. Much as Albert wanted Sylvia with him, he recommended that she not travel alone: "the times are very evil" *[23 July 1941]*. Still managing to be optimistic, Albert thought that Sylvia could travel in early 1942 when other missionaries were planning to return to New Guinea. Even though Anna had just written to say that she could not help Sylvia with her debt, she should come anyway if she had the chance. The Board had other ideas, however. In August 1941, it revoked Sylvia's permit to travel.

Albert didn't know about the Board's action when he wrote his 1941 birthday letter to Sylvia. How painful for Sylvia to read it, knowing the now baseless hope he held on to. As it had the year before, the letter showed how thoughts of her could reveal parts of him that were usually hidden. Sylvia had asked him how he would spend a day with her. He would, he said, prepare the day before by brushing and combing his hair. His houseboy would iron a fresh shirt and trousers. In America, he would have kissed her as soon as they met, but he could not do that in New Guinea: "No missionary ever kisses his wife in the presence of natives (a fiancée would be the same)." Next,

I'd like to take a walk to the sea shore and sit on a rock near you to regain that sense of spiritual affinity which

is rather vague at this remote distance. I don't know as though I'd want to talk very much, at least for a time. Of course, I'd be admiring your coiffure and attire. Then I'd want to get into a hiking outfit and climb a mountain for a picnic lunch on the soft grass in the shadow of a giant of the forest. I'd want to know what life has meant to you during the last four years, your problems and how you solved them. I'd also want to unburden and tell you of my rendezvous with humanity here in Papuan lands, of my discouraging and weak moments, of my joys, and above all of God's wonderful guidance and protection.
[19 October 1941]

"Rendezvous with humanity": a compelling phrase that must have attracted Sylvia's attention. Albert recognized the change in himself. As a young man, single-mindedly pursuing his own agenda, he cast people aside if they were in his way. Now, he had learned he couldn't reach the people he most wanted to reach without meeting them part way. He had also opened himself to Sylvia to a degree that he may have never done with anyone.

Being invited to imagine a day with Sylvia may have also encouraged Albert to express his frustration with her more fully than he usually did. In the very next paragraph after the description of the imaginary day, he called her "the sister of 'doubting Thomas.'" Was the request for the description of the day a test? Sylvia had suggested that they wait to get married until he returned home. They hadn't seen each other for four years. She was not even 20 when he left. Albert continued, "You are not certain that we would be truly happy if you came to New Guinea and we married. May I ask, do you think that we would have been truly happy if we had married in '37?" *[19 October 1941]*. True happiness in marriage, he said, comes over time, when two people have learned to live together.

Then came Pearl Harbor, December 7, 1941. There was now no chance that Sylvia could travel. Most of the mission women in New Guinea were evacuated to Australia because of the attack. Albert wrote to Sylvia about the new, harsh reality of their relationship in his Christmas letter. He was remarkably calm, certain that what had happened was God's will ("I am happy and grateful to God") even though he now had no idea when Sylvia and he might see each other again, let alone marry. He ended, "I hope and pray that we may continue to correspond" *[25 December 1941]*. Only one more letter and one short note of hers reached him.

The hope of Sylvia's coming could no longer sustain Albert. Because of the war, there were no new pictures of her that would show him how her hair looked or the kinds of clothes she wore, no news of where she was teaching, no possibility of talking with someone who had just seen her. Albert's faith both complicated matters and gave him a perspective from which to act. It made the difference for him when he could not be with Sylvia, as it had with his father's death and with his mother's refusal to approve his going to New Guinea. He could not have Sylvia now, but he was still living out his vocation. That made his longing for her tolerable. Earlier, he had reminded both Sylvia and himself that if she had refused to come to New Guinea at their last meeting, "it would have grieved me more than a little," but he would not have changed his mind. Now, his decision was being tested and he stood firm. The consequence was emptiness, but he could bear it.

Albert tried to reassure Sylvia and perhaps himself with a New Year's telegram: "HEALTHYAND BLESSED AND JOYOUS NEWYEAR." It must have helped, for she wrote back to Albert (in a letter that was returned to her because it couldn't be delivered), beginning with a favorite quotation from one of his letters:

"What is a year in the lives of two who live and love! It
is like the beauty of dawn before a brighter day. And dawn

in New Guinea is very short, you will believe me when you see it. But the days are long and filled with work. That is the way our lives will be. We are still in the dawn—our day and our work lie before us."

She went on, full of idealistic optimism about their love and its ability to survive, regardless:

> Do you remember writing that—on August 28, 1940? It's beautiful, Albert, a piece of poetry in prose. And evidence of a big spirit and a large faith in the writer. Many people—mostly those who do not know me very well—think I am very foolish to wait for you. I guess it's because I'm selfish. . . . But I know why I'm waiting. The year you spoke of is gone, and now it looks very likely that more will go before our dream is true, but, God willing, I can wait. Can you? But I know your answer. That is one thing I'm confident of now.
>
> Half a world and a war between us whichever way you go. It's not exactly a happy prospect, but would you be interested in knowing that you have never seemed closer to me than you have this fall and winter—closer even than our Two Weeks in 1937? This is a deeper affinity, a truer one. *[11 January 1942]*

And yet, the uncertainty in the following months must have been difficult. They had never been able to count on regular communication, and in 1942, their letters to each other arrived even more irregularly. Albert knew that his letters would be censored if he said anything of consequence. He now wrote half-page letters that were specific only about events such as the six puppies that were born to his bull terrier.

Albert never received the letter that Sylvia wrote in the summer of 1942, saying she was breaking off the engagement. When another typical letter arrived from Albert in November, she knew that she had to write him again. Her feelings had changed, and she had to be honest with him. More than five years had gone by. What was the relationship based on now? What was it ever based on besides their shared fervor for mission work? She was as direct as she knew how to be to the man to whom she had committed herself for the past eight years:

> Last summer when I came home from being away visiting for a few days there was a letter from you. And as I read it, I was suddenly faced with this flat statement from inside of me somewhere—my inner consciousness, I suppose—"You don't know him anymore. You aren't in love with him. It's wrong for you to let him continue thinking that you are." It was like having cold water thrown in my face, or suddenly have your clothes forcibly torn off you leaving you standing there naked. The more I thought about it, considered it, prayed over it, and talked to my mother and dad about it, the more it seemed to be true. You, for a time, seemed like a stranger; now that I've developed more perspective on my feelings, I want more than ever to do simply this: to call off our formal engagement and to wait until we see each other again . . . . You see, Albert, frankly, I'm not at all sure that you really love me—or am I wrong? . . . . I still have your ring, tho I'm not wearing it.
>
> I read the other day a statement something to this effect, that it is a great love that can continue even without encouragement or without hope of fulfillment. That is the way I would like to love and, frankly, that is the way I felt our love was, tho I never consciously put it into words. And now I'm not at all sure that I have ever been in love,

but rather more in love with the idea. I want you to know that it's not the war and the seeming hopelessness of our getting together that has brought this on. Nor am I in love with anyone else.

And tho I wish with all my heart that you had come out [an Australian government agent had urged Albert to leave, but he had refused], I'm very proud that you stayed where your duty is, where you are needed, and that you did not let your personal considerations cause you to weaken on that point. *[1 November 1942]*

Sylvia's idea of what she "should" think dominates in this last paragraph. Might she also have thought as I do, once again, God wins? Couldn't she come first at least once?

Not too long afterward, Sylvia met Harold, who had red hair and worked at a local florist's. Soon, she accepted an engagement ring from him. Her housemate, a colleague at Willmar High School, remembers being startled to find Sylvia at her door, asking to share her bed for the night because Harold needed Sylvia's. It was too late for him to return home. The friend became angry. She felt that Sylvia had not given Albert a chance. Harold was not good enough for her, but Albert sounded just right. Although Sylvia was now engaged to someone else, she wasn't ready to cut her emotional tie to Albert. She kept the letters from all those years of separation. Perhaps she didn't really love Harold; perhaps she had a sense that the story of Albert and Sylvia was not yet over, and she wanted to see what was going to happen.

IT IS IMPOSSIBLE TO TELL from Albert's letters to Sylvia and his family how much he knew of what was happening in the war in 1942. Albert may have had a shortwave radio, but it would have had to be battery-powered because he had no electricity, and he would probably have run out of batteries long before. On Valentine's Day, Albert wrote Sylvia, "We have been able to carry on as usual. I still eat three meals a day, make chocolate pudding, visit the natives, teach school, etc. etc." Later, the chickens were still laying eggs, and his dog had six puppies. By mid-year, he had run out of stamps and simply wrote "No Stamps Available" where the stamps should have gone on the envelopes. The letters were delivered. By November, he had run out of processed sugar, making his own by boiling sugar cane.

His diary for May records that an American bomber was forced down near Raipinka. Two of the crew stayed with Albert, bringing welcome news from home. American servicemen visited regularly that year; bombers flew overhead when there was fighting on the coast. In July, when Albert walked to Madang to see a dentist and to buy any supplies he could find, he saw the effects of the January 21 bombing of Madang (which had been preceded the day before by the bombing of Rabaul, the capital). Madang town was deserted; only a dog wandered the streets. In late 1942, 15 Lutheran missionaries were taken prisoner, along with 140 Roman Catholics. Two of the few missionaries remaining were killed by the Japanese in early 1943. Rev. Henkelman, Albert's mentor while he was on Karkar Island, disappeared at about the same time. Albert probably learned what had happened to his colleagues on the coast only after he himself had left New Guinea in January 1943.

In September 1942, two of the American missionaries that Albert knew best returned to the States, the same two missionaries that Sylvia had heard about and mentioned in one of her two surviving letters from this time. Albert told Sylvia he had "no great anxiety about the future." In the same letter, he stressed the extent to which life was continuing as usual. That afternoon, a Sunday, he gave aspirins to a young man who said his friend had pneumonia, repaired a football for the students, and salved the bruises of a woman who had been beaten by her husband. He was struck by what the preacher in that morning's service had said about temptation. "One who stands fast in temptation," is like "a tree that is well rooted and

therefore withstands the storm. The tree may sway, but does not fall"
[13 September 1942].

Periodic opportunities to return to America arose, but returning now
would have been giving in to temptation. At the same time, he missed Sylvia
so deeply that his usual clarity of purpose and action were confounded: "Your
words, deeds, joys and sorrows of the year, being unknown, confuse reality
and hamper profound living" *[15 November 1942]*. He had no way to know
that she had written him just two weeks earlier to break off the engagement.

Then, Albert had no choice but to leave. On January 17, 1943, an
American lieutenant ordered Albert out of the country. For historians
looking back on the war in the Pacific, the Battles of the Coral Sea and
Midway Island, fought in May and June of 1942, were the turning point
for the Allies. But in January 1943 the Japanese still controlled strategic
points in New Guinea, as well as Burma, Singapore, Borneo, the Solomon
Islands, and Netherlands Indies (now Indonesia). If they could get to Port
Moresby, on the south coast of New Guinea, they would have a perfect
launching point from which to invade Australia. As part of their plan, they
had seized Buna on the north coast in July 1942 before the Allies could
fortify it adequately. From there, they intended to proceed the 150 miles
south to Port Moresby on the Kokoda Trail—over the extremely rugged,
jungle-covered Owen-Stanley Mountains.

It took the Allies until the end of January 1943 to rout the Japanese
from Buna. The cost for returning to the status quo of six months earlier
was high for both sides: one-third of the 23,000 Allied troops were killed,
and three-quarters of the 16,000 Japanese. Had they not been defeated, the
Japanese would soon have starved to death; some resorted to cannibalism.
Since the Allies had a methodical plan for recapturing parts of New Guinea
essential to protect Australia, the fall of Buna may have been the signal for
Allied soldiers in the Upper Ramu that fighting would intensify in their
area. The few missionaries remaining, like Albert at Raipinka, were in the

way, having outlived their usefulness to soldiers new to the area as people who knew the terrain and the locals.

There was at least one other reason to remove civilians. In January, the Allies received information from New Guineans who did reconnaissance work for them (thus constituting a vital part of Allied strategy), that Japanese soldiers had begun to build a road from Madang to Lae. It would cross the Finisterre Mountains, go up the Ramu valley and then down the Markham River valley to Lae—an insane idea because of the rugged terrain. If they were successful, they had an alternative route besides the sea with which to bring in troops and supplies. (The road building project failed: by June 1943, the project was abandoned, with the road only half completed. It never reached the Ramu valley.)

Albert records in his diary that he had less than a day to pack, once he had received his orders. My aunt Nancy remembers him saying that Japanese soldiers were only 17 miles away. Perhaps they were scouting a route for the road. He left at noon on January 18 for the two-day walk to Bena Bena, a settlement with an airstrip near the Highland town of Goroka. From his diary that day, it's clear that he was leaving people to whom he had become deeply attached:

> The heathen, the helpers and wives lined to bid me farewell. The heavy atmosphere of gloom that prevailed about the station could have been cut with a knife. When I wanted to bid farewell to Kewegku whom I had nursed, I could not utter a word, as my heart was filled to overflowing with grief and sorrow. Children and others whom I had once helped gave me small "bilums" [woven bags], perhaps some had been pneumonia patients! These were their expressions of gratitude.

The lieutenant who had ordered Albert out also promised to look after his helpers and the station.

In 1943 and early 1944, the Allies continued their drive to push the Japanese off the island. Some of the battles were victories as punishing to the victors as to the enemy, fought in horrendous jungle conditions (the Australians, defending Wau, January 28-30, 1943); others were complete routs (all 12 Japanese destroyers and transports sunk by the Americans in the Battle of the Bismarck Sea, March 3-4, 1943). With dispatch, the Americans moved up the north coast of the island: Lae fell on September 15, and Finschhafen on October 2—although the Japanese retreated to the top of 3,000-foot Sattelberg Mountain, managing to hold off the Americans for another month. At the same time, the Australians were moving up the Markham valley, planning to cross over to the Ramu valley, a drive they completed in March 1944. By the time the Americans got to Madang in April, the Japanese had already left; they remained in the Rabaul area until the end of the war, although much weakened.

My description of Allied and Japanese actions does nothing to convey the effect of the war on New Guineans, caught in the middle of fighting of no concern to them. From the Lutheran Mission's perspective, New Guinean evangelists from the coast who were living in the Highlands were particularly vulnerable because they were so far from home and family. According to one account of a Japanese bombing raid on the Ega station in the Chimbu area, the Australian authorities forced them to leave the station and to live in villages. They had to remove their European clothing. Although they were later allowed to return to their native villages on the coast, many died along the way. The trauma that the war caused cries out in this account written by a New Guinean pastor. Albert translated it from Kotte for his own account of the effects of the fighting in New Guinea:

> Your bombs, your mortars, and your men overwhelmed
> us. Our villages, our gardens, as well as some of our people,
> were destroyed and battered. We were driven back to
> the habitat of the animals, the wild pigs, rats, birds, and

cassowaries. We ate their food, vines and leaves. We pleaded with the boulders to open that we might hide in them, but in vain. . . . We saw things that not even our heathen ancestors saw. Our legs shook, our knees turned to water, and we could not control our excretions. We say that this should never again come to us. Therefore, you people in high positions, place a barrier in the path of war that it may never come again.

UNLIKE THE NEW GUINEANS, Albert had the good fortune of being allowed to leave. On January 20, a Douglas transport plane flew in to Bena Bena to pick up Albert, another Lutheran missionary, and seven Roman Catholic missionaries, taking them to Port Moresby, on the south side of the island. One of the Catholics had been in New Guinea for 30 years. Albert was convinced that their being removed was the "work of the Devil." Once they arrived in Port Moresby, no one knew what to do with them. Because the Catholics were Germans and because the "inland authorities" had provided no credentials for Albert, everyone was placed in a barbed-wire enclosure not far from a similar enclosure for 40 Japanese prisoners.

Albert recorded what happened in his diary. First, he protested mightily, showing his American passport and enumerating all the Americans he had fed and cared for in the preceding year: "That was as much as an American Passport signed by Cordell Hull meant to an American in a time of war in a village that was pulsating with American airmen and American planes and equipment!" Although they were let out of the enclosure to have dinner with the military police, they had to spend the night outdoors in the open enclosure. If they were bombed (they were told), they should lie on the ground. Albert had a mosquito net in his luggage, but the Catholics had none and spent a miserable night. The Secret Service interviewed them the following day, and Albert and the other Americans were released that evening with apologies by an officer who said he had simply followed orders.

The very next day, they were put on board a ship bound for Australia, including the 40 Japanese prisoners. For safety, a small destroyer was in the lead. The American and Australian soldiers on board told stories about the war, concentrating on atrocities on both sides. One told of capturing three Japanese, lining them up, and then shooting each one between the ear and eyes, then throwing their bodies to the side of the road. American soldiers with serious wounds were made to walk for up to six hours before they received medical attention. Another theme was the devotion of the New Guineans to the Australians and Americans. Albert heard about men who carried wounded soldiers on stretchers for as long as 12 hours, first, up mountain paths, then down again.

After a day's travel, they sighted the Australian coast. A day later, they landed at Townsville, on the north coast of Queensland, where they boarded a train for Brisbane, staying with Australians who had been missionaries in New Guinea. Albert spent about three weeks in Brisbane, waiting for arrangements to sail back to the United States. He visited missionaries, preached sermons, and talked to school children about New Guinea. They sailed from Brisbane on February 20, Albert writing in his diary that he played checkers with an "American Negro" (a "new experience"!). Submarines were reported in the area.

On March 12, Albert landed in San Francisco. He sent telegrams to Anna and to Sylvia in care of her father, not knowing where she was, and certainly knowing nothing about Harold. With her new address in hand, Albert wrote her on March 15, saying, "I have so many things to tell you and a few little things from three countries to give you, but when? You say it!"

Five months earlier, Sylvia had written, firmly breaking off the relationship. Then this letter arrived. Although she might have concluded that Albert was being arrogant, disregarding her painful letter, I think it much more likely that she realized he had never received her letter. Why not at least give him a chance? It didn't take Sylvia long to decide, and Albert arrived in Willmar by bus the last weekend in March.

Albert's diary is maddeningly understated about the most important event in his life since his decision to go to New Guinea. Sylvia entered the room where Albert was passing the time with her roommate Margaret Kemp: "The first time I had seen her in six years!" The two went to a concert that evening and then, "we talked." On March 26, Sylvia broke off her engagement to Harold and accepted Albert's offer of marriage.

According to Albert's diary, he and Sylvia visited friends two days later, and when they returned to the house, "Margaret and Mrs. Robbins had strewn rice on the davenport and placed a toy parson there. Had a long serious talk with Sylvia and we understand! <u>A most memorable night!</u>" After a two-day trip to Minneapolis, Sylvia returned alone to Willmar, and Albert made his way to Talmage in time for Anna's birthday on April 1. Albert and Sylvia saw each other once more before the wedding—for Easter—although they wrote almost every day. They were married on June 16, and Sylvia's letter calling off their engagement reached them on their honeymoon. By September, she was pregnant with their first child. Nine months earlier, Albert had not known whether he would ever see Sylvia again.

WE LOVED THIS STORY. I still tell it often. For all my uncertainty about Sylvia's true feelings in many areas, I have always believed that she felt she married the right man, however emotionally distant he could be. For his part, Albert never wavered during their long separation. That they actually married after this separation showed us that the relationship was meant to be. True love had won, and perhaps it would for us as well.

Had Sylvia settled down with Harold, she might still have been able to live her dream of a beautiful life. She would have had to do it, however, in a small Minnesota town, discarding dreams of something much bigger. I think she knew that she needed a larger stage from which to express herself. Marrying a missionary, continuing as a teacher, living and rearing children in a land that could hardly be more different from the rolling farmland of southeastern Minnesota—these were challenges great enough even for her boundless energy and deep commitment. To a remarkable degree, she was also able to keep alive her dream of living beautifully as she had originally conceived it, in the attractiveness of her home, the clothes she made for herself, and the music she played and sang.

Chapter Seven

Even the strongest among us grows a bit faint.

I wasn't planning to write this chapter. I intended to touch briefly on Albert's and Sylvia's first two-and-one-half years of marriage. Then I was going to skip ahead and give a nod to Albert's nine months alone in New Guinea, before Sylvia joined him with my brother and me in October 1946. I wanted to get to Sylvia's exuberant first months in New Guinea as quickly as I could: Albert had had enough space in this book. I assumed that my memory of my parents' stories of this time—that they had everything they wanted, and that it was simply a matter of time before they would both be in New Guinea doing what God had intended for them—would be enough. There is some truth in what they said. The first years of their marriage seem almost idyllic, even with several moves and a three-month separation because of Albert's speaking commitments in California. They had two children within fifteen months, and they felt the kind of unity that makes a marriage.

But my memory knew only part of the truth, and I was not prepared for what their letters from these early years revealed. Albert's mother continued to resist his return to New Guinea, at least as intensely as eight years earlier, and Albert showed that he was his mother's son as much as ever. His unwillingness to bend was, if anything, more intense than it had been previously. He had had six years of mission experience under quite difficult conditions, but he had come through it well and knew without a single doubt that he was doing the right thing.

Neither was I prepared for how daunting it had been for Albert to return to New Guinea just after the war ended. He and his colleagues returned to nothing. They said so repeatedly. Albert kept writing that being there was dream-like. They heard horrible stories from the New Guineans about the privation they had endured, and they saw their mission stations in ruins. Albert wrote in a magazine article soon after he returned, "Even the strongest among us grows a bit faint." Their one ray of hope was that many of the New Guineans with whom they had worked still retained their faith.

And then there was the difficulty of communicating with Sylvia. Both she and Albert had known that they would be separated for several months while Albert made sure that their home was ready to be lived in comfortably. Albert was completely unnerved by the irregular communication, however. He wrote every other day for at least half of the nine months until Sylvia could join him. Sometimes he wrote every day. But two months passed before he received anything at all from Sylvia besides a brief telegram when he arrived. He was certain of her commitment. Or was he?

I BELIEVE THAT ALBERT always intended to return to New Guinea after the war as soon as the Australian government would permit it. Sylvia had no doubts either. However, Albert's mother was freshly resolved that he and Sylvia live close by, perhaps discounting any wishes Sylvia might have had to live closer to her family since Albert had been gone for so long. In the fall of 1943, Anna went over Albert's head a second time, to Richard Taeuber, Executive Secretary of the Board of Foreign Missions, writing that she would rather see Albert dead or turned to stone than have him return to New Guinea. Albert implored her to stop writing such letters and to try to see his decision as God's will. At other times, he argued with her. Once when we were staying with Anna, the fight between them was so intense that Sylvia hurried David and me outside for a walk so that we would not hear the shouting. Telling a daughter-in-law this incident many years later, Sylvia said that she had asked herself, "What have I got myself into?"

Although Sylvia and Albert spent the first years of their marriage in the United States, they moved frequently, and Albert accepted multiple speaking engagements away from home. Then and throughout his life, he may have turned down a speaking invitation, but if he did, I never knew about it. During their first year together, they moved to St. Louis so that Albert could attend classes in theology at Concordia Seminary, and their first child, David Michael, was born there, May 27, 1944. That summer, Sylvia and David lived first with Anna and then with her parents in northern Minnesota. Albert was traveling, speaking in the Midwest and West, a pattern he would repeat whenever we lived in the United States. During three-and-one-half weeks in California, he spoke in 23 churches, discussing the work of the mission, along with the Japanese treatment of captured missionaries.

For the first and only time during their lengthy separations, Sylvia wrote as regularly as Albert did. She always included something about David's progress. Whether he really was an unusually good-sized, attractive, and sweet-tempered baby, everyone said so. When he was six-weeks-old, Sylvia wrote, "David is changing and growing. I wake up in the mornings and he's lying there kicking, cooing, and smiling contentedly to himself. His eyes are so bright and black at that hour and his smile so quick and ready that he seems ready to talk any time" *[12 July 1944].*

Since it was not yet clear when missionaries would be permitted to return to New Guinea, Albert and other missionaries were told to find churches in which to work. Several small congregations in Nebraska were interested in Albert, as was a German-speaking congregation in Missouri. The California Synod suggested that Albert do mission work in the Los Angeles area, and at the end of July 1944, the Synod issued him a call. Albert wrote Sylvia: "I can see only those thousands of new homes going up on the west coast and people who should have a church home" *[11 August 1944]*. The challenge appealed to both Albert and Sylvia. They decided to accept. Again, Anna objected: they should have accepted one of the calls they had received from rural churches in Nebraska.

In October, they moved into an apartment in Inglewood, in west central Los Angeles, then to an apartment in Monterey Park. Albert walked from one door to the next in every neighborhood in the area, asking people if they were Christians and whether they had a church home. By mid-November, he had contacted a large enough number of people so that he could rent the American Legion hall in Studio City, and 22 people attended his service. He continued his outreach efforts in greater Los Angeles, and in February 1945, he held services in San Gabriel.

Even though the work in California engrossed him and even though he, Sylvia, and David delighted in one another, thoughts of New Guinea were never far from Albert's and Sylvia's minds. When Albert was speaking in Glendale, he visited the parents of a young soldier he had buried. He also maintained contact with his missionary colleagues. Ann Wenz, whom Albert had known in New Guinea, wrote to say that she had heard unofficially that her husband Wilbur had been killed by Japanese soldiers. (Later, she learned that he had been beheaded.)

There are two letters from Lydia Fliehler, whose husband Paul had been superintendent of the mission before the war; she had not seen him since mission women had been ordered to leave New Guinea after Pearl Harbor. In April 1944, when she first wrote Sylvia and Albert, she had had no word of him. She was afraid that he had been on the Japanese ship that was carrying missionary prisoners up the north coast of New Guinea. American planes had strafed the ship earlier that year. When Mrs. Fliehler wrote again in December, she knew by then that Paul was dead, marched off into the jungle by Japanese soldiers, never to be seen again. Both her letters are headed, "Not I but Christ." She knew no other way to make sense of such a loss than to see it as part of some larger plan that she couldn't understand.

The Japanese imprisonment of American missionaries and their subsequent experience of being bombed by American planes was a galvanizing narrative for mission-minded people. These missionaries had given their lives; no sacrifice was too large for those who remained to carry on the work. I can see how this clear focus appealed to Albert's single-mindedness, how personal concerns, such as the effects of one's actions on one's spouse or children, were secondary. Mission work demanded one's all.

Albert didn't learn the details of the imprisonment and bombing until he returned to New Guinea. In 1944, he probably knew only that the bombing had killed seven missionaries, and that a total of 11 Lutheran missionaries were killed in New Guinea during the war. Many times over, Albert must have thought that he too could have been in that group of prisoners if he had continued to live on the coast as when he first arrived in New Guinea. I'm sure that he and Sylvia contributed as much as they could afford when *The Lutheran Missionary* launched a drive for $14,000 ($126,800 in 2008 dollars) to support new missionaries who could replace those killed during the war. The money was raised by the following year.

Albert's intense feelings about the comrades he lost were heightened by his frustration at not knowing how or when he could return to New Guinea. In January 1945, Albert and five other missionaries received copies of a letter sent to the American Lutheran Church by Otto Theile, the main spokesman for the New Guinea mission in the Lutheran church in Queensland. Theile was eager for mission work to begin. He was also frank about the politics involved. The Methodist Church of Australia intended to begin work in the Highlands, near what had been Lutheran Mission territory before the war. Would the Lutherans accept them as neighbors? Theile urged the Americans to say "Yes."

Theile explained his thinking. No matter when the Lutheran Mission could return, it would be short-handed because German missionaries would not immediately be welcome. If other Protestant missions, such as the Methodists, began work, that would help to keep the Roman Catholics and the Seventh-Day Adventists at bay. Even though in the short run the Methodists might be rivals for the souls of the New Guineans, their help was more important in keeping Lutheran Mission fields strong in the long run. Theile's letter also included important information about the relationship between the Australian government and missions in general: missions were now to be completely in charge of education, a factor that greatly strengthened the role of missionaries in building a civil society in New Guinea *[3 January 1945]*.

Soon after Japan surrendered to the Allies in August, Theodore Fricke, who succeeded Richard Taeuber as Executive Secretary of the Board of Foreign Missions, and John Kuder, the new superintendent of the mission, spent four months in New Guinea, surveying the damage done by the war. Their first day in Lae, a young boy whom Kuder had known in the Highlands greeted them joyfully, the first among many such welcomings that encouraged them to continue. The stories of loss and destruction were the same wherever they traveled. People were often in poor physical condition because their gardens had been destroyed during the war. Some New Guineans had been killed because they refused to disown their connections to missionaries. The Japanese had also killed more than 300 missionaries from various denominations, and they had destroyed many villages and most mission stations.

Their first Sunday in Lae, Fricke and Kuder worshipped with over 200 people. Schools had managed to remain open and functioning, and people still sang from hymnbooks and read from their Bibles in Jabem, the local church language. In Amele, a village near Madang, the two Americans baptized 60 people and confirmed 90. Although Christian practices had not always been maintained, the faith was still strong in many places. On his return, Fricke wrote a book about the trip with a title that summarizes perfectly his and Kuder's perspective on the Christians they met: *We Found Them Waiting.*

Besides using the trip for fact-finding and encouragement, Fricke and Kuder looked for ways to re-establish the physical presence of the mission. They were literally working from the ground up and had to think big. They bought an entire hospital from the American army in Finschhafen, the settlement where Albert had studied Kotte in 1939. Using their connections with the government, Fricke and Kuder obtained permission for David Rohrlach, a young Australian who had been one of the mission-boat captains before the war, to come to Finschhafen to help them. Rohrlach had a bonanza for them. Accepting their invitation, he wrote that he had stored goods "in the large Army warehouses, the largest being 690 feet long, 40 feet wide. We received printing supplies, food, jeeps, trucks, bulldozers, graders, concrete mixers, a saw-mill, roofing iron, timber and lots, lots more." Moving all this material was easy. He had nine young New Guinean men working for him and unlimited use of the Army's three-and-one-half ton trucks—and gas from their pumps, which they left unattended.

ALBERT WANTED TO BE IN THE FIRST GROUP of missionaries to go back to New Guinea after the war, but his application was denied for a few months. In December 1945, five months after I was born, he finally received permission to return. His leaving then meant that we would not be able to leave with him. Albert and Sylvia would have approached this issue only in practical terms. The separation would be difficult for both of them, but there was no other solution, given the urgency Albert felt in returning to New Guinea. Who would restore Raipinka if not he? How could a young American woman who had never roughed it bring two young children to live in a house with no furniture, no running water, and no dependable food source other than what the villagers would sell them? New Guinean village women had always lived that way, and Albert had learned to do so, but he would not expect it of Sylvia, nor would she expect it of herself.

So, after 14 months in California, the entire family moved to Albert Lea, Minnesota, now the home of Sylvia's parents. The three of us would stay with them until we too received permission to travel. Albert must have regretted leaving his fledging churches in California. But he had no doubts that New Guinea came first. California was always only interim work.

Albert paid one last visit to Anna. Sylvia, who also believed that it was God's will for them both to go to New Guinea, begged him to try not to lose his temper while talking with her *[3 January 1946]*. If Anna came around, they could all leave with a light heart. She did not come around, and Albert left anyway. She was senile the next time he saw her, in 1954, a condition some family members believed was brought on by Albert's return to New Guinea. I'm inclined to agree with them, given the unbending intensity of her opposition. I see her senility as one more cost of Albert's vocation. It's likely that he too heard his relatives' comments, accepting them with the stoicism with which he accepted so much in his life. He probably didn't feel guilty; he felt he had done what he could in his relationship with his mother.

Albert sailed from San Francisco on January 24, 1946, this time with ten other missionaries, arriving in Sydney, Australia, after two-and-one-half weeks, and then flying to Lae, New Guinea, a week later. In 1937, his roundabout boat trip from Sydney to Madang via Rabaul had taken two weeks; this time, the plane trip to Lae took a day-and-a-half, with only an overnight stay in northern Queensland. Albert told Sylvia he was "thrilled" to be returning, even though he wished that we were with him *[29 January 1946]*. The mission had lost no time in trying to recruit other workers for the field, whether ordained or lay. *The Lutheran Missionary* kept up an active campaign for personnel: "5 plantation managers, 2 stenographers, 4 women for girls' schools, and 31 ordained missionaries," according to the August 1945 issue. Other issues called for nurses. Throughout 1946, the *Missionary* focused on the need and plainly assumed that readers would respond. All of the faithful were to ask themselves, "Does the Lord want *me* to go?"

Albert wrote Sylvia a long letter before he had even settled in. So much had changed in New Guinea during the three years since he had left, he told her *[23 February 1946]*. The Australian army was about to relinquish control of the island to a civil administration, but it was still very much in evidence, with the battleship *Canberra* anchored in the Lae harbor. The town itself had been destroyed. Europeans—whether government officers, returning miners and traders, or missionaries—all lived in rough wood frame buildings with roofs of thatched sago palm leaves. There was no running water, so Albert and the others showered by pouring buckets of water over themselves, the water piped in by the army from a hill six miles away. Albert told Sylvia how happy he was that she would be joining him eventually, but that Lae was no place for a woman and small children now.

There was much to learn about the suffering during the war. August Bertelsmeier, an Australian who had managed one of the mission plantations before the war, told Albert that he was taken prisoner when the Japanese first landed in Madang in December 1942. He spent his first week tied up, without shelter and with only an egg sandwich to eat. Throughout 1943, he and other missionary prisoners were held in several different places in the Madang area. They subsisted on bats, snakes, insects, and lizards when there was no other meat, and on whatever they could grow themselves or receive (or steal) from the gardens of New Guineans.

In February 1944, Bertelsmeier was one of 213 missionary prisoners, Lutheran and Roman Catholic, who were ordered to board a Japanese troop transport that would move them up the north coast to Hollandia in Netherlands New Guinea, the western half of the island. All of them were lying on deck the first morning when American planes flew over, firing bullets "that came like hail from all sides." Ninety-two survived the attack, although most of the prisoners were wounded. Seven bullet wounds fractured Bertelsmeier's leg. When the prisoners were put ashore in Hollandia, the mission doctor, who happened to be on board and was only slightly wounded, set Bertelsmeier's leg and then splinted it. One priest had to have his leg amputated. First the men got the priest drunk, and then the doctor gave him what little anesthesia he had. Bertelsmeier watched while the doctor sawed off the leg.

Perhaps Albert felt guilty for not having suffered as had his fellow missionaries during the war. He had had shelter and enough food when he was still at Raipinka, and, when ordered to leave by an American officer, he endured only the indignity and fear of a single night outdoors in an American stockade in Port Moresby, with no protection from possible Japanese bombers. But it's more likely that Albert's survival reinforced his conviction that the work in New Guinea was the work he should be doing, and he should do it at any cost.

Albert wanted to re-establish his personal relationships as soon as possible. A young man from Finschhafen, the home area of many of his evangelists in Raipinka, brought news of who was alive and now living back in their villages. Albert's dog Panther was still in Bena Bena, where Albert had left him in 1943 when he was forced to leave the country. The miner who told him so said that Panther was still looking for Albert: he went up to every white man and smelled him, then ran away. As far as I know, Albert and Panther were never re-united.

Mission work as a contest for souls was another theme of Albert's first letter to Sylvia from afar. Albert confirmed Theile's concerns a year earlier that no time was to be lost in returning to New Guinea. Albert had already learned that the Seventh-Day Adventists were back at work in the Highlands, "so it is imperative that we get in there to keep them from stealing our sheep [that is, the New Guineans already converted or who might be converted as Lutherans]" *[23 February 1946]*.

Albert found the same faithfulness in villages that Fricke and Kuder had found a few months earlier. On his first Sunday back, he and the other missionaries walked six miles to a village church. During the service two men "who had conducted themselves in a manner that was unbecoming to Christians" but who had now resolved to live differently were formally welcomed back into the congregation. Albert was most impressed.

Afterward, the pastor invited the missionaries to lunch. The meal was such as Albert had never been served in a New Guinean home. Had they been in a village, they would have sat on the dirt floor of a house, eating either with their fingers or perhaps a spoon. Here, guests sat at a table covered by a white tablecloth, with dishes and silverware for everyone. Although the fruit and vegetables were typically New Guinean—taro, slices of pawpaw and bananas, then tomatoes—the edges of the cucumbers were serrated, and the guests were served Spam fried in canned butter, a staple of postwar European food. Albert didn't want to think too much about how it had all been procured, commenting only that, as the Australian army was leaving, they left many things behind, and "the first one who comes along gets it" *[23 February 1946]*.

Albert's disorientation intensified two weeks after he arrived when he and two other missionaries went by boat up the coast to Finschhafen where David Rohrlach would give them supplies for their stations from those he was storing. With its deep, protected harbor, Finschhafen was a well-established government outpost. Lutherans felt a special connection to the area because the first German Lutheran missionaries had landed down the coast at Simbang in 1886.

The area bore no resemblance to the quiet and beautiful Finschhafen that Albert had known when he studied Kotte in nearby Heldsbach in 1939. The Japanese had seized it when they overran that part of New Guinea in early 1942. Regaining it was part of General Douglas MacArthur's strategy in pushing back the Japanese after the Battle of the Coral Sea. From that vantage, he could gain control of Rabaul, the major port that the Japanese had seized on the island of New Britain, when they began their assault on the islands around New Guinea in 1942. The Americans and Australians won back Finschhafen in 1943, quickly turning it into a major staging area for the continuing offensive on the Japanese army.

Situated on the easternmost part of the Huon Peninsula, Finschhafen was said to have become the third largest military port in the world. By the time Albert arrived, most of the soldiers had left, but a thousand were still stationed at the base. He was astonished by the four- and six-lane highways and their constant traffic of ten-wheeled trucks. Before the war, the road had been only rutted tracks.

Most moving to Albert were the 10,000 crosses in the cemetery, symmetrical rows of them marking the burial places of 10,000 American soldiers who had died in battles all over the South Pacific. In an article he wrote at the time, he conveyed his attitude toward these young men: "A few years ago these Johns, Henrys, and Carls walked the streets of a thousand American towns and cities, drove cars, kissed their mothers, wives, and sweethearts, loved and were loved. But when their country called, they left, they fought, and they never came back." Here, they could be honored only by simple, wooden crosses painted white. At home, he wrote, they would have had granite monuments.

To Sylvia, Albert wrote that only the ocean remained the same at Finschhafen. It was still pale blue early in the morning, and it still darkened as dusk came on *[6 March 1946].*

Living in such close quarters with soldiers in the American army frequently brought out Albert's judgmental and puritanical side. The army tried to make life tolerable for its thousand soldiers, one chief means being movies that the visiting missionaries were invited to attend any night at the theater on South 12ᵗʰ Street. Albert appreciated the diversion, but he found the movies as well as the reactions of the soldiers intolerable. *Two Girls and a Sailor* starring June Allyson, Gloria DeHaven, and Van Johnson, was "quite decent" because what happened sexually was left to the audience's imagination. The soldiers loudly and vividly provided the missing action, however: "like bulls ready to jump over the fence." He felt that he had sinned by staying in the theater and not protesting. He prayed (successfully) for the courage to stay away the next night when the movie was *People Are Funny*, even though all the other missionaries flocked to it *[12 March 1946]*.

For Albert, the best thing about being in Finschhafen was being reunited with the evangelists, teachers, and students who had worked so faithfully with him in Raipinka, all young men in their 20s and 30s. He had named only a few of them in his letters before the war, but now each one was exceptional: "one of my best students," "one of my very good friends," or "one of my very able evangelists." All of them had names.

The first to visit him was Enalekic, one of the teachers. He and others had managed to stay at Raipinka for a year-and-a-half after Albert left. Albert's house had not been bombed, although the government buildings in Kainantu, the nearby government outpost, were destroyed. Enalekic said that Albert's belongings were safe in the attic, although another evangelist said later that nothing was left in the house. All the livestock—sheep, goats, chickens, and cattle—were gone.

When the evangelists from the coast finally walked back to their home villages from Raipinka, three of them died along the way. Enalekic told Albert that the Australian army had conscripted his students at the school. The boys had to walk to coastal towns, such as Lae and Port Moresby, and many became sick. Some died, including Aupec, who, Albert said in his recounting, had been his favorite. Aupec's faith had become the most important thing in his life. When he was Albert's student at Raipinka, he didn't want to go home for Christmas vacation because, he said, everyone in his village was heathen. Albert said he would "never forget" Aupec's prayers when he led devotions. As a mark of Aupec's affection for Albert, he had walked with him to Bena Bena when Albert flew back to the States in 1943 *[10 March 1946]*.

Next came Helupe, the evangelist whose two young children had died in 1941, one after the other. He reported that relatives of Baseng, who had been Albert's cook, offered him a wife, but Baseng said no, he would rather return to Raipinka with Frerichs. Helupe said he too would return. Albert recognized the deep personal connections he had with these people: "I am realizing more and more how close I have been drawn to these simple people." He was sure that Sylvia would eventually feel the same way *[10 March 1946]*.

Describing the New Guineans as "simple" may sound condescending, but it was indeed an honest feeling on Albert's part. It would be many years before he thought of New Guineans as equals. To Albert, one of Aupec's best points was that he never talked back. At the same time, he would not have forgotten his conclusion eight years earlier that he and young men such as Aupec had a "similar soul pattern." Aupec was a child of God as much as he was. Seeing these faithful evangelists again, learning about the suffering that the war had caused, and learning that Aupec and others had died, brought home to Albert the deep bonds that he had formed with them as people sharing a common faith that was as meaningful to them as it was to him. They had indeed been his "rendezvous with humanity," as he had written to Sylvia in 1941.

ALBERT AND OTHER MISSIONARIES began to take trips out from Finschhafen to assess the war damage themselves and to connect with villagers again. Their first trip was to Sattelberg, a beautiful place high in the mountains above Finschhafen, and "the pride of the Lutheran Mission." Christian Keysser, the pioneering missionary who had arrived forty years earlier, founded it. Japanese soldiers had retreated to it after the Allies had forced them out of Finschhafen in 1943. Now, there was only "desolation and ruin." The Allies had dropped a ten-ton bomb near the church, completely destroying it and making a crater 20-feet deep and 40-feet wide. Albert thought it would take at least six months of hard work before the station was again livable *[12 March 1946]*.

From Sattelberg, Albert walked an additional seven hours to see Tiliec, another of his "best" teachers. Tiliec, not knowing that Albert was coming, was not in the village. One of the old chiefs compared Albert's sudden presence to the first time they saw Keysser, a comparison Albert found highly flattering. Other old men and women approached him "with a twinkle in their eyes" saying that they had been baptized by Keysser. The next day, Albert found Tiliec in a neighboring village and met his mother, who "was as proud of her evangelist son as any mother at home would have been." While he hoped that Tiliec would return to Raipinka for the reason that "he had been called to that work and his heart was in it," he acknowledged that only Tiliec and his family could decide where he would work.

Other New Guineans had not remained faithful. Three Sattelberg elders told Albert and another missionary about people who had fallen away from the faith. The head elder had begun to act in a manner inappropriate to the kind of group leadership that the missionaries had espoused, based on what they understood of the communal nature of village life. This man was now "lording it over the rest so much that they could not tolerate him. He said he was taking the place of Missionary Keysser and that no baptism should be held unless he gave permission." Albert commented, "Of course this is contrary to our principle of letting the congregation decide such questions." Even worse, the elder's son now led the "heathen" dances that had been reinstated in many villages *[8 March 1946]*.

Traveling to mission stations and villages also enabled Albert to see more of the destruction caused by the war. Allied bombing left huge craters in and around the village of Boleng-baneng, near Sattelberg. The villagers told Albert that the Japanese army was "a horde of soldiers gone mad because of the lack of food and supplies, hence they ate anything: grass, pulp from trees, roots and even rats, that is, after they had plundered the natives' gardens and killed and eaten the natives' chickens and pigs."

Over and over, Albert found that he could not answer the New Guineans' questions about the war and its aftermath. The Japanese were not Christians, but the New Guineans assumed that the Americans and Australians were. Why would Christians kill other people this way? Why did there have to be so much destruction to drive away the weakened Japanese army? Why did Allied soldiers throw so much food away? Weren't they themselves hungry? Albert himself was bewildered by the American army's actions. Once, he and another missionary picked up half a truckload of cookies that had been thrown away. In a single shed, he found "15 gal. aluminum boilers, hoes, axes and all kinds of tools, manure forks, rope, scales, dish pans, pails etc." *[31 March 1946]* With the American army getting ready to leave in mid-April, there was much to scavenge.

Albert and other missionaries who had been in New Guinea before the war had joined a functioning organization. Their homes had been comfortable enough, they had livestock, and they could grow anything in their gardens. Now, there was no home, no church, no school, and nothing to live on except what the armies left behind. The lives of the people that the missionaries had come to help had, in many cases, been ruined by the armies of the countries of these very missionaries. In the article in which Albert had admitted that, "Even the strongest among us grows a bit faint," he tried to convey the immensity of everyone's feelings. While a missionary "is standing on the site of his former home trying to fathom the completeness of the destruction, natives around him weep as though their hearts would break." Albert's sole comfort was that the "spiritual house" had not been destroyed; the "material house" could be re-built. His article ended with a call for men and women: "Come over here and help us!"

I wonder now why Albert didn't tell us about these experiences of New Guinea after the war, clearly among the most difficult and moving of his entire life. Perhaps it was because Sylvia hadn't been there with him to see what he saw, and so, since she was the family's main storyteller, the stories didn't get told. Perhaps it was some of the same reticence I remember as a child of four when our family visited John Haferman, a missionary who was then, in 1949, living at Narer, on Karkar Island, where Albert had lived during his first year in New Guinea. Mrs. Haferman was serving rice at the table, and Rev. Haferman passed the bowl to us without taking any, saying, "I've had my rice." I asked Mother later why he would say that when he obviously had *not* had his rice, and she explained to me that he was one of the missionaries who had been taken prisoner by the Japanese. They had had little to eat besides rice.

Albert would have happily acknowledged that writing letters to Sylvia was one of his main anchors in his disorienting return to New Guinea, even though he never knew when he would receive a letter from her. Only when he had been in New Guinea a month—a full two months since they had seen each other—did her first letter reach him. True, he had received a two-word radiogram, "Happy love," in his first week in Lae, a reference, I think, to the lovers in Keats's "Ode on a Grecian Urn." Frozen in time, their love can never be challenged. Keats calls it "happy love." Albert kept the radiogram and read it over and over, perhaps hoping that more words would magically appear and grant him the same certainty that the lovers on the urn experience.

As Albert did when Sylvia and he were separated before the war, he hung onto physical particulars that helped him to feel connected to her. In Lae, he wore the last of the shirts that she had ironed. He wanted her hair to be the same as when he had left. It seemed harder for him to keep his connection with David and me, even though he wanted to very much. He wrote that he looked at the babies he saw in the arms of their mothers, trying to see us in them, unsuccessfully. He knew that we were growing and changing every day but that he'd still recognize us when he did finally see us. He said several times that it seemed a dream that he had a wife and two children.

The one bit of humor in these early letters emerged from his description of how he shortened some army pants he had salvaged. He was using a treadle sewing machine and turned the wheel that powered the treadle in the wrong direction. Once he corrected the direction, he hemmed the pants to the length he had cut, only to realize that they were too short. One missionary teased him about his "Betty Grable" legs, and Albert wanted assurances from Sylvia that his legs were manly. He did admit that wearing shorts that began six inches above his knees made him feel "sparsely dressed" [14 March 1946].

By mid-March, Albert was feeling desperate without a letter from Sylvia. One of Albert's letters was filled with his uncertainties about their relationship and whether he was good enough for her. Once, seeing Albert writing his every-other-day letter, a fellow missionary asked him, "Why do you write, you don't get results?" Albert showed a picture of Sylvia to an army sergeant, who "found her quite the thing." The sergeant then said he had a question for Albert, but Albert stopped him, saying that he knew the question would be: "Frerichs, how did you do it?"

The letter ended with a disturbing dream Albert had had. He was in Nebraska, saw another woman, and couldn't resist marrying her, even though he knew "it wasn't the thing to do." They were married for two days, although Albert didn't "live" with her. Then he saw Sylvia again and knew immediately that he wanted his marriage annulled. He considered buying all the copies of the Nebraska City newspaper that carried the wedding announcement and then asking the paper to print a new edition without it. He also planned to stand before his congregation and confess the sin of having married the other woman. Albert continued, "I then went up to you, looked down to the ground and said that I'd be your dog if only you'd take me back." Sylvia was willing, and Albert awoke, bathed in perspiration *[17 March 1946]*.

Just as Albert forgave Sylvia for what she had done to him in becoming engaged to Harold, so she forgave him in the dream. He must have been deeply ambivalent about whether he was worthy of her—her beauty, her easy way with people, her intelligence and refinement. Could she truly love a Nebraska farm boy? The question is mine, but I believe it was also Albert's. To show his independence from her, he married someone else in a dream, but neither the marriage nor the dream could last. He could have had the dream without telling her about it. Yet perhaps he told her because he wanted to show her how deeply she had always affected him. Yes, he had chosen to leave America, knowing that his wife and children could not travel with him and that when they did undertake their journey, it would be immensely difficult without him. Even so, she and they were never far from his mind. Yet, why did Sylvia not write? It does not seem enough to say that she was never a disciplined writer, and that she had two young children to care for.

Sometime in May 1946, Albert received his permit to travel inland. But getting permission to travel was only part of the problem for him and the other missionaries. The slow and uncertain communication with the United States meant that scheduling the arrival of the wives with readying the stations for them would be very difficult. In early April, the men learned that two wives were planning to board the next ship crossing the Pacific, even though the house at the station of one of the men had been destroyed, and the house at the other man's station was not yet livable *[7 April 1946]*.

The long wait for their wives strained relationships among the missionaries. By early April, Albert had been having disagreements with the four other missionaries with whom he was living. He attributed the irritability springing from all of them to the fact that three of them were still waiting for their permits to travel. One argument concerned the number of days during which a woman is fertile each month. Two men insisted that it was only two days. Albert produced a medical book that said three days, "and then when you allow for the fertility of the male cells it extends over a seven-day period" *[3 April 1946]*. Repentant the next day, Albert wondered how good a Christian he really was if he was arguing all the time, thinking that he was better than the other men in the house.

John Kuder, the mission superintendent, particularly irritated him. Albert thought Kuder spent too much time reading novels and love stories. He even read them at the table when the men took their meals together. Albert thought Kuder should have been reading the Bible instead and praying more since his job affected so many people. To redirect his own energy, Albert focused on himself, "taking myself by the collar." Albert said he was the vinegar in the old saying, "You can't catch a fly with vinegar" *[4 April 1946]*.

No LETTER SURVIVES describing what Raipinka was like when Albert returned. From letters that he wrote to Sylvia and Anna in June, the evangelist seems to have been correct in saying there was almost nothing left of the main house apart from its shell. By then, Albert and his workers were building beds for the rest of the family. He was also soldering a hole in the water tank, and two workers were building a barn for some goats that Albert expected to buy. There would soon be chickens, perhaps from nearby villagers or from the government agricultural station not far from Kainantu. Only part of his cast-iron wood stove remained, now in a shed some distance away from the main house. By building a fire under the stove as well as in its interior, Albert could make the oven reach baking temperature.

Even though the physical circumstances of his return were more difficult than what he faced at his first station on Karkar Island, the emotional quality of Albert's letters from this period at Raipinka is completely different. Now, he was not an alien. He was returning to his home, even if damaged, to people he loved, and to work he knew he could do well. Very soon after his arrival, Albert began traveling to villages in his circuit, walking because the American army had commandeered all his horses. Perhaps he could buy or trade something for a horse that year and Sylvia could bring a saddle *[10 June 1946]*? Many of the relationships Albert had established before he left in 1943 remained strong. His early return after the war must also have been compelling for the Kamanos. By mid-June, just a few weeks after his arrival, 500 people were attending Sunday services *[24 June 1946]*. Eight-hundred attended the first Sunday in August, and 75 adults were enrolled in catechetical instruction to prepare for baptism.

After re-establishing the congregation and visiting other villages, the next priority was to build a schoolhouse. By August, he had enrolled 150 boys. He had enough slates for everyone, but not enough desks or buildings in which to install the desks. He enrolled every person who wanted to learn, however, knowing that some would drop out, as they did. In addition to the basic courses, Albert wanted the boys to understand that, as people living in a country governed by Australia, a member of the British Commonwealth, they too were ruled by King George VI. He found a handsome picture of the king, and as soon as the boys could sing "God Save the King," the picture was hung prominently in the schoolhouse *[4 August 1946]*.

The beginning school boys (probably young adolescents) were too numerous, in contrast to a disappointing enrollment of young men in their twenties in the advanced school. When Albert left in 1943, the school had enrolled 45 advanced students. At most, he could now count on 12. The young men's decisions not to return to school were evidence of Satan confusing them, Albert told Sylvia. One said that he might return after his wife had her baby. Another said that he wasn't "getting enough of this world's goods" while he was in school. Another said he was always sick. The boys from the village of Sebenofila wouldn't come because the Rihona boys wouldn't come *[4 August 1946]*.

One young man said that he couldn't attend the school because he had taken a second wife, and Albert forbade him to enroll. Albert nevertheless offered him a trial period of a few months, hoping he would send his new wife back to her family. The same problem arose with members of the baptismal classes, male and female, who were in polygamous marriages. During the war, many of the older "boys" took additional wives. Chief Menteno, whom Albert had known before the war and who had five wives, was now in one of the classes. According to mission policy, no one could be baptized or be in school if he or she were in a polygamous relationship. Some missionaries would not even allow polygamists to enroll in baptismal classes. Albert's reason for bending policy was straightforward: "Where are they going to get the strength to put away their extra wives" if not in a baptismal class? He counted on each man's having a favorite wife, and only she would be chosen "when it comes to a show-down." Once the class was established, he would separate the polygamists and the "monogamists."

Albert must not have been completely comfortable with his ideas about the issue, saying that polygamy was a problem "to which no one had given the last answer" *[11 August 1946]*. He would have known by then that marriages in New Guinea tribal cultures were economic and social relationships much more than personal relationships, and that the goods exchanged solidified them. Interfering in such relationships was interfering in a stable social fabric. On the other hand, he also saw how women were abused in polygamous relationships.

It's impossible to tell how often wives were abused then, or now, because polygamy is still legal in the independent nation of Papua New Guinea. I heard horrific stories about the treatment of women when I was growing up. Linda Harvey Kelley, another American who lived with her missionary parents in an area southwest of Raipinka during the 1960s, was strongly enough affected by the fates of young girls in polygamous marriages that she resolved to write about them. *Toropo: Tenth Wife* is her novel based on the lives of girls she had known. One twelve-year-old wife hanged herself. Another drowned crossing a river carrying a heavy load of sweet potatoes on her head. One husband pursued his runaway wife and chopped her in two. Albert wanted to save young women from such fates. He also would have known what happened when wives left a polygamous relationship, even if the husband dismissing her were following a missionary's injunction. Such women didn't automatically have a place in the families to which they returned. How does a person of conscience, religious or not, navigate in such complexities? It must have been some relief to Albert to have a clear mission policy even if the policy did not solve the problem of the status of women in traditional New Guinean society.

The decisions that Albert made about his own life were much simpler. He seemed always to be in motion, having limitless energy to do the work necessary to rebuild Raipinka. He wrote disdainfully of another missionary who also served in the Highlands. Some trouble had currently placed him under the care of the mission doctor on the coast. To Albert, he was a "weakling" *[11 August 1946]*. Ten days later, the government officer at Kainantu asked Albert whether he would be willing to pick up the official's jeep in Goroka and drive it back to Kainantu. Albert walked 65 miles to Goroka in one-and-a-half days (and probably drove back in a few hours).

If it were necessary, Albert could live off the land. By the end of August, he had not received supplies for three months. His gardens were doing well, the chickens were laying, and he was about to start milking the goats. The government agricultural station officer sent over coffee periodically, but Albert had no way to replace staples such as flour, sugar, canned butter, meat, and cheese. He ground some of his corn so that he could make cornmeal mush for breakfast. Sometimes the miners gave him their extras, advising him to do as they did: go out to Lae or Madang and sit on the doorstep of Mandated Airlines until someone flew in with what he needed *[21 August 1946]*.

The ongoing disagreement with his mother would not resolve. In September, he wrote Anna, "I would be much happier if you would say that you were in favor of my going to New Guinea. Why not get this thing cleared up while we [Sylvia and Albert] are both living here. You perhaps think that you will never give in. But the thing is, I'm here for the second time. God didn't put anything in my way to keep me back!" *[20 September 1946]*.

The knowledge that Sylvia would soon be with him sustained him. With the house more or less restored, the gardens producing, and healthy livestock in their pens, he was ready for us. He wrote that he'd fly directly to the United States if he could, but then, how would he get back? He imagined dropping in on us unannounced. Sometimes his letters imagined what all of us would be doing if we were there with him.

And then, on August 27, mission headquarters sent word that Sylvia and the children would be sailing from the United States on September 20. How excited Albert must have been! He planned every detail of our arrival. Sylvia was to send him a radiogram from Australia, to tell him when we'd arrive in Lae so that he'd have enough time to walk the five days to Lae to meet us. But Sylvia had much less notice about leaving Sydney than either of them had expected. Her radiogram arrived on October 25, a Friday, saying that we'd be in Lae on the 27th. Albert somehow caught a plane to Lae on the 26th *[4 November 1946]*.

Almost exactly ten years after Sylvia and Albert had met in the Oddfellows Home in Northfield, Minnesota, they were finally together again and with their children in New Guinea, ready to begin living out their mutual dream.

Chapter Eight
The wind makes music in the fine needles of our trees.

Sylvia's letters to her family during her first five years in New Guinea repeatedly convey her conviction that she was doing exactly the right thing. She was with the man she loved, her children were prospering, and something new was always around the bend. She and Albert, working together, were, from their perspective, providing greater value than anything else they could have done: they were bringing the Gospel to people whose lives it would immeasurably change, for the better.

For nine months as a single parent, Sylvia and two children, aged one and two, stayed with her parents, probably without enough space and money to feel comfortable. From Albert's letters to her, I know that she contracted mumps during this time, and that David and I both had measles. Her sole outlet was to direct a choir in a country church on Monday evenings. She would not have had much time to herself and was probably usually exhausted.

Sylvia's stories about her trip across the Pacific with two small children were as much a part of family lore as were the stories about Albert's call and their reunion after six years. The stories reminded us that our parents were blessed by a calling larger than any of us. They could overcome any obstacles. They were heroes. We were proud to have parents who were heroes, a pride that was diluted for me only after college. I was usually with people who had never heard of New Guinea and knew next to nothing about missionaries. My parents, their work, and my own experiences became increasingly difficult to explain, and I became less sure of who I was.

SYLVIA, two other women traveling to join their husbands, three missionary couples, 13 single men and women, and seven children sailed from San Francisco on September 28, 1946. The *S. S. Monterey* was still a troop ship, not yet converted back to civilian use. Even though young children were on board, the railings and other prewar safety measures had not been restored. David was a strong and energetic two-year-old, and thus a constant worry for Sylvia, while I was not yet walking and could more easily be contained. In Sylvia's stories about the trip, David provided one of the main sources of humor by constantly looking for his father. Any man could be Daddy, "from our little Filipino room steward and Negro table steward to one of the Catholic priests on board," Sylvia wrote her family *[4 November 1946]*. David would run up to them, throw his arms around their knees, and shout, "Daddy!" Embarrassed but amused, Sylvia would explain.

For the three-week trip to Sydney, Sylvia shared a cabin with the two other wives traveling alone, one of whom also had a small child. Their company was more important than any privacy she might otherwise have wished for, especially since living conditions were difficult. Quite likely, the cabin was below sea level, with no portholes. There was a ventilation system, but, of course, no air conditioning, as they headed toward the steamy heat of the Equator and the South Pacific. The cabin contained six bunks that were stacked only four feet apart, and so the women could not sit up straight without hitting the bottom of the bunk above. I slept in a baby bed. The cabin mates had their own sink and toilet, but they had to share a bathtub with three other cabins whose occupants were careless about cleaning it for the next use.

Sylvia was seasick frequently. It overwhelmed her, to the point that she had to rely on the other women to care for us. Once, taking David to the ship's doctor for some minor need, she began crying, and the doctor, entering the office, said to his nurse, "It's the mother who needs treating, not the child!"

Sylvia was grateful for the small community of missionaries on board, a source of comfort and a continuing reminder of why she was doing what she was doing. They met for devotions, morning and evening: singing hymns, reading the Bible, listening to a short sermon, and praying. Afterward, some of them told the others more about what they would encounter in New Guinea. One morning, Louise Kuder, Sylvia's cabin mate and the wife of Albert's Field Superintendent, talked about "the trying period of adjusting to the adverse culture of the New Guineans," based on her prewar experience. The missionary group also had to decide what contact they would have with the secular culture on board. The biggest temptation for the single mission people was dancing. They tried it, "got carried away" (according to one of the missionaries), and were told to stop, no doubt by one of the ordained men. Perhaps they held their partners too closely, or dipped too low, or twirled too quickly. Missionaries of that time, including Albert and Sylvia, felt that they had to set themselves apart and above, both from their own culture and that of the people they were serving. The resulting loneliness was a given.

The group finally arrived in Sydney, not knowing when they would be flying on to New Guinea. After a long week, Sylvia was told that she had three days to get ready. The three of us were allowed 45 pounds of luggage among us. Everything else that Sylvia had packed would be shipped to New Guinea, then flown to Raipinka. It had taken seven months for Albert's freight to arrive from Sydney *[4 November 1946]*, and it took that long for hers as well.

The Air Niugini planes that fly from Sydney to Lae today are the same Boeing 737s used for travel in the continental United States. The three of us, however, flew on a DC-3, the plane that David and I first took to boarding school. These reliable but slow planes must stop often to refuel.

Ours stopped three times between Brisbane and Port Moresby, including an overnight in Cairns, now the gateway to the Barrier Reef. Sylvia wrote her family that she was sick "at least a dozen times," and David often shared the bag with her.

After a 27-hour trip including the overnight, we landed in Lae. Albert, who had two days' notice of our arrival, had reached Lae the day before. Sylvia and Albert's separation this time had lasted nine months, and their embrace at the airport must have carried the weight of all those nine months and the relief of their being together again. To her parents, Sylvia wrote, "Everything was wonderful—more so than it had ever been." The next day, we took our last plane ride of the trip, on a Dragon, a small English bi-plane that, besides the four of us, also carried a new cast-iron woodstove for Sylvia *[4 November 1946]*. Only the Dragon's sheet metal and plexiglass separated us from the outside air and the jungle-covered New Guinea mountains.

Two Australian families met us at Kainantu, the government outpost three miles from Raipinka. There were also some 500 New Guineans (the guess was Sylvia's), in their ceremonial finest—"paint, headdress, drums, and all." The jeep carrying us along the three-mile lane to Raipinka proceeded slowly, following in the wake of the New Guineans, dancing ahead to lead the way. Sylvia said little more than this about the tumultuous greeting, probably because what she was seeing was too extraordinary to take in. She had wanted a beautiful life, but she had not anticipated the strangeness of this beauty.

Among the crowd were school boys, dressed perhaps in a shirt and the customary *laplap*, clean and looking healthy. Most of the exulting dancers were Kamanos from the small villages that surround Raipinka, not unlike the men and women who crowded around Albert's horse when he first rode up to Raipinka.

Where could her gaze rest when hundreds of women's breasts of all shapes and sizes surrounded her? The regalia people wore and their bodily decorations must have fascinated her. She would have noticed that the men, especially, carried themselves with presence, wearing their magnificent headdresses, made of feathers from birds of paradise and other birds, shells, beads, and fur of the *kapul* (a tree-climbing kangaroo). Boars' tusks curved out of the noses of many of the men, and the bracelets on their arms were made of shiny beads and shells. Women wore jewelry in their noses and ear piercings, thick necklaces of shells, and grass skirts with elaborately woven bands, sitting easily on their hips. Those with babies carried them in *bilums*, woven net bags that hung down their backs from a band around the forehead. The crowd chanted the same few phrases and a melody over and over. Men accompanied the chant, beating on *kundus*, hourglass-shaped drums hollowed out of hardwood, a stretched snakeskin forming the drumhead on which they beat.

When we arrived at Raipinka, we first listened to speeches and then prayers. Next, Helupe, the senior evangelist who had worked with Albert from his first years at Raipinka, presented Sylvia with a blue bag containing twelve shillings, more than a year's salary for him. Sylvia was humbled *[4 November 1946]*.

Two weeks later, Sylvia wrote her family that she had "fallen completely in love with this place." The climate averaged between 60 and 70 degrees Fahrenheit year-round. She agreed with a visiting Australian medical officer who pronounced it "the most equable in the world." Another missionary wife living elsewhere in the Highlands called it "perpetual spring," the same response Albert had had to living at Boana in 1938.

Being surrounded by so much beauty was the most auspicious beginning possible for Sylvia. The Kainantu valley is spacious and open, much of it covered by greenish-yellow kunai grass, which commonly grows six-feet high. The casuarina trees that the Europeans imported from Australia and

planted in the 1940s (and still plant) thrive in the somewhat dry conditions
of the valley. Their needles are gray-green, and, together with the green-
yellow kunai grass and the dark tan of two rivers, create a muted, calming
landscape, a quite different feel from the overwhelming dark green of the
jungle so characteristic of Albert's first home on Karker Island and of much
of the rest of New Guinea. Off in the distance are the Finisterre Mountains,
a "terrific fascination" for Sylvia, the same massive range that dominates
the horizon as one approaches Madang or Finschhafen by boat. Because
Raipinka is on a hill at one end of the valley, this entire scene can be taken
in almost without turning one's head if one stops to look. Sylvia wrote:

> Our hill is the third highest in the immediate territory.
> It and the next higher hill are grassy and originally, treeless,
> but there've been many trees planted on our place, but the
> highest hill which is just north is covered with dense jungle.
> Our yard is the flat circular top of the hill and there are
> two lanes lined with rather short pine-needled trees leading
> up from the jeep road which comes up from Kainantu.
> The lanes, by the way, are named Albert and Sylvia by my
> romantically inclined husband . . . .
>
> There's something new to be seen each day, especially at
> sunset when the sun picks out some ridge or hill or tree that
> I've not seen before. Sunsets are glorious and as we eat supper
> sitting in front of a south window, we watch the sky put on a
> panorama of color that ranges all the way from deep reds to
> deep indigoes with blue and white thrown in. We can hear
> the rushing of two rivers when everything is quiet on our hill
> and the wind makes music in the fine needles of our trees.
> Though I've seen just one other white person since I came to
> Raipinka I haven't thought of being lonely. There is too much
> to watch and marvel at and learn. *[15 November 1946]*

Such beauty helped Sylvia to take the house on its own terms. She must also have wanted to reassure her family that she and their grandchildren were safe and had what we needed. She did not tell them what the house did *not* have: electricity (and therefore no refrigeration), adequate running water in both the kitchen and the bathroom, comfortable furniture, or curtains on the windows. The house was "comparable to a large well built lake cottage—not the mansions, but we have seven rooms with wide verandas almost all around." Like the floors, the walls were hardwood, hand-sawn and unpainted. Sylvia liked their contrast with the lighter hardwood that framed the doors *[4 November 1946]*. She kept the hand-sawn wood floors clean by having one of the house servants wash them every day. Albert and his men had made all the furniture except for one wicker chair: "two single beds, a youth bed and a baby bed, all with woven strips of bamboo to make a spring, three cupboards, four tables and four chairs." There was also a galvanized-iron bathtub, a treadle Singer sewing machine, and a collapsible four-octave Army organ, which Albert had brought in from Finschhafen, along with four mattresses.

The vegetables and fruit were daily reminders of what the rich, volcanic soil in the Kainantu valley produced even with its dry climate. Sylvia listed the vegetables available to us: "tomatoes, peas, corn, potatoes, cabbage, Chinese cabbage, squash, green and yellow beans, cucumbers, turnips, and these delicious yams—not a bit like what you think they are, but rather three or four times as big and of a granular white texture . . . . Our fruit consists first and foremost of bananas. Right now we have eleven big bunches of various types on the back porch" *[15 November 1946]*. The vegetables came from villagers who brought them in for her to buy, or from the gardens Albert had begun when he returned. With no refrigeration, fresh meat was available only when Albert butchered, which he did twice during Sylvia's first three weeks. She canned any meat that we couldn't eat within a few days. More commonly, our meat was "tinned," either corned beef or salmon.

Baking cookies and cakes was a challenge: Sylvia had to adjust recipes to accommodate powdered eggs and milk, but modifying recipes to allow for the altitude was annoying at first. She needed to add at least one-quarter more liquid than the recipe called for. If she had to be more precise, she decreased the baking powder and sugar and increased the flour according to specific formulas. Since a wood stove can easily become too hot, she learned the tricks about regulating it so that her bread, cakes, pies, and cookies didn't burn to a crisp.

Above all, Sylvia's two children were prospering. Her first letter to her parents began, "The youngsters settled down as though they knew this was home without our telling them, and it's been wonderful to see how they've relaxed and blossomed out" *[4 November 1946]*. Days later, David and I were "eating like horses." I was getting fat and finally, at 15 months, learning to walk *[15 November 1946]*.

My favorite of Sylvia's early letters was written five months later, to her sister Margaret and family. It exudes energy and optimism. Margaret was the next oldest sister; Sylvia saw her as a rival, even though their lives were quite different. Margaret was prettier, had a better singing voice, and was an artist. As the second daughter during the Depression, Margaret had not been able to go to college; instead, while Sylvia was waiting six years for Albert, she had married her high school sweetheart, and by the time of this letter, already had three children and the beginnings of a house she and her husband were building. Sylvia saw her as more conventionally successful than she would ever be. In this letter, Sylvia did her best to convey the richness of the life she had begun.

Everything was an adventure, and everything had a story. Nothing was like the sleepy town of Albert Lea where Margaret lived. One Monday morning in March 1947, Sylvia was kneading her bread and about to start on a meat pie when a plane buzzed the station. Someone was coming to visit or the plane was delivering freight. In case it was a visitor, Albert sent several young men down to Kainantu with a horse. No visitor; instead, half the freight Sylvia had packed and shipped to Chicago the previous September, along with five Christmas packages.

The first thing Sylvia saw was four men carrying one of her barrels. They had cut down four young trees, making a rectangular frame the size of the barrel and held together with bush vines. They carried the frame and the barrel for three miles, "over muddy, rutty, slippery roads that go up and down steep inclines with little or no grading" *[2 April 1947]*. Although Sylvia was impressed by this feat, she also thought the men were just doing their job. She already accepted the division of labor in colonial New Guinea. White men never carried loads such as this; even so, Sylvia said she "almost felt guilty."

One of the Christmas packages was from Margaret, and Sylvia thanked her effusively for the coloring books, phonograph records, bath soap, and cans of tuna fish, which she was planning to save for a special occasion. The bath soap inspired her to describe their bathtub and Albert's resourcefulness in making it work:

> We have one, I want you to know—bigger than yours
> at 821 but it isn't porcelain. It's galvanized iron, I think—
> abandoned two or three times by Albert's predecessors and
> again by the Army—once it was used as a duck pond, but
> each time my thrifty husband has retrieved it, cleaned it
> up and brought it in. This time it was pretty badly dented
> up but he hammered it out pretty well and painted it with
> aluminum paint so it's really not bad. Then he connected
> up the base from the loud speaking system of a B-25
> [bomber] from the faucet to the tub and connected up
> the drain so we have running water into the tub and we
> just pull the plug like you do and all the water runs out.
> We aren't living in the sticks out here!

Albert found one more way to use a bomber part. David needed a deflector on his toilet seat, and Albert came up with just the answer. The mouthpiece on the B-25's speaker system was made of rubber and shaped like a funnel. Albert cut it in half and nailed it in place. "What an inglorious end for a piece of a mighty bomber!"

Sylvia also wanted Margaret to know they had visits from good friends. This time, the guests were John and Louise Kuder, the mission superintendent and Sylvia's cabin mate, who came for three weeks the day after the cargo arrived. Missionaries treasured visits from other missionaries. They could be themselves as with no other people. The miners panning for gold in nearby rivers were sometimes vulgar, and government officials, while friendly, were supposed to keep their distance, treating missionaries from all denominations equitably. Few missionaries lived close to one another, unless they were in one of the coastal towns. They visited one another infrequently: travel by foot or horseback was slow, and by plane, expensive.

Visitors stayed as long as they possibly could. The Kuders' visit was Sylvia's first chance to use her lace tablecloth, good dishes, and silver-plated tableware, carefully packed in one of those barrels carried up the hill to Raipinka. The dishes were Candlewick: glass, edged with small glass balls. Even the glasses rested on a ring of glass balls as their bases. Pink rosebuds in the newly arrived bud vases set off the table with a fresh bouquet of gladiolas on the side.

Wherever Sylvia lived for the rest of her life, her glass dishes and place settings of silver plate, accented with flowers, accompanied her. The dishes and place settings crossed the Pacific nine times and moved six times within New Guinea. Sylvia used to claim that nothing ever broke except for the handle on one coffee cup. Although we loved the dishes and place settings, none of us wanted them when we broke up Sylvia's last apartment. We live differently and have different tastes than she did. My youngest brother Peter has the dishes, packed away and never used. I have the place settings in their battered wooden box. Once in awhile, I open the box and think this time I will want to use its contents. I never have. The silver plate is light, and the pattern is fussy. The place settings don't connect me to my mother.

For Albert, a visit from a fellow missionary, particularly the head of the mission, presented an opportunity to study mission work at the village level. Albert and Kuder planned to go off on a week's trip. For Sylvia in her letter to Margaret, the trip illustrated the precariousness with which we lived, a fact she tried not to think about. The afternoon before the men were to leave, a government officer made a special trip up the hill to tell everyone that a Kamano had broken out of the *calaboose* in Kainantu, stolen a police "boy's" uniform, his rifle, and ten rounds of ammunition. He was said to be *longlong* (crazy), therefore dangerous, and was seen traveling on the road that the men would be taking the next day. The men decided to leave anyway. Facing danger was part of their lives, as it was for their wives. The following Sunday, with the men still gone, the *kiap* sent word that the escaped prisoner had been sighted near Raipinka. Three teachers and another police boy stood guard over the house that first night, and the police boy remained there until Albert and Kuder returned, four days later. Several weeks later, the prisoner was caught in a village 60 miles away.

Sylvia's children were a part of any letter she wrote. In one, she asked about shoes for me that she knew had been mailed several months earlier from the States but that had not yet arrived. She had no recourse if they didn't come: there was nowhere to buy them in New Guinea. Albert had replaced the stitching in my only pair of shoes, but the heavy waxed thread was worn through. Sylvia now tried to sew a piece of leather over the toes of the shoes to make them last a little longer.

Even though in later years we were barefoot as often as possible, Sylvia wanted us to wear shoes wherever we went because we might contract hookworm from the larvae which can live in human feces and in soil contaminated by feces. If a person comes in contact with the larvae, usually through the soles of the feet, the larvae enter through the skin, eventually passing into the digestive tract where they attach themselves to the wall of the small intestine and mature into adults. A long-term hookworm infection, untreated, causes severe abdominal pain and an iron deficiency. Living at boarding school, where we were barefoot much of the time and never contracted hookworm, probably won us the right to go barefoot at home. By then, Sylvia would also have had a better sense of the extent to which hookworm was a risk for us (she would have seen that New Guineans also have outhouses), and we would have had a better sense than young children have of where to put our feet. Perhaps because of the shoes, I was particularly on Sylvia's mind. At 19 months, I was 35 inches tall and weighed 35 pounds. She was proud of how tall and plump and healthy I was:

> Her cheeks are almost square and you can grab a
> handful of fat anywhere on her body. Her legs are chubby
> and cute as they can be and her hands still look as if they
> were screwed on. She still has about 3 chins and I wish
> you could see the color in her face. Her cheeks and lips
> are red as can be and her eyes have a gleam on them that
> wouldn't be there if she weren't in the pink of condition.

I never tire of reading this description of my young self and of how much my mother delighted in me.

This letter to Margaret also contains the beginnings of my relationship to New Guineans through Sylvia. Somehow, even before I was two, I learned that I could get away with teasing the men who gathered regularly outside the house. As Sylvia said, "She'll stand and look at a crowd of dirty, naked (almost) men, most of whom undoubtedly have half a dozen murders etc. to their credit, but whose hearts are in their eyes as they look at her. She'll all of a sudden grin with that little devilish gleam in her eye and say, 'Naw. . .' and then run off and leave them cold. She won't let them touch her."

One of my earliest memories is of Sylvia snatching me out of the lap of one of those half-naked, dirty men. Even though I was probably perfectly safe, Sylvia could not imagine her young daughter in close contact with men who were visibly dirty and whom she knew had almost certainly killed and eaten other people. From the swift decisiveness of her action, I learned what she too must have believed: that I should fear them, and that it was excusable—even necessary—to deal with them so sharply.

Sylvia saved the best for the last in this letter. She knew she would often have to be on her own with us children, but I doubt she gave much thought to the range of skills she would have to develop. The pastor's daughter who, as a teenager, had spent Saturday afternoons listening to the Metropolitan Opera, had a new-found resiliency, which came out especially when Albert was gone. If he wanted to visit the entire area for which he was responsible, he could count on five weeks of travel on foot and by horseback. To make it easier on his family, he split it up into blocks of two weeks and one week away, with a few days at home in between.

Sylvia had been there three weeks when Albert left on his first trip. The missionary was always responsible for the New Guineans who lived on his station. With Albert gone, Sylvia was in charge of the 270 or so New Guineans who were associated with the station. Most were students, some with their families. School and worship went on without her supervision, but she would have been called on for any problem—a sick child or a domestic dispute. As Sylvia said, "While he's gone, I'm a combination of a little of everything." In particular, there were the animals:

> The horse that Albert took to Goroka got a bad saddle sore on his spine—the thing is so bony I don't see how he escaped this long! So I pour sulfa powder into the sore each day. I'm prepared to take care of the pigs if they should catch the hog malady that's getting all the natives' pigs—their throat swells up and they die. I hatched out

my second batch of chicks awhile ago and I had one of the "pickaninnies bilong goat" butchered the other day because it had evidently been caught in the middle between two male goats who were taking it out on each other's heads. And our prize imported-from-Australia rooster which disappeared just before Easter was found drowned in a native "sit-hole," "house peck-peck," latrine, outhouse, or what have you." *[2 April 1947]*

OUR FAMILY LIVED AT RAIPINKA for five years, years that contained some of Albert's proudest accomplishments. He was "one of the most successful of the American Lutheran Church's missionaries in New Guinea" said a 1950 news release in his hometown paper.

Albert documented his impressive gains in his annual station reports to mission headquarters in Lae. Between 1948 and 1950, the number of New Guineans in his district receiving instruction for baptism almost tripled, from 2,400 to 6,200, and his 1950 report predicted 1,000 baptisms for 1951. In 1948, there had been 14 teachers in his district, and in 1949 there were 32. However, one-quarter of the students who began the school year at Raipinka stopped attending before the end of the year. He acknowledged that it was one thing to establish a school and quite another to retain students. Albert also busily extended Lutheran influence in the Highlands. He searched for and found land suitable for another mission station, later to be called Tarabo, in the area around Mt. Michael, where some New Guineans had never seen a white man.

In 1951, the Australian magazine *Pix*, a publication similar to the American *Life* magazine, featured Albert and his work in a photo layout. The National Lutheran Council sent a film crew to Raipinka to shoot *Trail Blazing in New Guinea*, a dramatization of mission work, which also featured Albert. As did Hollywood, Albert had a village built for the movie.

The houses had woven bamboo walls and thatched roofs and were enclosed in a stockade. He arranged for Kamano men to stage an attack on it, which they did with gusto, storming the stockade and once inside, burning down the houses. The point was to show how Kamanos lived before missionaries began their work, and thus to gain additional donations.

Colleagues within the mission respected Albert equally highly, electing him to its Executive Council and then, choosing him to be Acting Superintendent while the Kuders went on furlough for a year. His new position meant that we had to move in 1951 to Lae, the mission's headquarters after World War II.

The proudest moment for both Albert and Sylvia during those five years at Raipinka was undoubtedly the dedication of the new church in 1949, which replaced the quaint structure that Albert and his men had built in the early 1940s. A photograph of it shows a square building with walls of woven bamboo and a thatched roof. A house in a Highlands village would have looked just like it. Its unique touch, which Albert was proud of, was a skylight made from the glass cockpit of an American bomber that had crashed half-a-day's walk from Raipinka in mid-1942.

The new church that they were building, Albert and Sylvia wrote in one of their quarterly letters to their supporters, was "a real church, one with a metal roof, board sides, an altar, and a bell" *[March 1948].* Donations from churches in Ohio, Iowa, Nebraska, and New South Wales had made the bell possible as well as the church's "art glass windows." Just before the dedication, Albert wrote to George, "Between you and me, it is the finest church in the mission to date" *[27 February 1949].* Still in use today, it stands solid and strong.

ALTHOUGH SYLVIA'S LIFE during the Raipinka years was not as dramatic as Albert's, it was more complex. Her multiple roles and allegiances called forth her engaging personality, intelligence, talents, and energy, and she functioned well. From the letters, Sylvia emerges as the more traditional parent, that is, the parent who most consistently wanted to transmit the values with which she had been raised. Yes, she believed that the Gospel should be brought to New Guineans, but her children were right there in front of her. They needed to be kept safe and healthy. They needed to know they were American, and they needed to be educated as well as they would have been had the family remained in the United States. The major difference between Albert and her was that his daily life as a missionary reinforced the rightness of his choices. Sylvia's daily life—with her children at its center—meant that she regularly had to deny what she felt. She couldn't always act in the best interests of her children. I believe she managed this dissonance by avoiding it as much as she could. These early experiences were practice for how she would feel when she sent her children off to school at too young an age.

Sylvia kept herself separate from New Guineans more than most of the missionary women did. I think she did this deliberately, not to be discriminatory, but because she felt there was so little of her left once she had met her family's needs and fulfilled her obligations to teach in the local school, hold baby clinics, and supervise her household help.

Her inattention to language study is one instance of the separation. She was never fluent in Kotte, the only New Guinean language she tried to learn in any depth, although I must add that her first Kotte textbook was written in German, which she had never studied. Sylvia's failure to become fluent in any New Guinean language set her apart from the people that Albert (and presumably she) worked with. Unlike Albert, she could not develop the close relationships with New Guineans that came to mean so much to him. As it was, her behavior set a pattern for us. Following her lead, we limited ourselves in the quality of the contact we could have with New Guineans. None of us learned Kotte or any other language, except for Tok Pisin, the *lingua franca*.

When Sylvia was interviewed for church archives in her retirement and asked whether she had any friends among the New Guineans, she said, "I did in later years more so than I did at first. There was just too great a gulf between us. At Raipinka, I would have wives of the [New Guinean] pastors, and wives of the teachers come up for coffee or tea. At first, they were afraid to come into our house [New Guineans and Europeans did not mix socially]." Her response is understandable, but other retired missionary women interviewed for the same project spoke differently. One said that "really living with the people" was most important. Another stressed, "You have to learn how they feel, why they feel the way they do and that doesn't happen overnight." Another said that she became close to New Guineans because she saw so few white people, and that her young son was for a time afraid of whites because, except for his parents, he had seen only New Guineans.

IN OUR TIME AT RAIPINKA, Sylvia cultivated her interests as best she could, her expressions of living beautifully. Our 1950 Christmas photograph *(see the cover)* shows how well she succeeded. Sylvia has on a lovely dress with puffed sleeves and a full skirt that sweeps the floor. There are candles on the fireplace mantel and a reproduction of a popular painting of Jesus hangs above the fireplace. The boards on the floor and wall were hand sawn and rough, but none of that shows in the photograph. We are an attractive, young family in a pleasant home, not unlike the homes found in any Midwestern city at that time.

Sylvia continued her keyboard skills by playing the four-octave Army organ, not too limited an instrument if you're playing a Bach prelude, but severely lacking if you want to capture the sweep of a Chopin nocturne or a Brahms rhapsody. A wind-up phonograph let us hear our small collection of 78-rpm records. Our short-wave radio finally arrived after 14 months in transit, but we had only a wind charger to power its battery *[March 1948]*. When it worked, Albert and Sylvia listened to news from around the world, usually from the Australian Broadcasting Commission. The ABC also broadcast serial dramas and classical music. Sylvia liked to tell us that it was she who discovered the opera singer Joan Sutherland, having heard her when she was still at Raipinka.

She could listen to Joan Sutherland while she kneaded her dough or sewed my dresses, but she had little time to read anything other than a children's book. Nor did the harsh light of a Coleman lantern invite relaxed reading. *Time, National Geographic*, and several church magazines arrived fairly regularly. Sylvia read the magazines, usually left lying open at an article she hadn't finished. I don't remember her reading the few "secular" books in our living room. In later years, David and I read the books over and over and devoured the magazines. Albert also read the magazines, along with the thick biblical commentaries and theological books in his study.

Sylvia and Albert lived in separate spheres. Even when Albert was home, he spent little time in the house or with Sylvia. She described his schedule for the previous day in a letter to her parents: "Albert was out at 6:30—or before for all I know!—in for breakfast a little before 8:00, off again and didn't come in for lunch til 1:45, off again and busy with natives—swarms of them—til 7:30 when we had supper. Then back to the office until 11:15" *[6 February 1949]*. She was writing the letter by Coleman lantern at 10:30 in the evening while Albert was still at the office. Perhaps this part of Sylvia's life, including its loneliness, was not so different from what her younger sisters in Minnesota were experiencing as their husbands worked long hours to advance their careers.

Using solely the letters or my memory from those years, no inferences that I could draw about their relationship ever showed anything to be wrong between them. Yet in the same letter, she goes on to say, "He's a nicer guy all the time—or I should rather put it I think he's nicer each new day (Sh! He seems to like me too so we're very happy.") The comparison catches my notice now. What was he like before (before what?) if he's nicer now?

When I married, Sylvia's advice to me, delivered in a matter-of-fact way that was nonetheless incisive, was "Don't come to me with your problems." I was on my own (no change there), just as she had been. Her other piece of advice was, "Learn to keep your mouth shut," a cynical summary of what she had to learn as a missionary wife. The public, vocal Sylvia did not keep her mouth shut. What could her life have been like, trying to build a relationship with a man who was usually preoccupied with his work, managing a household in a foreign and intrusive new culture, rearing young children, and trying to learn a new language? There must have been problems. By her own account in the interview after she retired, she said, "In a situation like that you settle your own problems where you are." You figure out what to do by yourself. You probably, also, go to great lengths to avoid conflict, mainly by keeping your mouth shut.

As a "European" woman, Sylvia was expected to hire two or three teenaged girls from local villages to help her out in the house. She and other missionary women saw this as an opportunity to educate young women in European ways, a valuable gift since there were still almost no schools for girls. When Sylvia arrived in late 1946, Albert had trained the young men ("boys") who worked in the kitchen. By mid-1947, Sylvia and Albert agreed that the boys should be in school, and that training and supervising the young women was Sylvia's responsibility since she was now more confident speaking Kamano phrases.

Sylvia made dresses for the three village girls they selected, so that the girls would not be working bare-breasted in her home. Never having had a door, they had never opened or shut one, nor had they ever turned on a water faucet. After two weeks of working with them, Sylvia wrote Albert's mother that they were much more careful about their work than the boys had been, but that their slowness frustrated her: "It took one girl almost two hours to scrub Albert's office floor—and his office is smaller than your bedroom!" Yet, Sylvia rebounded at once: maybe the girl was just being extra careful *[6 May 1947]*.

Another missionary woman described her own experiences to the interviewer for the Church archives. Their first morning on the job, she gave instructions to the two girls she had hired: make a fire in the stove to heat water. Instead, they built the fire *under* the stove. They were using the only frame of reference they knew—village life, with fires burning on the dirt floor of a house. Fortunately, the stove was resting on a piece of galvanized iron, and no damage was done.

Mondays were wash days—the entire day. I was too young to help when we lived in Raipinka, but I learned the routine very well in later years when I went home to Lae (or Rintebe or Finschhafen) on vacation. First, the house girls built a fire outdoors under a large copper kettle to heat the water. Especially dirty clothes were boiled in the "copper" before being scrubbed by hand on a wash board or tossed in the washing machine. An open-sided shed built specifically for the laundry housed a washing machine and a series of rinse tubs. The washing machine was a cylinder perhaps two-feet wide and two-feet high, made out of galvanized iron and supported by four feet, each about 18-inches high. The "machine" part consisted of a handle which was attached to a cone almost as wide and high as the cylinder. We took turns pushing this handle up and down so that the cylinder could move the clothes around in the soap and water. Then we put them through a wringer, turned by hand, trying not to catch our fingers between the two rubber rollers.

Next, we rinsed the clothes in three big wash tubs, the last of which had "bluing" in it, the predecessor to today's bleach. We wrung them out to our best ability and hung the clothes on clotheslines strung between posts. Doing laundry struck me as an egalitarian enterprise among women and girls, regardless of skin color or status, even though it was long, hard work. Once the laundry was dry, it had to be ironed. Neither Sylvia nor her helpers had that task until August 1947 when an iron she had ordered finally arrived. With no such thing then as permanent press fabric, our unpressed cotton clothes would have been wrinkled all the time and must have felt rough. The iron, powered by Coleman fuel, worked best on clothes that had been dampened with liquid starch and then rolled up to allow the starch to permeate the fabric evenly *[31 August 1947].* It usually took several days to finish the ironing, and then it was time for laundry again.

Sylvia established a well-baby clinic, and, later, other missionary women joined her to provide rudimentary but still worthwhile assistance in helping village women keep their babies healthy. The routine every week was the same: "hygiene lecture, baby's bath demonstration, and weighing and checking all the infants from the four closest villages" *[12 June 1950].* They also provided medication for simple sores and aspirin for fevers. These clinics became Sylvia's primary contact with village women. She was probably less comfortable when she walked down to Kainantu to visit the European women who lived there. Then, she was an object of endless fascination to the women and girls who crowded around her, eager to touch her fine, wavy brown hair, her skin, and her clothing. One day during a baby clinic:

> Suddenly everyone just got up and walked off. David ran to see what the attraction was and came back saying there was a woman over by the store just covered with blood. Sure enough—she had terrific cuts on her face and head—a young woman who'd been attacked by an older woman, both wives of the same man, who now wants to be baptized. He has to choose one wife to keep and he chose the younger, tho' we're told she's not been very faithful while the older one is a hard worker etc. Well, the older woman started fighting the younger woman and hit her with her bush knife—about 18 inches long—and

almost killed her. We put some bandages on her and tried to give her some medicine, which she couldn't have gotten much of because her jaws were so tightly closed. Albert came then and said he thought her skull was fractured, but we sent her down to Kainantu to the hospital—and she's still living. *[12 June 1950]*

Violence in polygamous relationships was common, usually between the husband and one of the wives. Here, however, the man's expectation of becoming a Christian had created the violence between the two women, one of whom would soon be abandoned because of mission policy. This obvious outcome of missionary intervention seemed not to have occurred to Sylvia, who commented simply, "This polygamy is a terrible problem."

LIFE AS A MISSIONARY'S WIFE seemed impossible at times. What toll did this take on Sylvia? Albert's many absences made difficult situations even more difficult. In November 1950, Sylvia was recovering from an infection in her big toe. My younger sister Angela, then three, had dropped a heavy camera while Sylvia was standing next to her, and it landed on her toe. She was already scheduled to fly out to Lae for routine dental work and was also able to see a doctor. The round of penicillin that he gave her did not help. The government doctor in Kainantu came to our house and removed the toenail, but then her entire foot swelled up and she couldn't walk. Albert was gone that week, during which I slipped on a wet tree root and broke my collar bone. Again, the Kainantu doctor came to the rescue by bandaging my shoulder. The following Wednesday, David developed a temperature of 105 F, and once more, the doctor was on hand.

Sylvia recounted this series of events to her Aunt Bertha at the end of a letter during which she thanked her aunt at length for the gift that she had sent recently. So the structure of the letter was: thanks; the details of the trying week; and then, with no transition, yes, Aunt Bertha, the new *Better*

Homes and Gardens magazines were arriving *[26 November 1950]*. Everything was once again in place in our lives. Sylvia's ability to frame a situation may be the primary reason why I remember breaking my collar bone in a matter-of-fact way. It was just one of those things that happened.

All of us would, occasionally, travel with Albert. It must have tried his patience that we slowed him down so much, but those trips are some of my happiest memories of Raipinka because of the way that David and I traveled. The New Guineans had built a canvas stretcher, called a sail, that four young men could carry on their shoulders. We sat or lay on it, our blankets, toys, and books close by to amuse us. From my perspective now, traveling that way seems so "colonial," reinforcing our separateness from and our sense of superiority over the New Guineans. But for me, as a child, I could see only that I was having fun.

We once traveled that way for 25 miles for a large baptism. David and I were happily sitting on our sail, and Angela, still a baby, was being carried in a wash tub. A pole had been slid through the two handles, and two men rested the pole on their shoulders while carrying the tub between themselves. The pole must not have been tied securely because when the men were carrying Angela through a particularly muddy area they slipped, and the tub capsized. Angela landed face down in the mud but unhurt, and we all continued on.

Albert had other villages to visit after the baptism. The rest of us started back to Raipinka. About 100 Kamanos accompanied us, Sylvia estimated. She was riding a horse and dismounted at an irrigation ditch so that the horse could be led across by one of the Kamanos. Instead, "somehow or other the horse sank into mud up to his stomach, laid his head on the ground beside the ditch, and looked much happier than when he was carrying me…. Finally, with a lot of shouting, pulling, pushing and prying they got him out" *[27 March 1949]*. Sylvia remounted him several miles later, when both horse and saddle had dried off.

Having a baby presented some of the biggest challenges for a missionary family. If they lived on an out-station, as most did, prenatal care was unavailable. Most women arranged to go to a hospital on the coast as much as six weeks before the baby was due so that they could obtain adequate care in a proper hospital during the time immediately preceding the birth. When Sylvia was pregnant with Angela and then with Jonathan, she could travel to a hospital fairly easily because we lived close to an airstrip. Angela was born in 1948 in the hospital in Finschhafen that the mission had purchased from the American army. Jonathan was born in 1950 in the government hospital in Lae.

Many missionary women were not so fortunate in their travel. Amee Brandt had a mountainous day's walk to reach an airstrip. Marion Walck returned home with her one-week-old baby by jeep until they had to cross a river. They transferred to a canoe, and, once on the other side, a weapons carrier that awaited them took them to the Finschhafen airstrip. They flew to Lae, then boarded a ship to Madang.

When Jonathan was born, Sylvia took me with her to Lae (why, I'm not sure) and left David and Angela with Albert. Darlene Diemer (the second missionary wife at Raipinka, beginning in 1948) helped out with Angela, and the young New Guinean women who worked in the house could easily care for six-year-old David. The children were well taken care of, according to Albert, but the change in cooking threw him for a loop. Although Sylvia had been working with the girls for several months, preparing food European-style was still foreign to them. They had learned how to cook pumpkin, and so, they served boiled pumpkin every day. One day Albert had had enough. He kept an eye on the garden, and snatched up and hid the next pumpkin that was ready to be picked. Without a pumpkin to cook, the young women made cabbage and beans. Preparing fruit presented no problem to them: they boiled it the same way they prepared vegetables, adding salt, of course *[26 May 1950]*.

NEITHER SYLVIA NOR ALBERT had much respite from the intensity of their daily lives. Sylvia and Albert took their only vacation during their five years at Raipinka when they traveled to Karkar Island in 1949 to see where Albert had lived when he first came to New Guinea—the time Sylvia pronounced it "the most isolated spot I've ever been at" *[4 November 1949]*. Shortly after we arrived, in 1946, Albert and his helpers built a one-room cottage a little distance up the hill from our house. He called it their "Honeymoon House." I don't remember their ever going there by themselves, but I do remember that all of us cooked dinner in the fireplace, played games, read, and sang songs there. Honeymoon House may have been one of Albert's efforts to show Sylvia that, regardless of how he spent most of his time, he still loved her, and he cared about spending time with his family. The house no longer stands, but Kamanos who are there now and were alive at the time remember it and can tell you where it used to be.

Sylvia and Albert lived together in New Guinea for 29 years, but not one of all their relatives visited. It was much more difficult and expensive to travel long distances then, and therefore much less common. None of their siblings was wealthy, and each of them had the expense of rearing a family. Some of them helped my parents financially; all of them wrote regularly. Unpredictable mail deliveries sometimes resulted in 25 or 30 letters arriving at once.

Mother in particular wanted us to know and feel that we were members of her larger family and of Albert's. She taught us the names of all our aunts and uncles and cousins, and we knew them by heart. Quite a feat, since Albert and Sylvia each had seven siblings, each one of whom had children. David, by now five, liked Uncle George, particularly the tractor in a picture of Uncle George on his farm. Sylvia passed on his questions to George and his wife Laura: "How fast can I go [when I drive it]?' "What if I go into the ditch?" "Can Cathy drive it too or do only boys drive tractors?" *[27 March*

1949]. These appealing questions gave George and Laura a sense of their young nephew, and Sylvia deliberately strengthened the connection.

Even with valiant efforts to maintain connections, Albert and Sylvia's seven- and eight-year separations from their families meant a gradual lessening of intimacy and of the possibility for deepening relationships. At least once, Albert and Sylvia clearly chose their work over their extended families. Eligible for a one-year furlough in 1953, they volunteered to remain in New Guinea for an extra year because so many other missionaries were scheduled for furlough at the same time. Later, Albert did not attempt to travel to the United States when his mother was dying, nor to attend her funeral, nor did Sylvia for the death and funeral of her beloved father. They orphaned themselves just as they orphaned their own children.

With Albert often away on mission matters, and with Sylvia's family halfway around the world, Europeans filled some of the need that Sylvia felt for being close to adults. Yet, just as you could have 11 bunches of bananas at a time on the back porch, or two dozen fertile eggs to eat before the yolks started to form chicks, or an entire butchered cow to eat or preserve before the meat spoiled, so, in New Guinea, you frequently had too many visitors, or none. House guests, invited or not, might stay for weeks, or months might pass before you saw another European.

Most of the time, however, missionary wives would have given anything to have more visitors. Interviews with eight wives, including Sylvia, make vivid the obstacles that they faced in their struggle with loneliness, in trying to spend time with someone else of their gender, race, and values. For eight years, Amee Brandt and her family had to walk wherever they went, as did their visitors, because they lived a day's walk from the nearest airstrip. Edna Scherle's husband was away from home for 250 days one year. Months and sometimes years passed without her seeing another white person besides her husband. Although their station was on the coast and only 30 miles from Lae, they might as well have lived on another continent. Travel by outrigger canoe was safe, but only if the ocean remained calm. Walking to Lae along the beach was another option, but that required crossing a river and a lagoon, both of which were habitats for crocodiles. Walkers always had to be prepared to wait for someone in a canoe to come along, and that person had to be willing to let you hop aboard. You might wait an hour, a day, or two days.

Raipinka was not nearly as difficult to get to as were the stations where Amee and Edna lived. Kainantu, with its airstrip and a jeep, was just three miles away. The agricultural station, Aiyura, was only a few miles farther. The Seventh-Day Adventist missionary had returned with his family after the war. With gold in the nearby rivers, miners were also frequent visitors. Most of Sylvia's letters describe recent visits to or from one of these groups. Visits were usually planned in advance, but everyone knew that you could stop in on anyone anytime, particularly if you were in trouble. Sylvia welcomed these occasions for being a hostess. Her first request to Aunt Bertha, two weeks after she arrived at Raipinka, was on behalf of the medical officer at Kainantu, who needed a pen and asked for a Parker 51, then considered one of the best ink-filled pens for writing by hand, as most people did with their correspondents *[14 November 1946]*.

Sylvia kept her distance from the Seventh-Day Adventists: like Albert, she did not consider them true Christians. They followed Old-Testament practices of worshiping on Saturday and not eating pork. Neither did they give Jesus the centrality that he deserved.

For a different reason, Sylvia was relieved not to see much of one of the miners who lived nearby. He had been there for 20 years and was said to have "two or three—or more—native mistresses who visit him regularly in his grass hut." Of him, she wrote to Aunt Bertha: "Prepare to be shocked. A native came to [the miner] evidently to sell some food and [he] had his [nursing] wife with him—she most likely carried the food. The miner saw her and asked the husband if he could get some milk from her—at a price of course. The native agreed, the miner got a cup from his house and the woman expressed a cup full. Whereupon the miner took the milk and drank it himself." *[10 May 1947]*. The Kamanos who told Albert the story asked if this behavior was "the white man's custom."

At times, Sylvia actually wanted fewer Europeans around. From April 1948 until February 1949, Max Diemer and his family lived with them while their house, which had been carried in pieces from Aiyura, the original location of the Lutheran mission station in the valley, was being reassembled. Another American couple lived with Sylvia and Albert at the same time; the husband was rebuilding the Diemer house while their own grass house was being built. After this couple moved out, they continued to have meals with our family. When both families finally left early in 1949, Sylvia and Albert had exactly one week to themselves before new people arrived. "Just as I was finishing baking bread, two Swedish tea rings, a double batch of brownies and putting a pork roast on for supper," Sylvia wrote her parents, "I saw two fellows come riding in" *[6 February 1949]*. They had crossed the Pacific with Sylvia and were certain she would welcome them, and she did.

Max Diemer was not as relaxed about the inconveniences of missionary life as were Sylvia and Albert. According to Max's autobiography, his first and most lasting impression of the house that he and his family would be sharing with the Frerichses and the other family was that the overhang on the porch made the entire house too dark inside. Sylvia told them at once that bath nights were Tuesday and Saturday, nine people taking turns in one tub. The house girls would carry in enough hot water from the laundry house to fill the tub once for each family. The toilet was a huge West Bend kettle that Albert had salvaged from the American army in Finschhafen. It was emptied each day by being carried outside through a small door in the bathroom wall.

Cockroaches were omnipresent, particularly at night. Albert had been away when the Diemers arrived, but on his first night back, Max heard a loud pounding as soon as the families turned off their Coleman lanterns. The cockroaches had emerged after everyone had gone to bed, and Albert was on his nightly "cockroach patrol," using one of his shoes as his weapon. None of the Raipinka letters describe Albert's cockroach patrols, and I don't remember them. Both Albert and Sylvia would have felt their families did not need to know the more unsavory, ongoing details of their lives.

Friction between the missionary families appeared in other ways. When the Diemers moved into their own house, the two families took turns separating milk each morning. Most of the cream was churned for butter, a welcome change from having to eat "tinned" butter, which was sometimes rancid. One morning, Darlene saw brown flecks in the butter that her house girls had churned. She looked a little closer and realized that a cockroach or two had fallen into the separator, and had been ground into the butter. She asked the girls to spread out the butter on a cookie sheet and to pick out of it as many brown flecks as possible. After that intricate task, they scraped up the butter and delivered it to the Frerichs household. Max doesn't mention whether his family used the same butter that day. Some of the focus and tone of Max's descriptions of his early Raipinka years in his autobiography may be attributed to the personal dynamics between two strong-minded men who had to work together when one was younger and less experienced than the other.

All missionaries lived communally. The tensions that such closeness creates were a peculiarity of mission life. Each missionary family had to prepare its annual budget for the following year for all the supplies that they needed, down to the number of new washcloths and pounds of nails. These lists were sent to the commissary in Madang, and a committee decided who would get what. Some of the supplies were purchased and some were donated by home churches. The November 1947 *Lutheran Missionary*, for example, recorded that churches in Dubuque sent 119 boxes of "Christmas Cheer," and churches in Pittsburgh sent 79. "Christmas Cheer" might be children's clothes, men's boxer shorts, pots and pans, canning jars, or hundreds of yards of fabric from which wives and daughters sewed their own clothes. Whatever the source of the purchases or donation, the recipients often disagreed with the allocations. Max's budget requested a reel lawn mower. With it, the young men who worked for him would no longer have to use a scythe to cut the grass. When the committee learned that there was already a reel lawn mower at "Raipinka 1" (Albert had one), they denied Max's request. Albert, asserting that his lawn mower had been a gift and was therefore his own private property, told Max that he couldn't use it.

The lawnmower story exemplifies the frugal lives that Albert and Sylvia and the other missionaries lived, usually without complaining. Their travel, housing, food, medical expenses, and children's education were paid for by the Lutheran Mission, and they also received allowances for each person in the family. They felt themselves to be well-provided for. In 1947, when John Kuder, the Mission's superintendent, was offered a raise by the Board of Foreign Missions, he said that he felt unworthy of it. He contrasted his salary with that of an evangelist's, one Australian pound per year; he was concerned about the increasing gap between salaries for European missionaries and New Guinean evangelists *[17 March 1947]*.

In 1949, Albert wrote to his mother and George that an Ohio church which they had never visited was assuming the family's "full support," of $1217 ($11,025 in 2008 dollars). Whether that was an annual sum or for a longer period is unclear. A 1949 financial report lists a missionary's salary as $161.47. Roland and Amee Brandt remember being paid about $300 per year. They and my parents both had a portion of their salary deposited in an American bank. When they ordered something from Montgomery Ward or someplace similar, they could then pay for it with a check drawn on an American bank. Neither family had much need for cash.

When George responded to Albert's letter about the support from the Ohio church, he must have replied that Albert wasn't making much money compared to what he would have earned as a pastor in the United States, because Albert wrote back, "There is quite a bit of difference between us and them. We don't need to buy a car and keep it up. The Mission pays for all our food and for our medical work. So you see the salary we get is pretty high" *[7 September 1949]*. Sylvia would have seconded his response. They had what they needed and more.

AND SO MY PORTRAIT of Sylvia as missionary wife and mother in these early years comes to an end. By looking at the arc of my mother's life as a whole, I have attempted to understand her feelings about the choices that she and my father made. There is no support for my conclusions in the letters that she wrote, where her tone is consistent: whatever challenges we all faced, we were up to them. We were doing the Lord's work, and he was looking out for us. Her love of drama and her sensitivity to how she presented herself to others encouraged her to turn the spiritual basis for her actions to her best advantage. The early letters are filled with good stories, but she always wrote them after a calamity had been overcome.

She seemed unaware of the darker undercurrent in her life—distancing herself from New Guineans, who paradoxically took precedence over her own children and all other family members—as both she and Albert lived each day to the fullest. I do not think it possible that she articulated her misgivings even to herself. She most certainly did not articulate them to her children. Her letters exhibit only a partial Sylvia. The quality of the public Sylvia, the one I had wanted to dissolve into as a child, was strong and remains with me despite what Alzheimer's disease did to her brain during her final 15 years. The ambiguity of her whole person softens the ambivalence that I feel about what my parents did.

Were Mother to read what I've written, she would say that she did what she felt she had to do to under the circumstances, given the choices she had made. I asked her once whether she had ever considered divorcing

Dad, fully expecting that she would say yes. She paused for a moment and then said slowly, in a convincing way that persuaded me that she was being honest, "No, I never did." Initially, she would resist having to say how she felt about whatever difficult topic was at hand. She alternated between being angry and depressed when Dad died at age 74, four years into their retirement from the churches they served after they returned to the States. Yet, when we suggested that talking to someone might help, she said, "I never had anyone to talk to. Why should I start now?"

If there were more time, if there were someone she trusted to whom she could speak, and if she weren't in the early stages of Alzheimer's, I believe Mother would have been willing to begin this journey into herself. Doing so would have felt like tearing off a scab—one that grows back as quickly as it's torn off and then must be torn off again and again until there is finally nothing left of it. The wound eventually heals from within. I know this experience because it has also been mine in writing this book. I am my mother's daughter.

At Raipinka station, the wind still makes music in the casuarina trees along the lanes named Albert and Sylvia. She never forgot the trees or the richness of her time in New Guinea. As a college student, Sylvia had dared to hope for a beautiful life. In so many ways she lived out that hope, in the context of the highest calling she could imagine.

Chapter Nine
Yu Tok Stret.

In June 1975, I returned to New Guinea to visit my parents and to see my old haunts. It was shortly before they retired and my first visit since my departure in December 1962. I had planned the trip for over a year, saving money and scheduling my travel for a few weeks before they would leave and the new nation of Papua New Guinea would be born. The Territory of New Guinea, the northeast quadrant of the island and a trust territory of the United Nations, was about to unite with Papua, the southeast quadrant and a colony of Australia, to become an independent nation. My parents had also planned their departure carefully. They felt it appropriate that they leave as the new nation formed. Their work was done.

We were all good planners, used to overcoming any obstacles in our way. This time, however, an event had occurred earlier that year, that even now, 35 years later, has left an open wound in the hearts of everyone in the family. David, the eldest child and the sibling to whom I was closest, was killed at age 30 on February 14, 1975, when the Mooney that he was piloting crashed into a butte near Chadron, Nebraska. He was flying in a snow storm that also iced the plane's wings, and he and his three passengers were killed.

Rescuers found the plane's wreckage up on the butte the day after the crash, on a Saturday. My brother Paul called me that afternoon to say that David was not just missing but dead. One of the anchors of my life was now gone forever. I felt hollow and numb. Nobody could replace David. In the months that followed David's death, I tried to make sense of it as a Christian. I knew with chilling clarity what I did not believe. I did not then and do not now believe that "God wanted him home," or "It happened for a reason," as some Christians would say. I do not believe it is God's will that a promising young life (David was a Captain in the Air Force) be cut off so abruptly and painfully. I do not believe it is God's will that his widow Jacquie and their two daughters, Jennifer aged five and Sarah aged three, had to struggle so profoundly to shape new lives in spite of the unspeakable emptiness that they felt. I do not believe it is God's will that our family, already emotionally crippled from all the separations, would now have an even greater loss to absorb.

What was there left for me to believe? Accidents happen. God doesn't have anything to do with their occurring. I do, however, have the promise and the experience of his continuing relationship with me, which underlies my actions, feelings, and perspectives. Eighteen years after David's death, during my divorce, I resolved to get rid of my faith. I would step out of my relationship with God. I would leave behind the grace available to me through the sacrifice of Christ his son. But I couldn't do it. I learned that my faith is not like a coat I can take off at will and hang in a closet, put away when I don't need it and available to me when I want it. I couldn't reason it away. It continues as it has since my childhood, an indissoluble part of who I am.

As the eldest living child, I felt I should be the one to call my parents to tell them about David's death. They had probably had a phone for the 11 years that they lived in Port Moresby, the capital city, and I had the number in my address book, but I had never called them, and they had never called any of their four children then living in the States. I no longer remember what an international call such as that would have cost; whatever it was, we all thought it was too much, a luxury we could not afford. Besides, over many years, we had become accustomed to communicating by letter. Typically, we did not have an intimate feel for the particulars of anyone else's life, but we had never had that. We knew our parents loved us, although I at least didn't think about what that meant in concrete terms beyond a letter or two each month that had always been our way of showing we cared about one another.

I called my parents late Saturday evening. The 15-hour time difference meant they would get the call after they returned from church early Sunday afternoon. I had no idea how to tell my parents that their eldest son, who was everything they had ever hoped for—tall, handsome, outgoing, capable, and a committed Christian—was now dead. Dad answered the phone, and I said simply, "Dad, this is Cathy. David is dead." And then I told him what I knew about what had happened.

My parents made arrangements to return to the States for the funeral as soon as they could. On their way, they stopped at St. Peter's to see Peter and Ruth, who were then students there. They felt they could not afford the plane fares for Peter and Ruth to come with them; my youngest siblings were left to grieve on their own for a brother they barely knew. My parents were probably using the same line of reasoning they had applied when Dad's mother and Mother's father died. We didn't interrupt our tours of duty for anything. Later, I wondered why I didn't go to our relatives, hat in hand, somehow collecting the money so that Peter and Ruth could be with the rest of us during this momentous time. Even though I knew I was resourceful, I was used to making do when it came to feelings and family relationships. I would not have thought it acceptable to ask for help.

David is buried in a small, quiet country cemetery that overlooks the undulating corn fields of Otoe County in southeast Nebraska. Dad's parents are buried there, our Uncle George, and, after David, Mother and Dad. I too hope to be buried there, as do three other siblings. We couldn't get a large enough plot to be right next to one another. We will be buried as we have lived, connected but also always separated. I am not sure enough about an afterlife to say with conviction that we will all eventually be reunited.

WHEN I RETURNED to New Guinea four months after David's death, I felt his loss over and over again. I stopped at St. Peter's, the high school we had attended in Queensland, Australia, where the teachers remembered him with affection and sadness as the captain of the "A" football team, Head Prefect, and solid citizen of the school. When my sister Ruth and I traveled around New Guinea, visiting places where I'd lived and gone to school, all of the missionaries and New Guineans who had known David wanted to talk about him. I appreciated that. It helped my grieving to see that he was special to so many people. The conversations also gave Ruth, the baby of the family, a clearer sense of her older brother. Above all, I felt great compassion and tenderness for my parents. After so many years of sacrificing their personal lives for the cause to which they had committed themselves, they were now denied some of the reward that was their due: the chance to make up for lost time with one of their children.

I remember my parents' raw grief at the time of the funeral. After that, when they talked about David's death, it was always within a traditional Christian framework: "The Lord gives, the Lord takes away. Blessed be the name of the Lord." They did not dwell on how David's death had cheated them out of the time with him that they had been counting on.

For me, David's death ripped the fabric of what I thought was a successful start to my adult life. I was 29, had been married for four years, held a good teaching job in a small college, and was about to adopt a child. I had never had a loss of this magnitude with which to contend. I learned that becoming an adult was about more than being successful. It was also about finding a way to acknowledge and live with all that life brings.

THAT FIRST VISIT BACK to New Guinea allowed me to extend and deepen my mourning for David. It also fulfilled the desire that was my primary reason for planning the trip. I needed to find out whether New Guinea was still my real home, even though I hadn't been there for 12 years. Visiting familiar people and places, I felt over and over that I still belonged, that I could claim this island as my true home. I was sure there would one day be a good reason for me to return.

More than 20 years later, reading my parents' letters, I first conceived the idea of writing a book based on their lives and knew that I had to return to New Guinea once more. It would be impossible to stay long enough to gain an authoritative perspective on the work that my parents and others like them had done, but whatever impressions I could gather would be valuable. They might even be enough to let me make my peace with my parents, my father already dead for 15 years and my mother failing.

And so, in the early morning of July 18, 1999, I stepped off the Air Niugini plane at Nadzab airport, now the main airport for Lae. It had long since replaced the little airstrip whose runway led straight to the ocean on take-off, the one from which a plane first carried David and me to boarding school. The humidity hit me first, the air so heavy that I couldn't take a deep breath without gasping. I relaxed as we drove into town, taking in the familiar landscape. New Guineans were walking along the sides of the road, as they always had, although now the road was paved. A billboard for Coca Cola (*olsem oltaim*—"always the same") startled me. There had never been public advertising in the New Guinea I knew. And it was written in Tok Pisin, its status as the *lingua franca* of the country now assured.

Other changes directly affected how I could live and what I could do while in New Guinea. Safety was now a prime concern for everyone, regardless of skin color. Daily, I was reminded that, as a single white woman traveling alone, I could not afford to hide behind my warm memories of a childhood in which my position was secure. What part of this country could I now claim as mine?

My re-education began my first day in New Guinea. My hosts in Lae were the older sister of a classmate from St. Peter's and her husband. Noela and Bob lived in a house whose yard was surrounded by an eight-foot fence topped by another foot of razor wire. They kept three guard dogs inside the yard itself for good measure. "Don't even try to go outside without Bob or me," Noela warned, as she noticed me admiring her colorful garden. "The dogs don't know you, and they'll attack you for sure." Next, she showed me a certain button on the wall next to the kitchen. "If anyone tries to break in, press the button and a guard from our security company will come immediately. The place where we lived before didn't have a system like this, and we were broken into four times." I nodded politely, trying to conceal my dismay.

Most of the expatriates (no longer called "Europeans") lived the same way if they could afford it. The minimum safety requirement for blacks and whites alike was an outdoor fluorescent light, which illuminated the house and yard all night. Next came a fence. Like other towns in New Guinea, Lae was plagued with *rascols,* young men who leave their villages to look for work in the towns, can't find it, and so break into houses or hold up vehicles on country roads. They will rape women or kill anyone in their way.

The New Guinea I was visiting seemed harsh and dangerous, so different from the security of my childhood world. The new prime minister of a country with resources of oil, natural gas, gold, copper, cobalt, nickel, copra, cocoa, and coffee to sell to the world admitted freely that the country was almost bankrupt. Because of widespread government corruption, little of the money the country earned reached the people whose labor had readied the oil, minerals, and produce for the world market. Everyone I talked to believed that much of the overseas aid for the people of Aitape, where the tsunami hit on the north coast of New Guinea in July 1998, never reached the devastated villages. The local currency, the kina, had been devalued: for only 35 dollars (U.S.), I could stay overnight in a comfortable seaside resort, and that included breakfast. The people caught in the middle were those who moved to towns. No longer having their gardens as sources of food, and having to rely on motorized transportation that they could barely afford, they turned to desperate measures.

During my visit in 1975, when Papua New Guinea was newly independent, I had believed that New Guinea would always have a place for me, but the new New Guinea kept pushing me away. I had grown up there and loved the country. Didn't I deserve a place there? I imagined myself living in Lae as I once did, perhaps teaching at a high school or the local university. Who would be my friends? What could I do to feel safe? There was nothing there on which I could build a life, had I wanted to. I was angry and sad.

On balance, however, most experiences were not so bleak. The day after I arrived, Noela, Bob, and I went to church at Ampo, the old mission compound outside Lae and now the headquarters of the Evangelical Lutheran Church of New Guinea. Yes, buildings were smaller and closer together than I had remembered, and sometimes rundown, but a hedge of croton bushes—bright red, yellow, and green—still surrounded the guest house, the center of so many missionary social gatherings. The corrugated iron roof of St. Andrew's Church is almost rusted through, but that Sunday morning, just as I remembered, the people decorated with flowers wherever they could. They put them in the bamboo vases that were attached to all the supporting posts of the church as well as in the openings of pipes that held in place the backs of the benches. Most were New Guineans, with just a sprinkling of expatriates. People walked through the jungle to attend church, as they always had, possibly arriving before the service began but just as likely to enter any time during the service. Now, though, the worship was in English, with the sermon also translated into Tok Pisin. When I was a child, the entire service would have been in Jabim, the main local language, which I never learned to speak.

On our way back from church, my hosts and I drove past a new sports stadium where 2,000 Lutherans had gathered to celebrate, for some six hours, the 113th anniversary of the nearby landing of Johannes Flierl, the first Lutheran missionary in New Guinea. Noela and Bob said this annual celebration was completely the idea of the local churches. There was not a white person in sight. My hosts also told me that the indigenous Lutheran church is responsible for most of the education that goes on in Morobe Province, in which Lae is located. The same indigenous church also runs a teachers college, a seminary, and a shipping company.

Thus did I gain at least a partial answer to a question I had often wondered about before my return to New Guinea. I had left 36 years earlier and was out of touch. Now that almost all the Lutheran missionaries had left, how strong was the indigenous church? I needed it to be strong. Otherwise, what was the point of the sacrifices that our family had made? I had heard that churches were doing well on the local level, but individual churches of any denomination didn't contribute financially to their national church organizations. The lack of financial support put national church leaders in a tenuous position. I couldn't worry about them. I was primarily interested in getting a sense of local churches because the legacy of longtime missionaries would be most evident there. My experiences in Lae and elsewhere confirmed their vitality. That part of the indigenous church was strong and helped me to make peace with my parents' choices.

A week after my visit to Lae, I was on Karkar Island, 50 miles off the coast from Madang, and my father's first posting soon after he arrived in 1937. I went there mainly out of curiosity, wanting to know what it had been like to live in such an isolated place. My hosts, Anna and John Middleton, gave me much more: a glimpse of the New Guinea of my own childhood—now, as then, sustained by the work of New Guineans and

Western money and technology. Along with their son and John's brother, the Middletons owned four of the coconut and cocoa plantations on the island. In Lae I felt as though I were a virtual prisoner in Noela's and Bob's fortified home. Here at Kulili Estates, I could live even more freely than I had as a child. The Middletons' home has never had a front door during all its 50 years; instead, one enters through a high, wide archway that leads into the dining room and to formal sitting areas. They can live with such freedom because they trust their staff, all New Guineans, who care for the house and grounds and have done so for many years.

Anna has long been a patron of New Guinea art, and carvings, weavings, and paintings fill their home. She talked about the "cultural damage" inflicted by missionaries who destroyed art that was part of heathen practices. My own two-bedroom guest house lay near the beach, and I slept in a bed with an ornately carved frame.

At the close of the twentieth century, how could a plantation whose owners were white and whose employees were black be sustained? My three-day visit gave me only a few glimpses of what a complete answer might be. On the one hand there were the obvious inequities. I had hot and cold running water and slept in my carved bed, while the workers used a large spring near their compound for their washing and laundry. On the other hand, there is almost no other employment on the island, and men can live on the plantation with their families rather than being hired out as contract labor as in the past. When New Guinea gained its independence, the Middletons became citizens as a sign of their commitment to the new country, something that only a small group of white people did.

For the year that Dad was on Karkar, from 1937 to 1938, he lived at Narer, at an elevation of about 2,000 feet. Anna Middleton drove me there over a heavily rutted road, dodging pigs that crossed the road at their whim. Anna explained, "The local council [dominated by white plantation owners] has decided that if you hit a pig while driving, it's the pig's fault."

Whites owned most of the vehicles on the island and therefore were the ones most likely to hit the pigs. This policy gave them an ingenious way to avoid payback, the traditional system of retribution for hurting or killing pigs or people. Anyone hitting a pig did, however, have the obligation to report the accident to the nearest village.

The station at Narer is so thickly surrounded by jungle that it is difficult to believe that any other place in the world exists. From one vantage point, I could see the ocean, and I imagined that the view gave my father some relief from surroundings that must at times have seemed claustrophobic. I could see why Mother found it so isolated when we visited in 1949. As Anna and I walked across a large, open field to the home of the New Guinean pastor, I could hear "The Old Rugged Cross" being played on a tape deck in a nearby house. Perhaps the owner had no other tape, but I chose to take the music as a small sign of someone's faith, a continuation of the legacy my father had helped to establish.

When we reached the pastor's home, word of our visit had preceded us. His wife and children were outside, and she told me that the pastor was not at home. I felt I needed to do or say something, so I asked his wife, children, and other onlookers to stand in front of the house while I took their picture. I was actually much more interested in the house than I was in them because I thought that was where my father had lived. The pastor's wife did not invite us in, and I didn't feel comfortable asking to see the house. Anna and I left. It was only later that I learned my father hadn't lived there. Japanese bombing had destroyed his house.

I thought that the best way to connect with my father's experience on Karkar would be to find people who remembered him. At church in a Lutheran settlement near the beach the day following our trip to Narer, I met a retired pastor who was nine years old when my father arrived. The pastor knew of his later work in the Highlands as a teacher and then as acting superintendent of the mission. Another man, Mailong Labong, had been a student and then a teacher at a high school that my parents opened in the Highlands in the late 1950s. When the church service ended, Mailong spoke in Tok Pisin about how valuable my parents' work was (*wok bilong ol i bin gudpela tru*), and how good it was that I had come back to visit (*mi amamas tumas yu kamup long dispela ples*). He added that there was still a great need for more medical personnel for the local Lutheran hospital, the only one on the entire island of 40,000 people. Mailong invited me to speak, and I thanked the congregation for their welcome (*tenkyu tru*) and told them that I had a son and a granddaughter and was a teacher. (*Ples bilong mi Amerika. Mi gat wanpela pikinini man na em i gat wanpela pikinini meri. Mi tisa.*)

The cordial reception at church that morning was repeated wherever I went, whenever I told people that my parents were missionaries and that I had grown up in New Guinea. The people I met thanked me for coming, wondered why I wasn't staying longer, and gave me gifts—all this, independently of whether they knew my parents. My return meant much more than I had imagined. I thought I was going just for myself. As several New Guineans told me, I was honoring my parents as well as honoring the people I met.

Most intensely of all my wishes and hopes, I had been looking forward to seeing Raipinka again, not having seen my first home in New Guinea for 48 years. The airstrip at Kainantu was now closed so I could no longer fly there (a bank had been built in the middle of it). Instead, the De Haviland Beaver dropped me off at Ukarumpa, the site of the first Lutheran station in the valley and now a little America, a large settlement of the Summer Institute of Linguistics, whose members have translated the Bible into over 100 New Guinean languages. In the village store, one can buy American cake mixes and salad dressings. The settlement includes a high school and guest houses where families stay when they visit their children every month. Younger children are educated in their homes on outstations;

the Internet and email make home schooling so much easier than when Mother was trying to teach David and me using "correspondence school" materials. Being a missionary in 1999 meant giving up much less than it had 50 years earlier.

My first moments at Raipinka were awkward. I didn't know whom to contact in advance about my visit, so no one knew to expect me. A crowd began to gather, and the man who had driven me from Ukarumpa tried to explain to them who I was. Blank stares. Suddenly, I recognized the casuarina trees, now 60-feet tall, that Dad had planted along the two driveways that he had named "Albert" and "Sylvia." I pointed to the trees, and in Tok Pisin I said that my father had planted them (*Papa bilong mi i bin plantim dispela diwai*). *Yu tok stret* (you're telling the truth), one of the men shouted, and everyone laughed, remembering my father and now knowing me. When the driver asked who would take me around (*Husat i luk autim dispela meri?*), three men stepped forward.

The German missionary living in our old home had just returned from Germany and had no interest in someone who had lived there 50 years ago. Nevertheless, I could see enough to know that the house, now painted yellow with red trim, was in excellent shape. With my three guides, I relished walking along the paths to the nearby houses of New Guineans, imagining that they were the same paths I had walked on as a child, narrow paths now worn inches down into the soil from years of use. The houses looked the same too, their walls made of woven pit-pit, a plant similar to bamboo but more pliable, and their roofs thatched with the kunai grass that carpets much of the valley. I asked my guides about Honeymoon House, the getaway cottage that Dad had built for himself and Mother, but that all of us used. They showed me where it had been, further up the hill, with a panoramic view of the valley.

Looking down the steep hillsides, I saw women working in their gardens, where every inch of arable land was cultivated to grow sweet potatoes, taro, tapioca, and sugarcane. By then, Esther had joined us. She was the granddaughter of Munepe Yafanko, who, Esther said, took care of me when I was two- and three-years-old. Would I like to see her again? Indeed, even though I had no memory of her. Esther led me down a path so steep that I could keep my balance only by concentrating on each step I took. There in her garden, I met Munepe. Her hair was completely gray, she moved stiffly, and Esther said she could barely see. She may not have remembered me, and I could hardly comprehend that this woman had probably indulged my every whim. Knowing that my mother had arranged for someone else to take care of me when she could not made me feel doubly cared for. Munepe cut some sugarcane, Esther peeled it with her teeth, and the three of us sat together for half an hour, chewing and sucking the cane. I felt content and complete, grateful for this intricately specific link to my childhood.

All the older men I met remembered my parents. They called my father "Pericks" (their language has no phoneme for English "f's") and described him as *longpela man* (tall man). Twice, I talked with Papa Mangi, the senior man of the valley. He was a schoolboy when Dad came to Raipinka in 1941, although he didn't stay in school long because Raipinka was far from his home village, and there wasn't enough food at the school for all the students. He remembered Dad going on "church patrol," walking all through the valley to make sure that the villagers were building churches and homes for the evangelists who would be moving there. Papa Mangi has always considered himself a Lutheran but he had never been baptized. He was going to rectify that two weeks after I left, even though he had two wives. One of the women in his clan explained to me that he needed both of them because he was an important man. When my parents were there, mission policy would have required him to give up one of those wives upon his baptism, but no one mentioned that possibility now. Church rules about polygamy were probably no longer so strict since polygamy is legal for native New Guineans. A year later, I learned that Papa Mangi had not yet been baptized.

I wanted to believe that life in the Highland villages was little changed from my childhood, even making allowances for a Barbie doll I saw near the entry to one of the houses and the Coca-Cola sign hanging on a "bush" trade store. In the few days I was there, however, I had to acknowledge the romanticism of my nostalgia. The road that runs past our old house and that we traveled on horseback or on foot is now paved, and vehicles of all sorts use it. While my guides and I were walking, a huge semi-trailer all but forced us off the road, a red sign on its front bumper reading "Explosives." It was headed for Porgera, several hundred miles to the west, the site of an enormous open-pit gold mine.

For all the changes, my visit to Raipinka strengthened my sense that my life had had a good beginning. I had lived in a beautiful place, and I had been lovingly cared for. Depth and integrity characterized my parents' relationship with the Kamanos. Fifty years later, the people remembered them vividly and fondly, especially my father. I needed this direct experience of the long-term effects of my parents' work.

A BROADER PERSPECTIVE of a different kind emerged from a talk with 15 university students and other young adults at Nagada, outside Madang on the north coast, the first mission headquarters. The afternoon gathering began as a writing workshop, organized with the help of Susanna Teta, a third-year accounting student at the Technological University in Lae, with whom I had been in contact by email before my trip. Susanna and I agreed that I would discuss with them how to write research papers.

Susanna had arranged for the meeting to occur in the church at Nagada. It was open on two sides, which allowed a pleasant breeze to blow through, offsetting the effects of the hot, humid afternoon. I began a little hesitantly: "When we have finished talking about doing research and writing papers, could we talk about some other things? You know that my parents were missionaries here, and I'm really interested in what you think now about the church and missionaries." I let out a breath. "Also, would you be willing to talk about things that can be a bit difficult, like your belief in God?" They smiled and nodded their heads. No problem. With their assurance and openness, they reminded me of Albert's students at Heldsbach in 1938. I seemed to be the only one with any concern that I might be prying. The workshop went well enough, considering the humid afternoon and my not having a clear understanding of the kinds of papers their professors expected of them. Six students remained after the workshop to talk. *(See photo on p. 152.)*

I began gingerly: "Missionaries come from cultures that are different than yours. Often, they think their ways are best. Have they tried to make you believe that?"

One young man responded, "I've heard that missionaries used to be that way. But those who followed the early ones learned from their mistakes."

Another said, "It's too bad the missionaries couldn't just have brought the Good News and left their materialism at home."

I tried another tack. "Is the Christian God a Western god?"

"Oh no," they said in unison.

"God is our father," a young woman continued. "Everyone in New Guinea believes in at least one god. You just have to decide which one. We have chosen the Christian God." She looked at the others. Everyone was smiling. "Why would you think the Christian God is any more your God than ours?" I reminded myself of what Susanna had previously told me. Everyone there was a third-generation Christian to whom missionaries were ancient history, a fact of life.

As an adult, separated from any regular contact with what was happening in New Guinea, I felt much ambiguity about mission work. The students read me correctly: I needed to be reassured of its value. The first man who had spoken reminded me of some of what missionaries had accomplished:

"At a mission school, you don't just learn to read and write, you learn right from wrong. Our grandfathers' main job was to fight enemies from other tribes. Now, most of the time, there is peace, and we can do things like go to school."

"Don't forget the medical work," another chimed in. "Where would we be in Madang if we didn't have the mission hospital at Yagaum?"

"We respect missionaries and their families. We respect you for coming so far." Everyone nodded, agreeing with Susanna's sister Elizabeth.

Susanna added, "We know that not all white people are the same. Some come to mine gold, drill for oil, or cut down trees. When they have what they want, they leave. But missionaries like your parents—they stayed. They learned our languages and our customs. We could tell they really cared about us."

The "cultural damage" that so concerned Anna Middleton wasn't an issue for these young people. They weren't particularly concerned that traditional art forms were disappearing. They weren't agonizing over whether a man could have more than one wife. They had always lived to some degree in Western culture. They welcomed it and the knowledge it brought, as long as they had a say in how it was used.

The student who had commented on Western materialism went on to try to identify the kind of help they wanted. "We know we as a country still have a lot to learn. But we don't want help that makes us dependent on another country or that just encourages corruption among our leaders because there is so much of it."

"What's an example of good foreign aid?" I wondered.

"The road from Madang to Ramu Sugar," he said quickly, and everyone nodded.

Susanna said her family was expecting me for dinner, and we walked slowly to her home, continuing to talk. "The first missionaries blessed the people they worked with," she said.

I was astonished. "What do you mean?"

"These missionaries wanted to be sure the natives were well educated. They helped them get good jobs and showed them how to be leaders," Susanna responded.

Now, I thought Susanna was idealizing missionaries for my benefit. But she was speaking in earnest, not simply saying what I wanted to hear. The next day, I asked a German development worker what she thought of Susanna's assessment of early missionaries. Lilo had worked in Papua New Guinea for 12 years and was somewhat skeptical of missionaries. She thought for a moment and said that perhaps there was some truth to Susanna's statement. Lilo had a more pragmatic explanation, however: the early missionaries had spent a great deal of time with the first converts, who had thereby received more extensive guidance and support than later converts did. Yes, she thought that was a blessing.

Susanna's mother had made a feast of fish, rice, and several kinds of vegetables, all cooked in coconut milk. Dessert was a pineapple cake. The day ended with a picture-book experience from the tropics. Susanna took me to my guesthouse across the lagoon in her family's dugout canoe as the setting sun silhouetted the palm trees and the flying foxes overhead—those large bats for which Madang is famous.

I fell asleep that night, tired but content. Talking with the students lifted a burden for me so profoundly that I felt it physically as well as emotionally. The students' ability to step back and reflect was exactly what I needed. They had developed their own understanding of themselves as Christians. They didn't feel bound by a missionary's teaching although they would listen to it. They didn't say in so many words, "People like your parents helped to create a civil society in New Guinea," but their examples pointed to that conclusion. Making my peace with my parents' work required that I could defend to myself what they did besides gaining converts.

The intensity of my needing to reassure myself shows in the analytical thinking I fell back on as I continued to reflect on our conversation. I reminded myself: the students didn't speak for all Papua New Guineans; what they said about missionaries did not apply to all missionaries or to any of them all of the time. I was undercutting my experience, even though that was what had really made the difference for me. My conclusions would not pass a logician's test for a sound argument. Did they need to? I told myself no. It was enough to have met Susanna, Mailong, Munepe, and many others, all of whom showed me that missionaries had made a difference for the good in people's lives. Those people can now pass this gift on to their children and their children's children.

THE GREATEST GIFT that the trip made possible for me was being able to see Papua New Guineans as equals for the first time. Although we didn't have many material goods by American standards when I was growing up, we had much more than any of the nationals. Our houses were much larger and made of sturdier materials, we had many more clothes, and we were educated in better schools. As children, we inferred easily that we were better than the people we were supposedly there to help.

We set ourselves apart, from the adults as well as the children. When we traveled overland as a family, David and I were carried on a sail by four young men. We were enjoying ourselves while they were working. Although we may have seemed to play on equal terms with New Guinean children, what I remember is that we were the ones who made the rules. We also often played by ourselves while the New Guinean children stood watching. I don't remember ever taking a meal with any of the children or their families. I had never shared a room with a New Guinean woman or girl until this trip.

Seeing that I was with equals helped me also to differentiate my parents' experiences from my own. Thirty-six years had passed since I had spent any significant time in New Guinea. I had matured as an adult, but my strongest impressions of New Guinea and of my parents as missionaries were still those of a child, hardened in my mind with no practicable way to change them. From conversations with my younger siblings, I could see that, by the time my parents moved to Port Moresby in 1963, their attitudes had changed from those they held when they first arrived, even as their roles changed. They gave the New Guineans the space to become equals. Now, I had the same opportunity. Living in Port Moresby in the 1960s and 1970s was quite different for Mother, Dad, and their three youngest children than it had been for us in the 1940s and 1950s.

Paul, Peter, and Ruth could live with our parents because there was a good school in Port Moresby for them to attend. The years before independence in 1975 were an exciting time. Peter remembers the opening lines of a song in a musical: "Papua New Guinea, your day has begun, / Nations are watching the rise of your sun... ." Since Mother and Dad were the Lutheran Mission's representatives in Port Moresby, they were often invited to ceremonial events marking the development of the new nation.

Mother, in particular, had lived in the shadow of the British Commonwealth long enough to develop an affection for the British Royal Family and the formality their presence required. When the Duke and Duchess of Kent stopped off in New Guinea, Mother and Dad were invited to meet them on board a British warship. The guests were in formal attire, including long white gloves for women. They climbed a steep gang plank and then a ladder up the side of the warship. Mother stepped onto the cramped deck without enough time to compose herself before being presented to the Duchess. She had practiced a curtsy, even though, as an American citizen, she was not required to curtsy. Flustered, she forgot. Nearer the actual day of independence in 1975, Queen Elizabeth and Prince Phillip visited. Again, Mother and Dad were invited to meet them. To Mother's chagrin, it was Dad who was placed in the receiving line for the Queen, while Mother had to be satisfied with being presented to the Prince.

Mother could also express herself in more meaningful ways. For a time, she presented a radio program that was broadcast throughout New Guinea, featuring her commentary on recordings of classical music. She organized several choirs, the most noteworthy performing Handel's *Messiah* every year at Christmas. Both New Guineans and expatriates sang in the choirs.

Of particular concern to Mother and Dad were the many young New Guineans arriving in the city from Lutheran areas in the north. Leaving traditional village life and their families behind, they were rudderless in this strange, new environment. They usually had no jobs and nowhere to live. They ended up in large, tribally mixed shanty towns on the outskirts of the city. Crime was rampant, and sometimes riots broke out. Husbands spent entire paychecks on alcohol and, given the traditionally low status of women in New Guinea tribes, neither law nor custom restrained the men from beating their wives.

Another concern for both Dad and Mother was the strength of the *wantok* system. Villagers were expected to share their goods with their relatives (*wantoks*). The system may have worked when everyone was living in their familiar villages, even though only at subsistence level. Now, however, New Guinea was moving to a cash economy, and villagers coming to Port Moresby could barely support themselves with whatever work they could find, let alone support relatives who remained in the home village or who appeared at their doorsteps, expecting to be taken in.

Mother's main focus was working with women and children. She could once again draw on the speaking and leadership abilities that she had developed at St. Olaf. She was active in the YWCA, teaching women to sew, all the while counseling them on social issues. Peter remembers Mother talking with groups of women after church, often for so long that he and Paul and Ruth, none of them yet in high school, would give up on being driven home and would walk the two miles in the humid noonday sun. During the family's last five years in Port Moresby, Mother served as the ombudsperson in Children's Court, consulting with the judge on the equity of sentences for juveniles. Ruth says that she was often the only expatriate in the courtroom.

As chief pastor at Good Shepherd Lutheran Church, Dad offered three services every Sunday—in English, Tok Pisin, and Kotte—and he held church-related meetings many nights of the week. Even as a boy, my brother Paul was impressed by Dad's willingness to let lay New Guineans preach rather than always leading the worship himself. "The sermons by lay leaders were good," Paul remembers. "They taught me to have confidence in lay leadership." Peter adds, "I have vivid memories of Dad literally taking a backseat in Church Council meetings, not saying anything." Now, the primary measure of his success was not, as it had been at Raipinka, how many people he baptized each year, but how successful he was in grooming others for leadership. Now, he had become a servant leader.

My parents had let go of the sense of separateness and superiority that I carried with me into adulthood, and that created the defensiveness I felt in explaining myself to my academic colleagues. Even Mother and Dad's articles for American Lutheran publications in the late 1960s and early 1970s reflected their new position. Now, they wrote about young New Guinean leaders, not about themselves and their adventures, as had been the case in the early years. When I lived with my parents, they had been the leaders, venturing into new territory, deciding how churches and schools would be run. Now, the Papua New Guineans with whom they had taught and worked had stepped out in front.

I THOUGHT THAT MY 1999 JOURNEY would be the last time I'd see Papua New Guinea. Then, one morning in March of the year 2000, I received an e-mail message from Heiner Stahl, the Lutheran missionary at Tarabo station, which my father had helped to found in 1950. Would I represent my father at the 50th anniversary celebration in the coming June?

The invitation held two big attractions for me. I had never been to Tarabo, but I suspected that its remoteness in the Highlands, three days' walk from Raipinka, would have kept it almost as untouched as it had been 50 years ago. Perhaps traveling there could satisfy my hunger for the Highlands of my childhood. Much as I loved returning to Raipinka, it had changed too much. The other reason to accept was to experience even more of the long-term effects of my parents' work. I invited my friend Lynn, an experienced traveler, to accompany me. Other expatriates with connections to Tarabo had been invited from the United States, Australia, and Germany, I learned later, but I was the only one who attended.

The old New Guinea was apparent to me during the several hours' drive to Tarabo from Goroka, the capital of the Eastern Highlands Province. I settled in to enjoy the countryside and to explain to Lynn what we were seeing. Villagers had spread out coffee beans on large plastic sheets along the side of the road to dry them in the sun. Although coffee beans were now the main cash crop of the area, other villagers were selling bananas, sweet potatoes, and taro. Somehow, the landscape didn't seem complete. What was missing? Pigs! "Where are all the pigs running loose?" I asked the driver. "All I can see are a lot of goats."

"Oh," he said, "these people are all Seventh-Day Adventists, and they're not allowed to eat pork. So they raise goats instead." I allowed myself a moment of superiority. At least the Lutherans had left the pigs alone. I wondered how goats could ever be as central to New Guineans' lives as pigs had been.

We could see gardens off in the distance, geometrically laid out on hillsides. Mt. Michael became visible not too far out of Goroka. Australians named it after Michael Leahy, the 1930s explorer. It dominates its surroundings in the way that Mt. Rainier does for Seattle or Mt. Blanc for Geneva. You catch yourself looking upward for it; if you can see it, you know where you are, literally and psychically. Fifty years earlier, my father had traveled here on horseback, the first white man many people in the area had seen. Our driver told us about a "big *rascol*" who had terrorized the area until recently, when the locals decided they were tired of being robbed on their roads or in their homes, and they killed him.

An hour or so out of Tarabo, we came to what was left of a bridge over a river 30 feet below; two-thirds of its planks were missing. In good New Guinea fashion, someone who needed boards for a fence or perhaps to shore up part of a house had taken them. I remembered how growing up in New Guinea has given me a love for the unpredictable. Lynn and I got out of the Nissan truck and rearranged the remaining planks so that the left front tire and the right rear tire had a plank beneath them at the same time while crossing most of the bridge (the plan was the driver's). He drove across, while we walked a safe distance behind.

At Tarabo, we found the station's gate locked, but only to give the 15 women who were welcoming us enough time to assemble. Their singing and dancing strengthened the same feeling that still resonated in me from the journey to Tarabo. I was living in 1950 and in 2000 at the same time. I had heard and seen all of this before as a child, but now some of the women wore Western-style dresses and some were un-selfconsciously bare-breasted. Lynn and I walked with the women to the Stahls' home. They hugged us, kissed our hands, and chucked us under our chins. "I haven't been the center of so much attention since I got married," Lynn exclaimed.

Everything that could be decorated on the station was covered with garlands of sugar cane, pineapples, cucumbers, ginger root, and gladiolas. Waves of visitors kept bringing gifts to Heiner and Ricarda Stahl: a three-foot bunch of bananas, stalks of onions wrapped in banana leaves, and a live chicken. On the sports oval below the Stahls' house, men had built long houses out of woven pit-pit and grass roofs to shelter the hundreds of guests expected, some from as far away as a two-day walk.

The four-day festivities began the next morning. We were awakened at six by unison singing from the surrounding houses: hymns had been set to traditional tunes from the area. By mid-morning, five groups of about 100 men and women arrived from different villages, all wearing elaborate decorations, singing and dancing their way to the ceremony. Extravagant headdresses on the men were ingenious combinations of the old and the new. One man combined bird-of-paradise feathers, *kapul* fur, cowrie shells, and many red and yellow chewing gum wrappers, carefully pleated on a band to outline his forehead. Another man wore a penis gourd, the rest of his body covered only with white ceremonial paint—except for the battered hiking boots on his feet. What could I do but look?

On a platform erected on the sports oval, chairs had been placed for various church and government dignitaries. They were not permitted to walk onto the platform; instead, they were carried in a decorated "car" mounted on two long poles and carried by ten men and boys. Before the speeches began, a tambourine band from Tarabo Girls' School played. The girls, all dressed alike in school uniforms, did simple dance steps while accompanying themselves to hymns they sang in Tok Pisin and English. The Western hymn tunes sounded thin and empty after the richness of the early morning singing and the traditional chants of hundreds of dancers.

Nobody had asked me to give a speech. But I had decided before I left the United States that if I were traveling so far to represent my father at a celebration, I would ask to speak and that I would do so in Tok Pisin, which everyone there would understand. The organizers told me I would speak on the second day. I began by explaining who I was and then I told the audience about my father's first trip to Tarabo, which he had recorded in his diary. Knowing that my listeners would enjoy hearing the details of the trip, I translated a diary entry about how the hooves of my father's horse Cal became sore on the rough road: *Hos bilong mi, nem i Cal. Rot i no gut, na fus bilong en i bin bagarup tru. Mi sori tumas long en.* Dad had found many sick people and regretted the small amount of medicine he had brought with him: *Manmeri long dispela ples, em i gat planti sik. Mi no gat marasin long dispela sik.*

Mi sori tumas. He and his men went to investigate the World War II wreckage of an American B-17 bomber outside a nearby village, a crash that had killed 12 men. I wanted everyone to know how much it had meant to my father when he could return several months later with Max Diemer, his colleague at Raipinka, to buy that very land for the station. He wrote in his diary that he would never forget that day: *Mi no bai lusim tingting long dispela de.*

I ended my speech by attempting to explain how my father felt about New Guineans. I was talking to myself as much as to my audience. I used a story that I knew they would remember, from the book of Acts in the New Testament. Philip, one of Jesus' original 12 disciples, was told by an angel to go south from Jerusalem to Gaza. Along the way, he met an Ethiopian nobleman who was reading from Isaiah as he was returning home after having worshipped at the temple in Jerusalem. Philip asked the nobleman if he understood what he was reading, and the man asked Philip to help him. Philip explained the connection between Jesus and the "suffering servant" in Isaiah. (*Filip telemautim gutnuis bilong Jisas.*) The nobleman was instantly converted, and he asked to be baptized. I said that my father had come to New Guinea in the same way that Philip had climbed into the Ethiopian's chariot. The only difference between the two men that mattered to Phillip was that Philip had the Gospel (*gutnuis*) and the Ethiopian did not. For my father, I said, New Guineans were his brothers and sisters (*barata na susa*). He wanted to do nothing more than to bring them the Gospel: *Papa bin laikim tru long telemautim dispela gutnuis.*

Afterward, both Lynn and I were presented with gifts. I was given the skin of an entire *kapul*, and we each received a woven basket, net bags, and a length of cloth with the Tarabo seal on it. Later, a woman thanked me for my speech, also telling me that my tongue was "heavy" (how slowly I spoke). Another woman told me that my speech had made her cry. She was telling me, I think, that she was moved simply because I had come there and because I had spoken in a language she could understand.

By late afternoon each day, the ceremonies were over, at least until nightfall. Rev. Stahl would invite Lynn and me to have tea with other guests on his front porch. On one of these afternoons, he was reminiscing about earlier missionaries: "One of them carved his name on the trunk of a sacred tree in this valley. The tree was hundreds of years old, and its trunk was four feet in diameter." We gasped. "Teaching a new religion doesn't give you license to be disrespectful of the one you're trying to replace," Stahl continued. "There's just no reason for acts like these."

Yet for me, there was one more reminder during the festivities of the ways in which missionaries still set themselves apart, intentionally or not. On Saturday, the anniversary plaque was unveiled. The names and years of all the missionaries who had served at Tarabo were inscribed on it, but the names of the New Guinean evangelists and pastors who had truly made a difference were not among them. Had Stahl not noticed the disrespect in that act of omission?

Throughout the days of the celebration, I met men who had had some connection to my father. One had worked with him in Port Moresby. Someone else had been named "Pericks" after him. Arapo, an old man, said, *Papa bilong yu, em i poroman bilong mi.* A linguist at Ukarumpa later told me that your *poroman* accompanied you through initiation, one of the closest relationships possible between two men. I inferred that Arapo was describing how close he felt to my father, and not that they had actually gone through an initiation together. I particularly appreciated meeting people like Arapo who were adults when they knew my father. Just as at Raipinka the year before, I could see that the association had been a good one.

I BEGAN THIS BOOK with questions that were really one big question: what lay behind my parents' decision to follow the calling to be missionaries? I have written about them here primarily as young adults, and I can hardly imagine that lives can be lived with such intensity and devotion. My parents were indeed following the "desire of their hearts."

But was it necessary to sacrifice their children in order to live out their calling? They would not have accepted this way of describing their choices. "Sacrifice" is an exaggeration, they would say. They were following Jesus' injunction to make disciples of all nations, knowing there would be personal costs. You benefited too, they would say. You experienced the magnificent varieties of life in the world. You learned to take care of yourselves. They would say they had given us two gifts that are beyond measure: their dedication as examples to follow during our growing up, and faith in God to guide our lives.

A sacrifice looks different to the person deciding to sacrifice and the person with no choice about being sacrificed. Genesis 22 tells the story of God commanding Abraham to sacrifice his son Isaac. Abraham dutifully takes his son to the mountain where the sacrifice will take place. At the last minute, an angel appears and provides Abraham with a ram caught in a thicket so that Abraham does not have to sacrifice his son. Abraham has proved his faithfulness to God merely by being willing to obey his command. God rewards him by allowing him to keep his son and by telling Abraham that he will "multiply [his] descendants as the stars of heaven and as the sand which is on the seashore" (v. 17). As for Isaac's perspective, we're told only that, as he watched his father preparing to sacrifice a burnt offering, he kept asking his father where the burnt offering was.

Abraham could have it both ways—keeping his son and obeying God. For many years, perhaps for all their years, Mother and Dad believed that they too had it both ways. Roland Brandt, one of the retired missionaries who has faithfully read this manuscript, offered a perspective for which my parents would have thanked him: "The missionary command of Matthew 28 ('Go therefore and make disciples of all nations') was very real for your parents, just as it was for hundreds, even thousands, of other missionary families in the modern missionary movement. The joy and assurance that came from obedience to that command enabled all of us to serve faithfully." My parents believed that the Lord would provide. If they couldn't take care of us, someone else would, or we would take care of ourselves. We would make it through. Would we really have traded the richness of our experiences for a predictable childhood in a small Nebraska town near my father's family or a Minneapolis suburb near my mother's?

I don't know. I understand now that I have lived most of my life, wanting to be able to, thinking I should be able to, answer "yes" or "no" to this question that my siblings and I have discussed so often. *What life would we have wanted if we could have chosen it?* My cousins had these "predictable" childhoods. I like and admire them. I can't imagine how I would be with a different childhood, one like theirs. Most of all, I have hoped that I would somehow find the ram in the thicket, and I would be at peace. Perhaps the answer lay in stronger faith or a different perspective.

But I have kept coming back to the reality of our adult lives. There has been no ram in the thicket. Only three of the seven Frerichs children have had our own biological children, although more of us may have been able to do so. It is as if we didn't have enough in us to recreate ourselves. We needed what little we had for ourselves. Sometimes, I blame David's death on the way we grew up. If he hadn't become such a daredevil in the freedom we took for ourselves at boarding school, perhaps he wouldn't have risked that plane ride in the storm. Dad died and Mother sank into Alzheimer's before any of the divorces and depressions occurred in the lives of their other children. The cost of our restless and rootless lives has been high.

I wish there had been a middle way that would have enabled our parents to live out their vocations as missionaries *and* to have given us more of their time more meaningfully. But a middle way was not possible: my parents' personalities, their understanding of their vocation, and the era in which they lived make that a futile dream. It would be so different now, with different attitudes about child rearing, more money for travel, and the Internet for instantaneous communication that erases distance. Growing up in such a setting, I would not have had to wish for a ram in the thicket.

My concern for how I feel sometimes seems self-centered to me. My parents' work helped thousands of people to live better lives. It was part of the foundation on which Papua New Guinea now functions as an independent nation. Don't those accomplishments dwarf what happened to seven children, to our parents themselves, and to their families of origin? Some Christians would be impatient with me. "God's ways are not ours," they would say. Now we see only "through a glass darkly." We can question all we want, and the answers won't necessarily be there. Others might point out that many people (most people?) have difficult childhoods: a parent was an alcoholic and abusive, they moved too frequently, etc. The difference for me and my siblings was the active presence of God in our lives. We were not to question decisions made in his name, and for many years, I did not.

Of this much I am sure: writing this book has been an experience of grace in the Christian sense, a transformation beyond what I or anyone could have predicted. Traveling back to Papua New Guinea, I learned enough to establish a personal foundation for writing this book. I could view my parents' work from my perspective as an adult, one that I could live with and be proud of. I had my parents' letters and other resources available to me. My university generously allowed me to use some of my time for writing, and I have taken full advantage of that gift. Family, friends, and colleagues became readers who were willing to accompany me on this path. I have written as myself rather than under the guise of a piece of chalk. I have been able to *tok stret,* and I became more of a person in doing so. Through understanding how I came to be sent away, I have been able to come home.

Family Trees of
Albert Frerichs and Sylvia Fritz Frerichs

Frederick Frerichs (1852-1937)
Anna Farenholtz (1873-1960)
> Mary (1892-1965)
> Anna Margaretha (1894; lived two months)
> Anna Elizabeth (1895-1997)
> Tina (1898-1997)
> Elizabeth (1900-1989)
> John (1902-1979)
> Daughter Frerichs (1904)
> George (1906-1983)
> <u>Albert</u> (1910-1984)
> Genevieve (1913-2006)

Charles Fritz (1884-1965)
Pauline Pederson (1891-1978)
> <u>Sylvia</u> (1916-1999)
> L. Eliel (b.1918)
> Margaret (1919-2009)
> Paul (1921-2009)
> Mae (b. 1924)
> John (b. 1927)

Harriet (b. 1929)

Nancy (b. 1934)

Albert Frerichs

Sylvia Frerichs

David (1944-1975)

Catherine (b. 1945)

M. Angela (b. 1948)

Jonathan (b. 1950)

Paul (b. 1955)

Peter (b. 1957)

Ruth (b. 1959)

Where Albert Frerichs and Sylvia Fritz Lived, 1937-1943

Year	Albert Frerichs	Sylvia Frerichs
1937	Hildreth, NE	St. Olaf College
	Madang, New Guinea	
	Narer, Karkar Island	
1938	Narer, Karkar Island	St. Olaf College
		Canton, MN
1939	Boana, New Guinea	Canton, MN
	Heldsbach	Kanawha, IA
	Madang	
1940	Raipinka	Kanawha, IA
		Willmar, MN
1941	Raipinka	Willmar, MN
1942	Raipinka	Willmar, MN
1943	Raipinka	Willmar, MN
	Talmage, NE	St. Louis, MO
	St. Louis, MO	

Notes

The letters and diaries of Albert Frerichs and the letters of Anna Frerichs and Sylvia Fritz Frerichs are in the author's possession.

Chapter One: An Autobiography of a Piece of Chalk

Page

2   "for seven or eight years at a time": Background material on KLS School and stories from other children and teachers are from *Katharine Lehmann Voices,* a booklet prepared in 1991 for the fortieth anniversary of the school. Photocopy in the author's possession.

3   "'and we didn't fight against doing it'": Sylvia Frerichs, interview by Anna Marie Mitchell, *American Lutheran Church Women in World Mission: An Oral History and Archives Project* (Minneapolis: The American Lutheran Church, Division of World Missions and Inter-Church Cooperation, 1987). Archives of the Evangelical Lutheran Church of America (ELCA), Elk Grove Village, IL.

3   "Japanese invasion of New Guinea in World War II": Lydia Fliehler, interview by Solveig Swendseid, *American Lutheran Church Women in World Mission,* ELCA Archives, 1987.

3   "Wifehood was far more important than motherhood": Helen Calloway, *Gender, Culture and Empire* (Chicago: University of Illinois Press, 1987), 184, 206.

23   "'Oh, I thought it was Cathy playing'": Sylvia Frerichs, "Cessna for Children 10:00 Monday,'" *The Lutheran Missionary*, November 1953, 10-11.

29   "as she scrambled quickly out of the mire": Barbara Carlyon, *My Name Was Ba,* unpublished autobiography, 68. Photocopy in the author's possession.

30   "of being forever in-between": The category "third culture kids" has been most fully developed in David C. Pollock and Ruth E.Van Reken, *Third Culture Kids: The Experience of Growing Up Among Worlds* (London: Nicholas Brealey Publishing/Intercultural Press, 2001).

Chapter Two: Won't you let me follow the desire of my heart?
Page

37   "no longer available to young men and women in the Midwest": The connection between missionaries and the immigrant experience was first suggested to me by Jane Hunter's analysis of the family background of American women missionaries to China at the turn of the twentieth century: *The Gospel of Gentility: American Women Missionaries in Turn-of-the-Century China* (New Haven: Yale University Press, 1984).

38   "economic conditions at the time left them little choice": Hertha Oestmann Remmers, compiler, *Frerichs Family History,* Lincoln, NE, 1997. Photocopy in the author's possession.

38   "and then the rye crop": Mack Walker, *Germany and the Emigration 1816-1885* (Cambridge, MA: Harvard University Press, 1964), 70-73.

38   "between 1845 and 1890": Robert H. Behrens, *We Will Go to a New Land: The Great East Frisian Migration to America 1845-1895* (Mahomet, IL: Behrens, 1998), 13, 45.

38   "to move around more": Behrens, 52-54.

39   "anyone who was not German": Behrens, 60.

39   "marrying 'out'": Behrens, 62.

48   "attracting people from nearby congregations": Behrens, 67.

48   "And haste the coming of the glorious day": Mary A. Thomson, "O Zion Haste," *Lutheran Book of Worship* (Minneapolis: Augsburg Publishing Company, 1975).

51   "And that was the beginning of coming here [Papua New Guinea]": Albert Frerichs, interview by Jonathan Frerichs, Kristen Radio, Lae, Papua New Guinea, 10 June 1979. Audiotape in the author's possession.

61   "the mission method": Roland Brandt and Amee Gunlikson Brandt, *Halfway 'Round the World and Back*. As told to Mary O'Brien Tyrell (St. Paul, MN: Memoirs, 1998), 49.

Chapter Three: I want to live in as beautiful a way. . . .
Page

66   "only five grew to adulthood": The family histories of Charles Fritz and Pauline Peterson Fritz are from John W. Fritz, *The Fritz Family History* (Mason City, IA: Stylus Graphic Services, 2005), 12-21; undated notes by Pauline Fritz; and Sylvia Fritz, "How I Happen to Be an American," freshman essay, St. Olaf College, 1934. Typescript in the author's possession.

Chapter Four: New Guinea or Bust
Page

87   "while still allowing the fish to be a fish?": Some of the material on characteristics of New Guinea cultures and all of the early history of the Lutheran Mission in New Guinea are taken from essays in *The Lutheran Church in Papua New Guinea*, ed. Herwig Wagner and Hermann Reiner (Adelaide, South Australia, Australia: Lutheran Publishing House, 1987): Christa Gerhardy, "Medical and Diaconal Work," 514-17; Gordon Gerhardy, "Some Specific Observations on Partnership Involving

the Australian Church," 85-88; Carl E. Loeliger, "The Traditional Contexts," 15-25; Herwig Wagner, "Beginnings at Finshchhafen," 31-39. Comments on the supernatural are from Conrad Phillip Kottak, *Mirror for Humanity: A Concise Introduction to Cultural Anthropology* (Boston: McGraw-Hill, 2007), 209-11. The Papua New Guinean viewpoints come from Ennio Mantovani, *Meaning and Functions of Culture: An Introduction for Melanesia.* Occasional Papers of the Melanesian Institute, No. 9. Goroka, PNG: 1995, 3-19; and Bernard Narokobi, "The Old and the New," in *Ethics and Development in Papua New Guinea,* ed. Gernot Fugmann. Point Series No. 9. (Goroka, PNG: Melanesian Institute, 1986), 7-9.

94 Kunze's work on Karkar is taken from Georg Kunze, *In the Service of the Cross on Uncharted Ways* (Barmen, Germany: Mission House, 1896-1901). Trans. and rpt. Madang, Papua New Guinea: Kristen Pres, 1997.

95 "teachers were not well prepared": Gerhard O. Reitz, "Partnership Across Oceans," in Wagner and Reiner, 163.

Chapter Five: A Similarity of Soul Pattern
Page

123 "and then nothing": Michael Leahy and Maurice Crain, *The Land That Time Forgot* (New York: Funk & Wagnalls, 1937; rpt. 1957), 9.

123 "stone axes and sharpened sticks": Leahy and Crain, 42-50.

124 "not far from what became Raipinka": Reitz, in Wagner and Reiner, 174.

124 "violence between villages": Ann McLean, "In the Footprints of Reo Fortune," *Ethnographic Presents: Pioneering Anthropologists in the Papua New Guinea Highlands.* Ed. Terence E. Hays (Berkeley, CA: University of California Press, 1992), 41-44.

124 "serving in Raipinka": The information that Reo Fortune met Albert in 1951 is in a personal e-mail from Caroline Thomas, University of Waikato, Hamilton, New Zealand, 19 November 2007. Ronald M.

Berndt mentions meeting Albert in "Into the Unknown!" in Hays, 70.

125 "before they remembered it": Catherine H. Berndt, "Journey along Mythic Paths," in Hays, 105-106.

125 "one or a few 'big men'": Kottak, 138.

126 "to continue to fertilize the ground": Ronald M. Berndt, *Excess and Restraint: Social Control Among a New Guinea Mountain People* (Chicago, IL: University of Chicago Press, 1962), 41-48.

126 "could not be used for sorcery": R. Berndt (1962), 50-57.

126 "she was almost unconscious": R. Berndt (1962), 317-29.

127 "distrust of one's neighbors": R Berndt (1962), 233-66.

127 "were due to violence": McLean, in Hays, 54.

127 "a man's penis to his wife, for example": R Berndt (1962), 269-75.

128 "was being stymied": Kurt-Dietrick Mrossko, "Missionary Advance to the Highlands," in Wagner and Reiner, 199-200.

135 "a more mature believer": R. Berndt (1962), 382.

138 "ended the civil administration in 1942": Robin Radford, *Highlanders and Foreigners in the Upper Ramu: The Kainantu Area 1919-1942* (Carlton, Victoria, Australia: Melbourne University Press, 1987), 174-78

Chapter Six: Half a world and a war between us whichever way you go.
Page

175 "three-quarters of the 16,000 Japanese": Samuel Milner, *Victory in Papua* (Washington, DC: USGPO, 1959), 367-78.

176 "reached the Ramu valley": John Miller, Jr. *Cartwheel: The Reduction of Rabaul* (Washington, DC: USGPO, 1957), 41-42.

177 "although much weakened": Louis Morton, *Strategy and Command: The First Two Years* (Washington, DC: USGPO, 1962), 566, 582-83.

178 "may never come again": Gapenuo, qtd. in Albert and Sylvia Frerichs, *Anutu Conquers in New Guinea,* rev. ed. (Minneapolis: Augsburg Publishing House, 1969), 28-29.

Chapter Seven: *Even the strongest among us grows a bit faint.*

Page

189 "gas from their pumps, which they left unattended": David Rohrlach, *Army Service and Adventures, 1942-1945, and Return to Mission Service,*" n. d., 17. Unpublished booklet in the possession of Peter Frerichs.

192 "while the doctor sawed off the leg": Bertelsmeier's account of his imprisonment is fleshed out with details from Reitz, in Wagner and Reimer, 179-83.

194 "they would have had granite monuments": Albert's description of the war cemetery at Finschhafen is taken from *Anutu Conquers in New Guinea,* 27.

199 "'Come over here and help us!'": Albert Frerichs, "Missionaries at Work Again," *The Lutheran Missionary,* June 1946, 2-3.

Chapter Eight: *The wind makes music in the fine needles of our trees.*

Page

220 "*Trail Blazing in New Guinea*": Directed by Arnold Maahs for Lutheran World Action, National Lutheran Council, 1950. Copy housed at ELCA Archives can be viewed at www.catherinefrerichs.com

223 "he had seen only New Guineans": These summaries are taken from interviews with Amee Brandt, Frieda Mild, and Edna Scherle, conducted by Anna Maria Mitchell, Solveig Swenseid, and Fern Gudmestad, respectively. *American Lutheran Church Women in World Mission,* ELCA Archives, 1989.

230 "then boarded a ship to Madang": Interviews with Amee Brandt and Marion Walck, conducted by Mitchell and Swenseid, ELCA Archives, 1989.

233 "You might wait an hour, a day, or two days": Interviews with Amee Brandt and Edna Scherle, conducted by Mitchell and Gudmestad, ELCA Archives, 1989.

236 "told Max that he couldn't use it": Stories of the Diemer-Frerichs relationship are from Max Diemer, *Diemer* (Las Cruces, NM: Lapun Publishing Company, 2001), 111-12, 129, 147.

Bibliography

American Lutheran Church Women in World Mission: An Oral History and Archives Project. Minneapolis: The American Lutheran Church, Division of World Missions and Inter-Church Cooperation, 1987, 1989. Archives of the Evangelical Lutheran Church of America (ELCA), Elk Grove Village, IL.

Behrens, Robert H. *We Will Go to a New Land: The Great East Frisian Migration to America 1845-1895.* Mahomet, IL: Behrens, 1998.

Berndt, Catherine H. "Journey along Mythic Paths." *Ethnographic Presents: Pioneering Anthropologists in the Papua New Guinea Highlands.* Ed. Terence E. Hays. Berkeley, CA: University of California Press, 1992. 98-136.

Berndt, Ronald M. *Excess and Restraint: Social Control Among a New Guinea Mountain People.* Chicago, IL: University of Chicago Press, 1962.

———. "Into the Unknown!" *Ethnographic Presents.* Ed. Hays. 68-97.

Brandt, Roland and Amee Gunlikson Brandt. *Halfway 'Round the World and Back.* As told to Mary O'Brien Tyrell. St. Paul, MN: Memoirs, 1998.

Brandt, Amee. Interview by Anna Marie Mitchell. *American Lutheran Church Women in World Mission.* ELCA Archives, 1989.

Calloway, Helen. *Gender, Culture and Empire.* Chicago: University of Illinois Press, 1987.

Carlyon, Barbara. *My Name Was Ba.* Unpublished autobiography. Photocopy in the author's possession.

Diemer, Max. *Diemer.* Las Cruces, NM: Lapun Publishing Company, 2001.

Fliehler, Lydia. Interview by Solveig Swenseid. *American Lutheran Church Women in World Mission.* ELCA Archives, 1987.

Frerichs, Albert. "Come over here and help us!" *The Lutheran Missionary,* June 1946, 2-3.

———. "Missionaries at Work Again," *The Lutheran Missionary,* June 1946, 2-3.

———. Interview by Jonathan Frerichs. Kristen Radio, Lae, Papua New Guinea, 10 June 1979. Audiotape in the author's possession.

Frerichs, Albert and Sylvia Frerichs. *Anutu Conquers in New Guinea,* rev. ed. Minneapolis: Augsburg Publishing House, 1969.

Frerichs, George. Undated notes in the author's possession.

Frerichs, Sylvia. "Cessna for Children 10:00 Monday.'" *The Lutheran Missionary,* November 1953, 10-11.

————. "How I Happen to Be an American." Unpublished essay. St. Olaf College, Northfield, MN, 1934. Typescript in the author's possession.

————. Interview by Anna Marie Mitchell. *American Lutheran Church Women in World Mission.* ELCA Archives, 1987.

Fricke, Theodore P. *We Found Them Waiting.* Columbus, OH: Wartburg Press, 1947.

Fritz, John W. *The Fritz Family History.* Mason City, IA: Stylus Graphic Services, 2005.

Fritz, Pauline. Undated notes in the author's possession.

Gapenuo. Qtd. in Albert and Sylvia Frerichs, *Anutu Conquers in New Guinea.* 28-29.

Gerhardy, Christa. "Medical and Diaconal Work." *The Lutheran Church in Papua New Guinea.* Ed. Wagner and Reiner. 513-54.

Gerhardy, Gordon. "Some Specific Observations on Partnership Involving the Australian Church," *The Lutheran Church in Papua New Guinea.* Ed. Wagner and Reiner. 84-98.

Golding, William. *Lord of the Flies.* New York: Coward-McCann, 1962.

Hays, Terence, ed. *Ethnographic Presents: Pioneering Anthropologists in the Papua New Guinea Highlands.* Berkeley, CA: University of California Press, 1992.

Hunter, Jane. *The Gospel of Gentility: American Women Missionaries in Turn-of-the-Century China.* New Haven: Yale University Press, 1984.

Katharine Lehmann Voices. Unpublished booklet, 1991. Photocopy in the author's possession.

Kelly, Linda Harvey. *Toropo: Tenth Wife.* Port Melbourne, Victoria, Australia: Rigby Heinemann, 1995.

Kottak, Conrad P. *Mirror for Humanity: A Concise Introduction to Cultural Anthropology.* Boston: McGraw-Hill, 2007.

Kunze, Georg. *In the Service of the Cross on Uncharted Ways.* Barmen, Germany: Mission House, 1896-1901. Trans. and rpt. Madang, Papua New Guinea: Kristen Pres, 1997.

Leahy, Michael and Maurice Crain. *The Land That Time Forgot.* New York: Funk & Wagnalls, 1937; rpt. 1957.

Lionni, Leo. *Frederick.* New York: Alfred A. Knopf, 1995.

Loeliger, Carl. "The Traditional Contexts," *The Lutheran Church in Papua New Guinea.* Ed. Wagner and Reiner. 15-30.

McLean, Ann. "In the Footprints of Reo Fortune." *Ethnographic Presents.* Ed. Hays. 37-67.

Mantovani, Ennio. *Meaning and Functions of Culture: An Introduction for Melanesia.* Occasional Papers of the Melanesian Institute, No. 9. Goroka, PNG: 1995. 3-19.

Mild, Frieda. Interview by Solveig Swenseid. *American Lutheran Church Women in World Mission.* ELCA Archives, 1989.

Miller, Jr., John. *Cartwheel: The Reduction of Rabaul.* Washington, DC: USGPO, 1957.

Milner, Samuel. *Victory in Papua.* Washington, DC: USGPO, 1959.

Mrossko, Kurt-Dietrich. "Missionary Advance to the Highlands." *The Lutheran Church in Papua New Guinea.* Ed. Wagner and Reiner. Adelaide, Australia: Lutheran Publishing House, 1987. 187-222.

Morton, Louis. *Strategy and Command: The First Two Years.* Washington, DC: USGPO, 1962.

Narokobi, Bernard. "The Old and the New." *Ethics and Development in Papua New Guinea.* Ed. Gernot Fugmann. Point Series No. 9. Goroka, PNG: Melanesian Institute, 1986. 7-9.

Pollock, David C. and Ruth E. Van Reken. *Third Culture Kids: The Experience of Growing Up Among Worlds.* London: Nicholas Brealey Publishing/ Intercultural Press, 2001.

Radford, Robin. *Highlanders and Foreigners in the Upper Ramu: The Kainantu Area 1919-1942.* Carlton, Victoria, Australia: Melbourne University Press, 1987.

Reitz, Gerhard O. "Partnership Across Oceans." *The Lutheran Church in Papua New Guinea.* Ed. Wagner and Reiner. 141-186.

Remmers, Hertha Oestmann, compiler. *Frerichs Family History.* Lincoln, NE, 1997. Photocopy in the author's possession.

Rohrlach, David. *Army Service and Adventures, 1942-1945, and Return to Mission Service.* n. d. Unpublished booklet in the possession of Peter Frerichs.

Scherle, Edna. Interview by Fern Gudmestad. *American Lutheran Church Women in World Mission.* ELCA Archives, 1989.

Thomas, Caroline. E-mail to author. University of Waikato, Hamilton, New Zealand. 19 November 2007.

Thomson, Mary A. "O Zion Haste," *Lutheran Book of Worship.* Minneapolis: Augsburg Publishing Company, 1975.

Trail Blazing in New Guinea. Directed by Arnold Maahs for Lutheran World Action, National Lutheran Council, 1950. Copy housed at the ELCA Archives can be viewed at www.catherinefrerichs.com.

Wagner, Herwig. "Beginnings at Finshchhafen." *The Lutheran Church in Papua New Guinea.* Ed. Wagner and Reiner. 31-98.

Wagner, Herwig and Hermann Reiner, eds. *The Lutheran Church in Papua New Guinea.* Adelaide, South Australia, Australia: Lutheran Publishing House, 1987.

Walker, Mack. *Germany and the Emigration 1816-1885.* Cambridge, MA: Harvard University Press, 1964.

Acknowledgements

It has taken me ten years to write this book. I may never have completed it without the assistance of the following people:

Wendy Wenner, Dean of the College of Interdisciplinary Studies, Grand Valley State University, encouraged me to make my writing part of my regular work. Her support continued, even when the manuscript took much longer to complete than either of us had anticipated. Gayle Davis, Provost at Grand Valley, approved a sabbatical for me for Fall 2004, during which I concentrated on this project.

Two retired missionary couples—Amee and Roland Brandt and Bernice and Norman Imbrock—read early drafts of the entire manuscript. They answered my questions, suggested sources, and corrected factual errors. All of them knew my family well when we lived in New Guinea and offered perspectives my parents would have had, if they were still alive. I am grateful for the foundation the Brandts and the Imbrocks have given to these pages, even when they didn't agree with my point of view.

My brother Jonathan and I argued our way through my early drafts. He has always championed our father's work. He also brought his perspective as a lay church worker with thirty years' experience, including time in New Guinea. The book is more balanced in its portrayal of our father because of his contributions. To Marian Atwood Frerichs, Jonathan's wife, belongs the credit for making sure that our parents' letters and other documents were saved when we were breaking up the household after our father's death in 1984. I could not have written this book without these materials.

Margery Guest and Diane Herbruck invited me to join their writing group a few years into the project. The discipline of showing up with something every two weeks kept me going. At various times, Jean Bahle, Carol Bennett, Laura Bennett-Kimble, Emily Suhr Doyle, Debra Freeberg, Hilary Harper, Mary Jane Pories, Gloria Strassburger, and Marti Ayres White have been part of this group. Almost every page of the book, including its title, bears the mark of these discerning and faithful readers.

Several editors entered the life of the manuscript at different stages. Alice Koller, Elaine Eldridge, Ron Dwelle, and Mary Ebejer all pushed me uncomfortably with their questions, besides showing me how to write better sentences. Their comments contributed greatly to the overall coherence of the book.

A 2009 exhibit at Grand Valley of my father's New Guinea photographs from the 1940s was well received by the Grand Valley community and encouraged me in the final stages of preparing the manuscript. Some of the photographs are included in this book. Thanks to Henry Matthews, Director of Galleries and Collections, for accepting my offer of the photographs and to Paris Tennenhouse, Exhibit and Collections Design Manager, for her imaginative conception of the exhibit. Thanks as well to Dawn Oelrich, Curator, University of the Sunshine Coast in Queensland, Australia, and to James Cowan, author and friend of Grand Valley, for their interest and cooperation in arranging for the exhibit to appear at Sunshine Coast in May 2010.

Roy Cole, Professor of Geography at Grand Valley, prepared the maps for the exhibit and the book. Sherry Barricklow and Karen Burchard, in Information Technology at Grand Valley, solved formatting problems for me. Maria Codega, graphic designer, taught me to notice the features of a well-designed book as I was exploring publishing possibilities.

Documents in the Archives of the Evangelical Lutheran Church of America in Elk Grove Village, Illinois, were invaluable in broadening my perspectives of missionaries and the Lutheran Mission in New Guinea in the 1930s and 1940s. Elisabeth Wittman, then Director for Archives and Chief Archivist, and Joel Thoreson, now Chief Archivist for Management, Reference, and Technology, responded graciously to my requests as well as suggesting sources of which I was unaware. Robert Wiederaenders, Archivist, Wartburg Theological Seminary, helped in similar ways. From Caroline Thomas, doctoral candidate at the University of Waikato, Hamilton, New Zealand, I learned about anthropologists' work in the New Guinea Highlands, 1935-1950, and my father's relationships with them. Robert Beasecker, Director of Special Collections and University Archives at Grand Valley, assisted me when I was attempting to understand why an American Army lieutenant ordered my father to leave New Guinea in early 1943, as the Australian and American armies were beginning their rout of the Japanese in World War II.

Other people—colleagues, friends, and relatives—read some or all of the manuscript. They asked good questions, corrected errors, pointed out inconsistencies, suggested sources, invited me to speak in their classes, and believed in what I was doing. I thank:

Patricia Blakely, Kathleen Blumreich, Dan Bobo, Carol Brundage, Barbara Goldhardt Carlyon, Nancy Fritz Christian, Julie Connors, Mary Brandt Croft, Carson Dron, Kurt Ellenberger, Harriet Fritz Esse, Angela Frerichs, Jacquelyn Roberg Frerichs, Lani Frerichs, Paul Frerichs, Peter Frerichs, John and Doris Fritz, Lois Goossen, Vernita Heinke, Cindy Hull, Ruth Frerichs Imbrock, Lowell Johnson, Roswitha Fugmann Kaul, Jennifer Frerichs Kirby, Carol Kountz, Stan Krohmer, Mary Lou McGue, Elizabeth Diemer McKee, Shaily Menon, Rosanna Meyer (now deceased), Nurya Love Parish, Kim Ranger, Tamara Rosier, Ellen Schendel, Fran and Burnell Schrotenboer, Mary Seeger, Marilyn Fritz

Shardlow, Gary Stark, Marita Mae Kuhlenengel, Mona Kuhlenengel, Mae Fritz Skindlov, Chris Smith, Elda and Ronald Soderquist, Denise Stephenson, Judith Stoutland, Kathleen Underwood, Ruth Van Reken, and the women of "Life Journey with Books," a book discussion series sponsored by the Grand Rapids Area Council for the Humanities.

The book's attractive design is the work of Peter Honsberger, Principal, Cold River Studio, in Nashville, Tennessee. It has been a true pleasure to work with him.

Catherine Frerichs
Grand Rapids, Michigan
2009

Breinigsville, PA USA
22 March 2010
234634BV00001B/22/P